BARRON'S

AIMS

HIGH SCHOOL EXIT EXAMS
READING AND WRITING

Arizona's Instrument to Measure Standards

Dianna Sanchez, B.S.
Camp Verde High School
Camp Verde, Arizona

BARRON'S

All inquiries should be addressed to:
Barron's Educational Series, Inc.
250 Wireless Boulevard
Hauppauge, New York 11788
www.barronseduc.com

ISBN-13: 978-0-7641-3496-8
ISBN-10: 0-7641-3496-5

Library of Congress Catalog Card No. 2006017664

Library of Congress Cataloging-in-Publication Data
Sanchez, Dianna.
     AIMS high school exit exams in reading and writing / Dianna Sanchez.
        p. cm.
     Includes index.
     ISBN-13: 978-0-7641-3496-8
     ISBN-10: 0-7641-3496-5
        1. Language arts (Secondary)—Arizona—Examinations, questions, etc.
     2. Competency based educational tests—Study guides I. Title.

     LB1631.5.S26 2007
     373.126′2—dc22   2006017664

PRINTED IN THE UNITED STATES OF AMERICA

9 8 7 6 5 4 3 2 1

Contents

Part One | **Understanding the Tests**

Chapter 1 | Overview and Test-Taking Tips

The AIMS Language Arts Exams are divided into two separate exams: reading and writing. In the past, the exams were given in February, usually toward the end of the month. The reading and writing exams are spread out over two days. One is dedicated to the reading exam, and one is dedicated to the writing exam. One of the most important benefits for you is that each test is *not timed.* That means that you literally have all day to complete the test, so there is no need to rush. However, keep in mind that each exam does have to be completed within one school day—you cannot go home and then return to school the next day hoping to complete your test. The following describes each exam in a bit more detail.

READING EXAM

This exam consists of multiple-choice questions only with four answer choices. You are asked to select the best answer and darken the corresponding letter on your answer document. On the reading exam, you will be required to read many different types of text, ranging from short stories to advertisements. The exam will determine if you can comprehend many different types of reading materials. Make sure to read the instructions for each piece of new text that you come across during the exam. Keep in mind that since the exam is not timed, you can read each passage as many times as you need. Just keep reading until you understand what the passage is saying.

TEST-TAKING TIPS AND STRATEGIES

As already mentioned, the reading exam contains only multiple-choice questions. Multiple-choice exams can work to your benefit if you approach them with a few tricks. For example, the first step is to read all the questions *before* you read the passage of text. This will help you to locate information in the passage that appears in the questions. You can write in your test booklet. So you should highlight, circle, and underline information within the passages. Prereading the questions will help you stay focused on the important information.

Another tip is to eliminate answer choices that you know are incorrect. For the AIMS reading exam, every question has four answer choices. As you try to figure out an answer, immediately cross off any choices that you know are wrong. The process of elimination can help improve your score. If you are able to narrow down your answer choices to two rather than four, you have a 50 percent chance of guessing the correct answer instead of a 25 percent chance.

The reading exam will likely ask you to define potentially unfamiliar words that appear within a passage. The best technique for figuring out these words is to use the surrounding context. Context clues help you to piece together the general meaning of a word based on what is occurring within the sentence. Even if you cannot specifically define a word, the context helps you to create a general definition.

Another useful tool is to substitute the answer choices within the sentence. Some of the choices will make little to no sense. You can immediately eliminate those choices. When you substitute a word that seems to work, highlight that choice and continue substituting all choices until you feel that you have arrived at the best replacement. Combining context clues and replacing the word will typically help you arrive at a well-educated guess.

As you read questions, make sure to pay attention to words that are in **boldface** or *italics*. These words are typically important and deserve extra attention. For example, a question may ask you to find something that does **not** occur within a story. The word "not" is boldface because it is an important word. The question wants to emphasize what type of answer you are supposed to looking for. Remember to read all questions carefully, paying special attention to words that are in boldface or in italics.

Another point to keep in mind while taking the test is how you bubble in your answers. Make sure that you completely darken your chosen response. Your answer document is scored by machine. If the machine cannot detect your answer, it will be marked as incorrect even if you have chosen the correct response. If you decide to change an answer, make sure that you completely erase your previous choice. If the scoring machine detects two answers, the entire question will be marked as incorrect.

WRITING EXAM

This exam will be given on a different day than the reading exam. For this exam, you will be asked to write a fully developed essay in response to the given prompt. The writing prompt may vary slightly from year to year, but the majority of the writing prompts are of a persuasive nature. You may encounter prompts that ask you to persuade your reader about why your campus should change a current school policy or if the legal driving age should be modified. Your job is to state your opinion and to provide examples throughout your essay that support your opinion. Upcoming chapters will go into much more detail concerning persuasive writing.

As with the reading exam, you have as much time as you need to complete the writing exam. On the writing exam, you are allowed to use both a dictionary and a thesaurus, which are added benefits. Your essay will be graded using the six-trait rubric (which is discussed in detail in upcoming chapters). Using a thesaurus and a dictionary will greatly improve the scores you receive for word choice and conventions.

The writing exam gives you space to prewrite and to complete a rough draft. Since this test is not timed, completing both the prewriting and the rough draft is in your best interest. Once you have proofread and edited your essay, you then write it in the space provided in the answer document for your final draft. An important guideline to keep in mind for the final draft is that *it cannot exceed two pages*. Any writing that goes beyond two pages will not be graded. Make sure you are saying exactly what you want to say in a clear and focused manner.

KEY POINTS OF THE AIMS EXAMS

- The reading and writing exams are given on separate days.
- Both exams are **not** timed.
- All questions on the reading exam are multiple choice.
- You may use a dictionary and a thesaurus for the writing exam.
- The test booklet for the writing exam gives you space for prewriting and a rough draft.
- The final draft of your essay cannot exceed two pages.

Now that you have a general idea of what to expect from the AIMS exam, the following chapters describe in greater material the material on which you will be tested. Each chapter contains sample questions, and there are three sample tests at the end of the book that you may take to gauge how successful you will be on test day. Let's get started!

Part Two | **Mastering the AIMS Reading Exam**

Chapter 2 | **Fictional Passages**

▀▀▀▀▀▀▀▀▀▀▀▀▀▀▀▀▀▀▀▀▀▀▀▀▀▀▀▀▀▀▀▀▀▀▀▀▀▀▀

The AIMS reading exam will test your ability to comprehend several different types of text. You will need to be able to understand fiction, informational text, functional text, and persuasive text. The following chapters will help to build your comprehension abilities. They specifically focus on these types of text to ensure that you do your best on test day. The reading exam is all multiple choice. This chapter and the next three contain several tips on how to take a multiple-choice exam effectively. This chapter focuses on fiction and strategies that are specific to understanding literature.

For many students, reading fiction is the most pleasurable type of reading. You get to enjoy a great story with interesting characters, plot developments, and action. However, understanding fiction can also be tricky due to figurative language, complex sentence structure, and subtle themes and messages. This chapter focuses on the issues that typically come up when reading fiction so you can better comprehend what you read on test day.

ELEMENTS OF FICTION

A good story contains elements such as plot, setting, character, theme, and more. The AIMS exam will ask you questions specific to these elements, so you must understand what each one entails. You will need to understand the following elements and how to analyze them within the context of a story:

1. Plot
2. Setting
3. Character
4. Conflict
5. Theme
6. Tone
7. Mood
8. Context clues and inferences

Plot

A simple definition of plot is a summary of the important events that occur within the story. Plot answers the question, "What happens in this story?" For example, you can give the plot of your day at school by summarizing what happened to you throughout the day. Plot is fairly simple to understand and is usually quite easy to identify within a story. However, plot is broken down into several specific elements:

1. Rising action
2. Climax
3. Falling action/resolution

These elements are usually put together into what we call a plotline. A plotline typically looks like this:

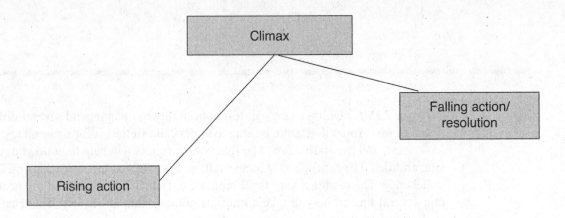

Rising action means the events in the story that build it up, making it interesting and exciting to the reader. Rising action can contribute to a sense of suspense, intrigue, or mystery. The job of rising action is to build up to the climax of the story, which is why you have been reading the story in the first place.

The climax of a story may be something like finding out who the murderer is, two people finally falling in love, or a student getting an A on a test. All of the events that took place in the rising action have now given us a climax, making the story worthwhile and rewarding to read.

The falling action follows after the climax and is typically toward the end of the story. The falling action ties up any loose ends that the story still may have. For example, if the climax is discovering who the murderer was, then the falling action is the murderer going to jail. Falling action gives closure to the story and should provide a satisfying end for the reader.

Setting

The setting of a story answers the questions "Where and when?" and "Time and place?" If you were reading a story about several teenagers who lived at a boarding school in the year 2006, the setting would be a boarding school during current times. The setting of a story is not limited to one location or time. Throughout the course of a story, the characters may travel, the author may choose to have characters in several different areas, and so on. Also, time may change throughout the duration of a story. For example, a story may begin with a character waking up in the morning, and the same story may end with the character going to sleep at night.

Character

The concept of character is exactly what it says—character. The characters are the individuals involved in the story. They create the action, dialogue, and relationships. A good author will use his or her characters to propel the story forward. Rather than the author creating the action by lengthy narration, the characters create the action by what they say and how they behave. Characters show you their personalities with their dialogue and actions. Keep in mind that the characters in a story do not always have to be human. Animals certainly may count as characters as well as whatever else the author decides to use to move the story forward.

Conflict

The conflict of a story is the problem that needs to be resolved. All good stories have identifiable conflicts. Imagine reading a story that did not have a problem that needed to be worked out. Would it be very interesting? Probably not. A good story revolves around an important problem that the characters need to resolve by the last page of the story. A story may contain multiple conflicts, just as it may have several settings and plots. For example, think of Shakespeare's *Romeo and Juliet*. If you have read this play, you know that many problems are occurring all at once. Of course, the primary problem is Romeo and Juliet's love for one another because they come from different families. However, there are also the problems of Tybalt's death, of Paris trying to woo Juliet, and of Juliet deciding whether or not to drink poison.

A good story will hold your interest by presenting multiple conflicts. If you think back to the picture of the plotline, the resolution of the conflict typically occurs during the falling action of the story. Logically, that should make sense because if the conflict has been resolved, not much is going to be left to develop the story, hence the falling action.

Theme

Although elements such as plot and character are easy to identify, theme can be slightly trickier. The easiest way to define theme is shown in the box.

> **Theme** is the underlying message or moral of the story. It is typically viewed as a universal truth, something that holds true for the majority of people. It is the significant message that the author wants you to understand. Theme is NEVER a summary of the story.

The example of *Romeo and Juliet* can be used to discuss theme. If you were to explain the theme of *Romeo and Juliet* by saying, "It's a story about two people who fall in love," you are already on the wrong track. As soon as you use the word "about" to explain theme, you are providing a summary for the story. Instead, if you were to say, "The theme of *Romeo and Juliet* is that true love can end in pain," you would be doing much better. Notice how this particular statement does not mention any specific characters or events. It simply makes a statement about something that the reader should learn or understand by the end of the story. Other themes of *Romeo and Juliet* could revolve around the issue of family rivalry getting in the way of love or the issue of the importance of friendship. Understanding theme takes practice. The more carefully you read a story, though, the easier identifying theme will be. Throughout the next few chapters, you will be given the opportunity to practice finding the theme of a story.

Tone

Similar to theme, tone takes a little bit of practice to feel comfortable with. Tone can be defined as the writer's attitude toward the subject and the reader. Tone is typically analyzed when reading fiction or poetry. Words such as compassion, irony, sarcasm, and bitterness describe a type of tone. For example, while reading *Romeo and Juliet*, you may say that an apparent tone is something like irony. Irony becomes evident at the end of the play after both Romeo and Juliet have committed suicide. The young lovers' deaths are ironic because now both families agree that they must reconcile their differences. If they had been able to do that before, both Romeo and Juliet could have lived happily ever after. Shakespeare has created irony through the actions of the characters and their behaviors toward one another.

Mood

Mood is simply the opposite of tone. While tone is the emotions that the *author* conveys in the piece, mood is the emotions that *you* (the reader) feel while reading the story. For example, if you think back to *Romeo and Juliet*, you are likely to experience many moods. During the scene when the nurse tries to persuade Juliet to marry Paris instead of Romeo, you may feel sympathy for Juliet. As you read the story of Juliet and understand that the nurse has been a dear friend to her and then does not offer support when Juliet most needs it, you might feel badly for Juliet. Mood can be extremely tricky. In essence, it is *your* emotional reaction to the story. However, you have to remember that the author definitely intends for you to feel a particular way. If you feel happy at the end of *Romeo and Juliet* because both characters have killed themselves, you are not assessing mood properly. This play is considered a tragedy for a reason. Shakespeare did not intend to have his audience rolling in the aisles with laughter at the end of the play.

Remember that you cannot say the mood of a piece is confusing or boring. You may have been bored while reading it, but chances are slim that the author set out to bore you intentionally. If your mood is bored or confused, you probably have some rereading to do. For example, if you have just read a poem that made absolutely no sense, you need to go back and figure out what the message (or theme) is first. After that, you can properly respond to the work, therefore interpreting a proper mood.

Context Clues and Inferences

Context clues and inferences are some of those things that you probably began to use as soon as you learned to read. Even if you do not consciously realize you are using them, you naturally use context clues and inferences to figure out the meaning of unfamiliar words, plot elements, and character elements. When you use context clues, you use the information from the story to fill in the missing gaps. For example, if you are reading a story and come across an unfamiliar word, you can use context clues to get a general understanding of what the word means. Read the following sentence.

The cloudy sky and the chilling rain created a <u>dismal</u> day.

As you read the sentence, you may or may not know what the word *dismal* means. However, even if you do not know the definition of *dismal*, you can put together a pretty good guess based on the other information in the sentence or by simply looking at the context clues. Based on the sentence, we know that the weather is cloudy and rainy. Typically, this type of weather is not described as cheerful or uplifting. When it is cold, rainy, and cloudy, being outside is usually unpleasant. By putting this information together, you should be able to form a general idea about what *dismal* means. It is definitely something unpleasant, maybe even miserable. If you were to look up the word *dismal* in the dictionary, you would find something like this:

Dismal: Causing or showing depression or gloom.

Even if you do not come up with a definition that is exactly like what the dictionary would show you, you can get pretty close by using context clues. The definition we devised based solely on context clues is not that far off from the definition we would find in the dictionary.

Throughout the reading portion of the AIMS exam, you will be asked to define selected vocabulary words that are found within a reading passage. Even if you are unsure of the exact definition, definitely use context clues to help devise a guess. Plus, the test is multiple choice, so you can pick the choice that you feel most resembles your guess. By reading carefully, you will be able to find hints that point you in the right direction of the correct definition.

Inferences are similar to context clues. However, they help you to understand a story on a deeper level than simply the meaning of particular words. For example, if you were reading a story about a young man who came home from school, ran straight into his room, and then loudly slammed his door, you could infer that he was angry. The author does not state, "The young man was very angry." Rather the author lets the character's actions and words let you figure out the young man's mood on your own. The exam will ask you to make inferences about characters, setting, and plot. Remember that characters, dialogue, and action all help contribute to making successful inferences.

REVIEW

When reading a piece of fiction, remember the following crucial points:

1. **Plot**
   - Be able to identify rising action, climax, and falling action
   - A summary of the important events
2. **Setting**
   - Time and place of the story
   - Remember that setting can change throughout the duration of a story
3. **Character**
   - The people that move the story forward by creating action, dialogue, and conflict
   - Remember that characters do not always have to be people; they can be animals or inanimate objects—whatever the author decides to use
4. **Conflict**
   - The problem that needs to be resolved by the end of the story
   - Resolution of a conflict typically occurs during the falling action of a story
5. **Theme**
   - The underlying message or moral of the story
   - Theme is *never* a summary of events
6. **Tone**
   - The writer's attitude toward the subject and the reader
   - There can be multiple tones throughout a story
   - Should be described by a word that reflects emotion or feeling
7. **Mood**
   - Your emotional reaction to the story
   - Should be described by a word that reflects emotion or feeling
   - Do not use words like *confusing* or *boring* to explain mood
8. **Context Clues and Inferences**
   - Use to define unfamiliar words
   - Careful reading will provide clues to strange words or concepts
   - Use characters, setting, and plot information to make inferences that will help you comprehend the story on a deeper level

Now that you are familiar with and have reviewed the basic elements of fiction, it is time to look at more advanced aspects of literature, particularly figurative language. After that, you will have the opportunity to analyze stories for plot, theme, figurative language, and so on.

FIGURATIVE LANGUAGE

You may be wondering, "What exactly is figurative language?" Figurative language is a tool that authors often use to lend creative power to their work. It is a way to describe ordinary events in creative, interesting ways. The first thing you have to grasp in order to understand figurative language is the difference between something that is *literal* and something that is *figurative*. Read the following sentences:

1. It is raining outside.
2. It is raining like the clouds just burst open.

Sentence 1 is an example of a literal sentence. Based on this sentence, if you looked out your window, you would see rain falling from the sky. The sentence says exactly what is happening without any extra fluff. In contrast, Sentence 2 is an example of a figurative sentence. If you logically go through this sentence in your mind and analyze the phrase "the clouds just burst open," you would probably understand that this statement is implying that it is raining really hard outside. However, can clouds actually burst open? Of course not, and that is what makes this sentence figurative. The sentence lets you know that it is raining very hard out but it is phrased in a descriptive, interesting way.

Keep in mind that figurative language typically compares two unlike things. This is what makes the description interesting. The author thinks of a way to relate two things that typically would not be connected.

Figurative language can make understanding literature difficult. When something is figurative, the meaning is not always clear. Careful reading and practice are needed to be able to identify figurative descriptions within literature. The following lists the most popular types of figurative language:

1. Simile
2. Metaphor
3. Personification
4. Hyperbole
5. Imagery
6. Allusion

Simile

A simile is usually the easiest type of figurative language to identify. A simile is a comparison using the words *like* or *as*. The following comparisons are examples of similes.

1. He ran as fast *as* a cheetah.
2. Her smile was *like* rays of sunshine.
3. The look in his eyes was as vicious *as* a hunting lion's.

Identifying a simile is easy because the words *like* or *as* tend to grab a reader's attention. In order to understand the implication of a simile, you have to ask yourself two questions:

• What are the two things being compared?
• What is the comparison suggesting?

Look back to example 1, "He ran as fast as a cheetah," and think about the two things being compared. You should recognize that the speed of a cheetah is being compared with how fast someone can run. The comparison suggests that he can run very fast. In order to grasp what the simile is saying, you must answer both of the above questions.

Metaphor

Unlike similes, metaphors can be difficult to recognize. A metaphor is a direct comparison between two unlike things. Authors such as Shakespeare are famous for their use of metaphors. A lot of original thinking and creativity are needed to devise meaningful metaphors. The following are examples of some metaphors.

1. "All the world's a stage." (Shakespeare)
2. He is a volcano ready to explode.
3. Love is a rose.

If you look at example 3, "Love is a rose," you should be asking yourself, "What does this statement imply?" You need to go over the same questions you ask yourself when you are analyzing a simile.

- What are the two things being compared?
- What is the comparison suggesting?

For this particular example, love is being compared with a rose. The comparison suggests that like a rose, love is beautiful and can bloom into something wonderful. At the same time, a rose also has thorns that can hurt, and love at times can be painful.

Look at the remaining examples. In the space provided, write what two things are being compared and the suggestion of the comparison.

1. "All the world's a stage."

   Two things being compared:

   _____

   Suggestion of comparison:

   _____

   _____

2. He is a volcano ready to explode.

   Two things being compared:

   _____

   Suggestion of comparison:

   _____

   _____

1. For the first sentence, you should have come up with something similar to the following:
   Two things being compared: <u>The world and a stage</u>
   Suggestion of comparison: <u>The world is similar to a stage because people perform on the "stage" or the world and act out their daily lives.</u>
2. For the second sentence you should have something like this:
   Two things being compared: <u>His attitude and an exploding volcano</u>
   Suggestion of comparison: <u>He is so angry that he's ready to explode.</u>

The more complicated the reading, the more difficult the metaphors are to understand. Some are easy to explain and analyze, while others can act as a hurdle to your understanding of the story. However, with careful reading and practice, you will be able to identify them.

Personification

Personification is giving an inanimate object humanlike characteristics. Remember that an inanimate object is an object that cannot feel emotion or pain. The following are some examples of personification.

1. The wind whispered in the night.
2. The river sang happily as it ran down the rocks.

In the first sentence, the implication is that the wind is blowing gently. This is an example of personification because the wind is not physically capable of whispering. Similar to the first sentence, the river in sentence two does not have the ability to sing. For personification, you must understand the two things being compared and the suggestion of the comparison in order to understand what the author is implying.

Hyperbole

A hyperbole is an extreme exaggeration that is used for dramatic effect. It is usually a statement that could never literally be true. The following are examples of hyperbole.

1. I cried a thousand tears last night.
2. I could eat a horse.
3. I went over that math problem a hundred times.

The above sentences are extreme in their descriptions. For example, could anyone ever really cry a thousand tears? Could someone ever really eat a horse? Could you really go over a math problem a hundred times? The answer is the same—probably not. An author uses hyperbole to emphasize something. In sentence 1, crying a thousand tears implies that someone is very sad. In sentence 2, being able to eat a horse means that someone is very hungry. Sentence 3 means the student reviewed the problem many times. If you come across a sentence that makes a dramatic comparison, chances are you are looking at an example of hyperbole.

Imagery

Imagery is a description that appeals to the five senses. Imagery focuses on the things that we can physically experience. The following statements are examples of imagery.

1. She felt the cool breeze blow against her face.
2. The sweet, juicy berries exploded in his mouth, staining his tongue blue.
3. He listened to the pleasant chime of the church bells as they broke the silence of the early morning.

Sentence 1 appeals to the sense of touch. Sentence 2 appeals to the sense of taste. Sentence 3 appeals to the sense of sound.

Authors use imagery to relate physical occurrences that we are capable of experiencing as human beings. They give power to the enjoyment of a story by letting the readers imagine that they are experiencing the same things as the characters.

Allusion

Allusions are references made to well-known pieces of literature, art, people, or historical events. If you are reading works by Shakespeare, Homer, or some other classic author, allusions may be difficult to understand. They may be difficult because allusions change as history changes. A person or work of art that was well-known in Shakespeare's time may not be recognizable to a modern-day reader. Therefore, a modern-day reader may not understand the implication of the comparison. The following are examples of allusions.

1. Her smile was like the *Mona Lisa's*.
2. The story in the newspaper was reminiscent of Cain and Abel.
3. He was a tragic hero, just like Odysseus.
4. It was as hot as the Sahara.

In order to understand the above statements, you need to understand what the *Mona Lisa* is; who Cain, Abel, and Odysseus are; and what the Sahara is. For example, the *Mona Lisa* is a famous painting of a woman with an intriguing, mysterious smile. The story of Cain and Abel occurs in the Bible and tells of two brothers, one who is extremely jealous and violent. Odysseus is an epic hero. If you are able to understand the reference, you will understand the comparison.

Make sure that you do not confuse an allusion with a simile. For example, when you read the fourth example, "It was as hot as the Sahara," your first response may be to label it a simile due to the appearance of the word *as*. However, keep in mind that you will not understand the comparison unless you understand the reference. If the sentence read, "It was as hot as the desert," then you can label it a simile because it does not refer to any particular desert. Just remember that as soon as a reference is made to any well-known location, person, piece of literature or artwork, it is an allusion.

Now that we have reviewed the different types of figurative language, it is time to practice! Read the following sentences. For each one, identify the following:

- Type of figurative language (simile, metaphor, and so on)
- Two things being compared
- Suggestion of the comparison

Answers are provided at the end of the section.

1. I have run a million miles.

    A. Type of figurative language: _____

    B. Two things being compared: _____

    C. Suggestion of comparison: _____

    _____

2. His face was set as stern as a soldier's.

    A. Type of figurative language: _____

    B. Two things being compared: _____

    C. Suggestion of comparison: _____

    _____

3. His voice shook the walls like the roar of Zeus.

    A. Type of figurative language: _____

    B. Two things being compared: _____

    C. Suggestion of comparison: _____

    _____

4. The stars shivered in the cold night.

    A. Type of figurative language: _____

    B. Two things being compared: _____

    C. Suggestion of comparison: _____

    _____

5. The morning is a blank canvas, waiting for you to create your day.

    A. Type of figurative language: _____

    B. Two things being compared: _____

    C. Suggestion of comparison: _____

    _____

6. The aroma of freshly brewed coffee wafted through the room.

    A. Type of figurative language: _____

    B. Two things being compared: _____

    C. Suggestion of comparison: _____

    _____

Key Points

Once you can identify and understand figurative language and comparisons, comprehending literature becomes much simpler. Keep in mind the following key points when interpreting figurative language.

1. The most common types of figurative comparisons:
    *   Simile
    *   Metaphor
    *   Personification
    *   Allusion
    *   Hyperbole
    *   Imagery
2. Figurative comparisons typically compare two *unlike* things, which creates a vivid description for the reader.
3. The difference between figurative and literal is that a literal description simply states the facts. A figurative description gives more detail and insight.

Answers for Figurative Language Practice

1. A. Hyperbole
    B. Running and a million miles
    C. Someone is tired or exhausted
2. A. Simile
    B. Face and solider
    C. His face is very stern, rigid, and unyielding—he looks very serious
3. A. Allusion
    B. His roar and Zeus
    C. His voice was loud and resembled that of the power of Zeus (king of the Greek gods)
4. A. Personification
    B. Stars and shivered
    C. The night air is very cold—cold enough to make the stars shiver
5. A. Metaphor
    B. Morning and blank canvas
    C. Each day provides a new start
6. A. Imagery
    B. Smell and coffee
    C. The air smells like coffee—we experience the physical ability to smell

READING AND ANALYZING LITERATURE

Now that you are familiar with the elements of literature and figurative language, it's time to practice and apply this knowledge.

Directions:	Read the following excerpt from Bram Stoker's *Dracula*, and then answer questions 1–10.

Dracula is of course one of the most famous horror novels that has ever been written. It tells the chilling tale of a blood-sucking monster from Transylvania. Dracula eventually comes to London, where he stalks and attacks characters, all with the intent of creating more vampires. The novel is significant for several reasons. Most importantly, it is a great story. However, the character of Dracula has become an easily recognizable villain. Everyone knows that Dracula is a vampire who bites individuals on the neck and then sucks their blood. It is because of this novel that we know who Dracula is today.

This excerpt occurs at the beginning of the novel. Jonathon Harker is currently traveling through Transylvania to visit Count Dracula. The count has just purchased an estate in London, and Jonathon intends to deliver paperwork that will finalize the count's purchase. As he travels through the countryside, Jonathon begins to realize that his journey is far from normal. At this point in the story, Jonathon is being transferred from one horse-drawn coach to another. The first coach has taken him through the Carpathian Mountains, and the second coach will take Jonathon the rest of the way to the count's castle. Jonathon is alone in the second coach. As he travels, he begins to doubt whether or not he should continue his journey. As you read this passage, keep in mind that Jonathon has no reason to fear the name "Count Dracula" itself. The count is simply a man who has purchased a home. His name does not signify a vampire or frightening creature . . . at least for now.

Dracula
by Bram Stoker
(Reprinted with permission from Dover Publications)

As I looked back I saw the steam from the horses of the coach by the light of the lamps, and projected against it the figures of my late companions crossing themselves. Then the driver cracked his whip and called to his horses, and off they swept on their way to Bukovina. As they sailed into the darkness I felt a strange chill, and a lonely feeling came over me; but a cloak was thrown over my shoulders, and a rug across my knees, and the driver said in excellent German: —

"The night is chill, mein Herr, and my master the Count bade me take care of you. There is a flask of slivovitz (the plum brandy of the country) underneath the seat, if you should require it." I did not take any, but it was a comfort to know it was there all the same. I felt a little strangely, and not a little frightened. I think had there been any alternative I should have taken it, instead of prosecuting that unknown night journey. The carriage went at a hard pace straight along, then we made a complete turn and went along another straight road. It seemed to me that we were simply going over and over the same ground again; and so I took note of some <u>salient</u> point, and found that this was so. I would have liked to have asked the driver what this all meant, but I really feared to do so, for I thought that, placed as I was, any protest would have had no effect in case there had been an intention to delay. By-and-by, however, as I was curious to know how time was passing, I struck a match, and by its flame looked at my watch; it was within a few minutes of midnight. This gave me a sort of shock, for I suppose the general superstition about midnight was increased by my recent experiences. I waited with a sick feeling of suspense.

Then a dog began to howl somewhere in a farmhouse far down the road—a long, agonized wailing, as if from fear. The sound was taken up by another dog, and then another and another, till, borne on the wind which now sighed softly through the Pass, a wild howling began, which seemed to come from all over the country, as far as the imagination could grasp it through the gloom of the night. At the first howl the horses began to strain and rear, but the driver spoke to them soothingly, and they quieted down, but shivered and sweated as though after a runaway from sudden fright. Then, far off in the distance, from the mountains on each side of us began a louder and a sharper howling—that of wolves—which affected both the horses and myself in the same way—for I was minded to jump from the coach and run, whilst they reared again and plunged madly, so that the driver had to use all his great strength to keep them from bolting. In a few minutes, however, my own ears got accustomed to the sound, and the horses so far became quiet that the driver was able to descend and to stand before them. He petted and soothed them, and whispered something in their ears, as I have heard of horse-tamers doing, and with extraordinary effect, for under his caresses, they became quite manageable again, though they still trembled. The driver again took his seat, and shaking his reins, started off at a great pace. This time, after going to the far side of the Pass, he suddenly turned down a narrow roadway which ran sharply to the right.

Soon we were hemmed in with trees, which in places arched right over the roadway till we passed as through a tunnel; and again great frowning rocks guarded us boldly on either side. Though we were in shelter, we could hear the rising wind, for it moaned and whistled through the rocks, and the branches of the trees crashed together as we swept along. It grew colder and colder still, and fine, powdery snow began to fall, so that soon we and all around us were covered with a white blanket. The keen wind still carried the howling of the dogs, though this grew fainter as we went on our way. The baying of the wolves sounded nearer and nearer, as though they were closing round on us from every side. I grew dreadfully afraid, and the horses shared my fear. The driver, however, was not in the least disturbed; he kept turning his head to left and right, but I could not see anything through the darkness.

Suddenly, away on our left, I saw a faint flickering blue flame. The driver saw it at the same moment; he at once checked the horses, and jumping to the ground, disappeared into the darkness. I did not know what to do, the less as the howling of the wolves grew closer; but while I wondered the driver suddenly appeared again, and without a word took his seat, and we resumed our journey. I think I must have fallen asleep and kept dreaming of the incident, for it seemed to be repeated endlessly, and now looking back, it is like a sort of awful nightmare. Once the flame appeared so near the road, that even in the darkness around us I could watch the driver's motions. He went rapidly to where the blue flame arose—it must have been very faint, for it did not seem to illumine the place around it at all—and gathering a few stones, formed them into some device. Once there appeared a strange optical effect: when he stood between me and the flame he did not obstruct it, for I could see its ghostly flicker all the same. This startled me, but as the effect was only momentary, I took it that my eyes deceived me straining through the darkness. Then for a time there were no blue flames, and we sped onwards through the gloom, with the howling of the wolves around us, as though they were following in a moving circle.

At last there came a time when the driver went further afield than he had yet gone, and during his absence, the horses began to tremble worse than ever and to snort and scream with fright. I could not see any cause for it, for the howling of the wolves had ceased altogether; but just then the moon, sailing through the black clouds, appeared behind the jagged crest of a beetling, pine-clad rock, and by its light I saw around us a ring of wolves, with white teeth and lolling red tongues, with long, sinewy limbs and shaggy hair. They were a hundred times more terrible in the grim silence which held them than even when they howled. For myself, I felt a sort of paralysis of fear. It is only when a man feels himself face to face with such horrors that he can understand their true import.

All at once the wolves began to howl as though the moonlight had had some peculiar effect on them. The horses jumped about and reared, and looked helplessly round with eyes that rolled in a way painful to see; but the living ring of terror encompassed them on every side; and they had perforce to remain within it. I called to the coachman to come, for it seemed to me that our only chance was to try to break out through the ring, and to aid his approach, I shouted and beat the side of the coach, hoping by the noise to scare the wolves from that side, so as to give him a chance of reaching the coach. How he came there, I know not, but I heard his voice raised in a tone of <u>impe-rious</u> command, and looking towards the sound, saw him stand in the roadway. As he swept his long arms, as though brushing aside some impalpable obstacle, the wolves fell back and back further still. Just then a heavy cloud passed across the face of the moon, so that we were again in darkness.

When I could see again the driver was climbing into the coach and the wolves had disappeared. This was all so strange and uncanny that a dreadful fear came upon me, and I was afraid to speak or move. The time seemed interminable as we swept on our way, now in almost complete darkness, for the rolling clouds obscured the moon. We kept on ascending, with occasional periods of quick descent, but in the main always ascending. Suddenly, I became conscious of the fact that the driver was in the act of pulling up the horses in the courtyard of a vast ruined castle, from whose tall black windows came no ray of light, and whose broken battlements showed a jagged line against the moonlit sky.

1 Within the sentence, "so I took note of some <u>salient</u> point," the word <u>salient</u> means:
   A hidden
   B obvious
   C bright
   D ghostly

2 The mood of this passage can best be defined as
   A suspenseful
   B magical
   C eerie
   D mystical

3 The setting for the majority of this passage is
   A mountains in the summer
   B a well-traveled road in the winter
   C mountains in the winter
   D a dark castle

4 Which of the following statements best reflects the fright Jonathon feels to the reader?
   A "The keen wind still carried the howling of the dogs, though this grew fainter as we went on our way."
   B "This was all so strange and uncanny that a dreadful fear came upon me, and I was afraid to speak or move."
   C "As they sailed into the darkness I felt a strange chill, and a lonely feeling came over me."
   D "Just then a heavy cloud passed across the face of the moon, so that we were again in darkness."

5 Within the sentence, "How he came there, I know not, but I heard his voice raised in a tone of <u>imperious</u> command," the word <u>imperious</u> means
   A frightened
   B hurried
   C bored
   D dignified

6 The purpose of this passage is to _____ the reader.
A entertain
B inform
C persuade
D educate

7 Within the sentence, "it must have been very faint, for it did not seem to <u>illumine</u> the place around it at all," the word <u>illumine</u> most likely means
A to flicker
B to light
C to hide
D to expose

8 The author uses the _____ and _____ to create an atmosphere of _____.
A wind, moon, anxiety
B horses, wolves, fright
C wolves, horses, agony
D driver, Jonathon, desperation

9 The statement, "Again great frowning rocks guarded us boldly on either side," is an example of
A simile
B allusion
C personification
D imagery

10 The details provided in this passage support the inference that the coach driver
A is a vampire creature
B can control animals
C can disappear
D is frightened of the wolves

Explanation of Correct Responses

1. **B** The word "salient" is defined as something that is noticeable or obvious. However, remember to use context clues to help you figure out a potentially unfamiliar word. We know that Jonathon is beginning to wonder if the coach is going past the same point again and again, so he determines to find a landmark to see if they pass by it again. Logically, he would be looking for something noticeable or something that he could easily identify. Therefore, the logical choice would be "obvious."

2. **A** Mood is the reader's reaction to the passage. When Bram Stoker was writing his book, he probably wanted to create a book that put his reader in suspense. This passage in particular utilizes the wolves, the reaction of the horses, and Jonathon's own fright to help create suspense for the reader. The other choices could work. Remember, though, you are always looking for the best answer in a multiple-choice situation. There is a sense of eeriness and mystical occurrences. However, the majority of the passage lends itself to a mood of suspense, making the reader want to find out what will happen next.

3. **C** Based on details that are provided in the book, we know that this passage is occurring on a rough road that runs through the mountains. We also know that it is winter because at one point, Jonathon describes the snow falling. Other details such as

the large rocks, the constantly ascending road, and the dense trees all contribute to the reader's understanding that Jonathon is traveling on a mountain road during the winter.

4. **B** By the time you have finished reading this passage, there should be no doubt in your mind that Jonathon is frightened and has had a nerve-racking journey. However, you need to be able to choose which details best contribute to the reader's understanding of the fact that Jonathon is frightened. Many elements add to this understanding, but your job as a critical reader is to determine which one is the most meaningful. Choice B is the correct choice because Jonathon clearly states his intense fright and makes it quite evident to the reader. The other choices also help to inform the reader that Jonathon is scared, but choice B is the best of the four.

5. **D** Once again, context clues are a crucial tool to use to help identify the meaning of the word. We know that the driver does not appear to be frightened of the wolves; therefore, he would not command them in a frightened or hurried tone of voice. The choice of "bored" does not make logical sense, so that leaves you with "dignified."

6. **A** The purpose of all fiction work is to entertain a reader. You will probably learn something new every time you read a story. However, the fundamental purpose of fiction is to entertain and not to necessarily educate, inform, or persuade a reader.

7. **B** You are by now sick of hearing about context clues, but once again, use context clues to identify unfamiliar words! The AIMS exam will ask you to answer plenty of questions concerning vocabulary words. Reading carefully for clues will help you do well on those particular questions. When you analyze the details of the passage, you understand that it is incredibly dark outside and that Jonathon is trying to see what the driver is doing relative to the blue flames. He notes that the light that the flame puts forth is very faint and does not light the surrounding area. Therefore, choosing a definition that pertains to the idea that the flame does not produce ample light is logical.

8. **B** The best technique to use when approached with a problem involving multiple blanks is to substitute all answer choices and see which one makes the most logical sense. For example, if you substituted choice D and the sentence read, "The author uses the driver and Jonathon to create an atmosphere of desperation," you would see that the sentence does not make complete sense. The first thing you should notice that makes this an untrue statement is labeling the atmosphere as "desperation." There is perhaps a mild sense of desperation throughout the passage but not enough to argue that it is the predominant feeling. Furthermore, if you thought that maybe the atmosphere was filled with desperation, the first part of the sentence would not lend itself to supporting that idea. A sense of desperation is not developed through the use of the driver. However, when you read the correct statement in its entirety, you can see that logically the horses and wolves contribute to an atmosphere of fright.

9. **C** The figurative element of this sentence is in the description "great frowning rocks guarded us." You should realize that you are looking at an example of personification because the sentence gives rocks humanlike characteristics. Rocks do not have the physical capabilities to frown or guard something, hence, you have personification.

10. **B** When a question asks you to make an inference, you are being asked to put together a logical guess based on provided details. In this case, Jonathon never simply states, "The driver seems to be able to control animals," but we can figure it out based on the details. The driver sweeps the wolves aside, and he is able to calm down the horses by whispering to them. These details support the idea that he can control animals. As far as the other choices are concerned, there is not ample enough support to deduce that the driver is a vampire, can disappear, or is frightened of the wolves.

Let's look at another passage pulled from a novel. Remember, the more you practice before test day, the better you will do.

Directions: Read the following excerpt from *The Jungle* and then answer questions 1–10.

This next passage is an excerpt from Upton Sinclair's *The Jungle*. This novel tells the story of a Lithuanian family immigrating to America in the early 1900's and the challenges they face adapting to a new culture and way of life. This novel was monumental in shaping America's policy concerning the meatpacking industry and how the government determined when food was considered acceptable enough to be sold to the public. The central character, Jurgis, relates his experience as a working man involved in the meatpacking industry and the horrors he witnesses both in the quality of food that is sold to the public and the conditions the workers themselves are forced to bear. It is through Sinclair's stomach-turning descriptions of poor food quality control that America revamped its food control policy, ultimately resulting in the formation of the FDA (Food and Drug Administration). This excerpt begins as the winter viciously sets in the city of Chicago. Jurgis and his wife Ona have been employed for several months now, and things have been going fairly smoothly for their family. The family has survived their first winter in Chicago but not without trial. Stanislovas, one of the young sons, endures painful frostbite during his first winter, and several family members become sick due to lack of protection from the cold. Regardless, winter is on its way in Chicago, and Jurgis discovers exactly how brutal the winter can become.

The Jungle
by Upton Sinclair
(Reprinted with permission from Dover Publications)

Now chill winds and shortening days began to warn them that the winter was coming again. It seemed as if the respite had been too short—they had not had time enough to get ready for it, but still it came, <u>inexorably</u>, and the hunted look began to come into the eyes of little Stanislovas. The prospect struck fear to the heart of Jurgis also, for he knew that Ona was not fit to face the cold and the snowdrifts this year. And suppose that some day when a blizzard struck them and the cars were not running, Ona should have to give up, and should come the next day to find that her place had been given to some one who lived nearer and could be depended on?

It was the week before Christmas that the first storm came, and then the soul of Jurgis rose up within him like a sleeping lion. There were four days that the Ashland Avenue cars were stalled, and in those days, for the first time in his life, Jurgis knew what it was to be really opposed. He had faced difficulties before, but they had been child's play; now there was a death struggle, and all the furies were unchained within him. The first morning they set out two hours before dawn, Ona wrapped all in blankets and tossed upon his shoulder like a sack of meal, and the little boy, bundled nearly out of sight, hanging by his coattails. There was a raging blast beating in his face, and the thermometer stood below zero, the snow was never short of his knees, and in some of the drifts it was nearly up to his armpits. It would catch his feet and try to trip him, it would build itself into a wall before him to beat him back, and he would fling himself into it, plunging like a wounded buffalo, puffing and snorting in rage. So foot by foot he drove his way, and when at last he came to Durham's he was staggering and almost blind, and leaned against a pillar, gasping, and thanking God that the cattle came late to the killing beds that day. In the evening the same thing had to be done again; and because Jurgis could not tell what hour of the night he would get off, he got a saloonkeeper to let Ona sit and wait for him in a corner. Once it was eleven o'clock at night, and black as the pit, but still they got home.

That blizzard knocked many a man out, for the crowd outside begging for work was never greater, and the packers would not wait long for any one. When it was over, the soul of Jurgis was a song, for he had met the enemy and conquered, and felt himself the master of his fate—So it might be with some monarch of the forest that has vanquished his foes in fair fight, and then falls into some cowardly trap in the nighttime.

A time of peril on the killing beds was when a steer broke loose. Sometimes, in the haste of speeding-up, they would dump one of the animals out on the floor before it was fully stunned, and it would get upon its feet and run amuck. Then there would be a yell of warning—the men would drop everything and dash for the nearest pillar, slipping here and there on the floor, and tumbling over each other. This was bad enough in the summer, when a man could see; in wintertime it was enough to make your hair stand up, for the room would be so full of steam that you could not make anything out five feet in front of you. To be sure, the steer was generally blind and frantic, and not especially bent on hurting any one, but think of the chances of running upon a knife, while nearly every man had one in his hand! And then, to cap the climax, the floor boss would come rushing up with a rifle and begin blazing away!

It was in one of these <u>melees</u> that Jurgis fell into his trap. That is the only word to describe it, it was so cruel, and so utterly not to be foreseen. At first he hardly noticed it, it was such a slight accident—simply that in leaping out of the way he turned his ankle. There was a twinge of pain, but Jurgis was used to pain, and did not coddle himself. When he came to walk home, however, he realized that it was hurting him a great deal, and in the morning his ankle was swollen out nearly double its size, and he could not get his foot into his shoe. Still, even then, he did nothing more than swear a little, and wrapped his foot in old rags, and hobbled out to take the car. It chanced to be a rush day at Durham's, and all the long morning he limped about with his aching foot; by noontime the pain was so great that it made him faint, and after a couple of hours in the afternoon he was fairly beaten, and had to tell the boss. They sent for the company doctor, and he examined the foot and told Jurgis to

go home to bed, adding that he had probably laid himself up for months by his folly. The injury was not one that Durham and Company could be held responsible for, and so that was all there was to it, so far as the doctor was concerned.

Jurgis got home somehow, scarcely able to see for the pain, and with an awful terror in his soul. Elzbieta helped him into bed and bandaged his injured foot with cold water, and tried hard not to let him see her dismay; when the rest came home at night she met them outside and told them, and they, too, put on a cheerful face, saying it would only be for a week or two, and that they would pull him through.

It was dreadful that an accident of this sort, that no man can help, should have meant such suffering. The bitterness of it was the daily food and drink of Jurgis. It was no use for them to try to deceive him, he knew as much about the situation as they did, and he knew that the family might literally starve to death. The worry of it fairly ate him up—he began to look haggard the first two or three days of it. In truth, it was almost maddening for a strong man like him, a fighter, to have to lie there helpless on his back. It was for all the world the old story of Prometheus bound. As Jurgis lay on his bed, hour after hour, there came to him emotions that he had never known before. Before this he had met life with a welcome—it had its trials, but none that a man could not face. But now, in the nighttime, when he lay tossing about, there would come stalking into his chamber a grisly phantom, the sight of which made his flesh curl and his hair bristle up. It was like seeing the world fall away from underneath his feet, like plunging down into a bottomless abyss, into yawning caverns of despair. It might be true, then, after all, what others had told him about life, that the best powers of a man might not be equal to it! It might be true that, strive as he would, toil as he would, he might fail, and go down and be destroyed! The thought of this was like an icy hand at his heart, the thought that here, in this ghastly home of all horror, he and all those who were dear to him might and perish of starvation and cold, and there would be no ear to hear their cry, no hand to help them! It was true, it was true—that here in this huge city, with its stores of heaped-up wealth, human creatures might be hunted down and destroyed by the wild-beast powers of nature, just as truly as ever they were in the days of cave men!

1 Within the sentence, "It seemed as if the respite had been too short—they had not had time enough to get ready for it, but still it came, inexorably," the word inexorably means
A harshly
B coldly
C inevitably
D unsympathetically

2 Jurgis's character can be best be defined as
A serious
B dedicated
C cowardly
D focused

3 The statement, "Then the soul of Jurgis rose up within him like a sleeping lion," is an example of
A simile
B metaphor
C allusion
D hyperbole

4 In the statement, "Then the soul of Jurgis rose up within him like a sleeping lion," what two things are being compared?
A sleeping and lion
B Jurgis and lion
C soul and lion
D Jurgis and sleeping

5 Which of the following statements best describes the hardships that Jurgis' family may face?
A "That blizzard knocked many a man out, for the crowd outside begging for work was never greater, and the packers would not wait long for any one."
B "He and all those who were dear to him might perish of starvation and cold, and there would be no ear to hear their cry, no hand to help them!"
C "Jurgis got home somehow, scarcely able to see for the pain, and with an awful terror in his soul."
D "There was a raging blast beating in his face, and the thermometer stood below zero, the snow was never short of his knees."

6 Within the sentence, "It was in one of these melees that Jurgis fell into his trap," the word melee means
A violent fight
B frightening occurrence
C dangerous riot
D confused struggle

7 The purpose of this passage is to _____ the reader.
A terrify
B persuade
C entertain
D educate

8 The statement, "When it was over, the soul of Jurgis was a song," is an example of
A simile
B metaphor
C personification
D imagery

9 The statement, "It was for all the world the old story of Prometheus bound," is an example of
A allusion
B simile
C imagery
D hyperbole

10 The mood of this passage is best defined as
A regretful
B sympathetic
C vengeful
D grateful

Explanation of Correct Responses

1. **C** Using the clues that surround the word itself, you should be able to arrive at choice C. The key clue to answer this question correctly is the phrase, "but still it came." This tells that winter is coming no matter what or that it is coming inevitably. The other choices do fit as replacement words, and they do define winter. However, you must use context clues to infer the correct answer.

2. **B** All of the provided choices could potentially work to describe Jurgis's personality. Remember, though, you are looking for the *best* answer. In this case, the best answer is *dedicated* because the passage shows Jurgis as a hardworking man who is intent on working and providing for his family. He braves snowstorms and brutal conditions to ensure that he can work to support his family.

3. **A** The key word in the statement is *like*. Remember that whenever you see the words *like* or *as* used in a comparative statement, you are looking at a simile.

4. **C** When you are analyzing the two things that are being compared in a simile, you are usually looking for the things that appear on either side of the words *like* or *as*. In this case, the statement is comparing the soul of Jurgis with that of a sleeping lion. Do not let yourself get confused by other possibilities such as sleep and lion. The soul of Jurgis is the focus of the sentence, so it has to be one of the two things being compared.

5. **B** One of the elements that the AIMS exam tests you on is your ability to identify quotations from a passage that support a specific idea. The concept of hardship is certainly made evident through the events that occur, but it is your job to pick the quotation that best shows the concept of hardship. All of the choices could arguably support this idea. However, choice B clearly shows how Jurgis's family will suffer.

6. **D** A melee is typically defined as an episode or occurrence that is filled with chaos and confusion. Once again, context clues give you indicators as to the definition of the word. This word occurs within the paragraph that describes a steer running loose. The room is full of steam, and the men cannot see the loose steer or one another's knives. Therefore, the situation would be full of chaos and confusion.

7. **C** Just like the passage taken from *Dracula,* the purpose of this fictional passage is to entertain the reader.

8. **B** In this statement, the soul of Jurgis is being compared to a song. There are no identifying words such as *like* or *as* in this statement. You should recognize that you are looking at a direct comparison, which is a metaphor.

9. **A** When you are analyzing a comparison that is an allusion, a key identifying element is a capitalized word. Even if you may not know what the reference to Prometheus entails, you can make a good guess based on your knowledge of figurative language. Clearly, the situation Jurgis is going through is being compared with the story of Prometheus, who was chained to a mountain and lived in torment.

10. **B** Remember that mood is the emotional response that a piece of work provokes in a reader. Based on the information concerning Jurgis, his job, and his dismal situation, the reader should feel sympathy for Jurgis and his family. For example, the feeling of gratefulness would not be an appropriate response based on the information provided. It would not be logical to feel grateful for Jurgis and his family when you take into account the fact that he is injured and that his family may starve.

CONCLUSION

These sample questions and explanations help you to understand the type of questions that will show up on the actual exam. The following chapters will focus on reading nonfiction texts, such as informational and functional texts. Part Four contains several sample exams where you can further test your ability to comprehend literary and nonfiction texts.

Chapter 3 | **Poetry**

━━━

P oetry can sometimes be challenging to understand. Poetry capitalizes on the use of figurative language (which was reviewed in the previous chapter) to send a powerful message or idea. Poetry also attempts to deliver that message using concise word choices. Poetry is an art form because the poet must find the words that say *exactly* what he or she wants them to say. What makes poetry challenging is simply trying to understand what the poem is about. The first time you read a poem, the meaning may go completely over your head, which is completely normal. Do not feel like you must understand the subtleties of a poem on the first read through. Essentially, poetry tests your ability to analyze language and both figurative and thematic elements. So let's begin to look at how to analyze a piece of poetry. Before you begin reading the sample poems in this chapter, let's first review some key points on poetry analysis.

KEY ELEMENTS OF ANALYZING POETRY

When analyzing poetry, follow these three steps all the time.

1. Always read the title first.
2. Read the poem several times.
3. Count the number of lines in the poem.

Always Read the Title First

This probably sounds extremely simplistic; however, it is very important. Many students tend to jump right into a poem, completely skipping the title. More than likely, the title of a poem will give you fundamental clues as to the meaning, subject, or message of the poem. If you do not read the title, the poem may become meaningless, leaving you in the dark.

Read the Poem Several Times

Due to the subtilies and nuances that many poems contain, you should read a poem several times in order to grasp everything that the poet wants you to take from the work. This can usually be accomplished only after several close readings of the poem.

On the first reading, simply try to get a feel for the language and the way the words flow and blend together. Do not worry about understanding the meaning of the poem just yet, simply become familiar with it. On the second reading, begin trying to piece together the message of the poem. Establish a general idea and read through it again, making sure that your interpretation makes sense within the context of the poem. Once you have figured out what the poem is about, begin noticing any figurative language that may appear and how that creates the tone and mood of the piece. In other words, you probably need to read a poem five to six times.

Do not feel foolish if you do not grasp a poem's meaning on the first attempt. Also, remember that the AIMS test is not a timed test, so do not feel rushed to get through a poem.

Count the Number of Lines in the Poem

This may already be done for you in the test booklet. If not, take a few seconds to number the lines. For example, if you have to number a poem, it should look something like this:

1 Roses are red
2 Violets are blue
3 My cheeks blush
4 When I think of you

Some questions will ask you to refer to a specific line number, so it pays off in the long run to number the lines. That way, you can quickly find the line you need without having to recount the lines every time.

As we look at sample poems throughout this chapter, keep in mind those three tips. They should be of great assistance throughout this chapter and, most importantly, on test day.

Before we begin analyzing, we need to review some vocabulary terms that are specific to poetry. A quick review will help you with several of the sample questions that will appear in this chapter.

POETRY TERMS AND VOCABULARY

Poetry has its own vocabulary. You need to understand the meaning of the following poetry terms because these words may be used in questions on the AIMS exam:

1. Stanza
2. Rhyme
3. Rhythm
4. Tone and mood
5. Theme
6. Form
7. Onomatopoeia

Stanza

A stanza is simply a group of lines in a poem. A stanza may consist of two, six, forty, or a hundred lines. There are no rules. The number is just however many the poet decides is needed. Stanzas are very easy to identify visually because they are very distinctive. You can quickly count up the number of stanzas in a poem without needing to read it. The closest thing that would resemble a stanza would be a paragraph. Locating a stanza is very easy because it has visually distinguishing features. Look at the following example of a poem consisting of two stanzas.

Study for the AIMS exam
Don't rely on your ability to simply cram
Make sure you get a good night's sleep
Otherwise you'll be in pretty deep

Be prepared to read and write
Keep a passing score in your sight
Come prepared and this test you can crush
Just make sure to take your time and not rush

By simply looking at the above poem, you can see that this poem consists of two stanzas. Each stanza contains four lines. You can see that a new stanza begins after the fourth line of the poem because of the space.

Rhyme

When in comes to rhyme in poetry, there are plenty of different ways that a poet may decide to integrate some sort of rhyme scheme into the work. Many people believe that any "good" poem has to rhyme because that is what makes something a poem. Although many good poems do indeed rhyme, many good poems do not rhyme.

When you discuss the rhyme scheme of a poem, you are not simply looking at just the end words rhyming. Since poetry is an art form, poets have devised such subtle ways to connect words that a reader may not even realize that a poem contains a rhyme scheme.

Rhyme schemes are always in a pattern. You usually need a certain degree of practice to be able to identify difficult rhyme schemes. Most likely, the AIMS exam will not ask you to identify a subtle rhyme scheme, but you do need to be aware that poems do not rhyme just at the end of each line.

Rhythm

Although rhyme may be easy to detect in a poem, especially one that has rhyming end words, rhythm tends to be a bit more tricky. You must remember that poetry is an art form that is meant to be read aloud. When you hear a poem that is read correctly, there almost seems to be a certain "beat" to it. This is what we call the rhythm of the poem.

Rhythm in a poem is much the same as in music. When you listen to your favorite song, you probably tap your foot to the beat. Poetry utilizes that same idea but more subtly. Rhythm in a poem can be established through emphasis on particular syllables in a certain order. It can be established through voice inflection. It can also be established through stressing words on particular lines, just to name a few strategies. Once again, the AIMS exam will probably not ask you to identify the rhythm of a particular poem. The better prepared you are, however, the better you will do on test day.

Tone and Mood

These terms should be familiar since they were already discussed in Chapter 2, "Fictional Passages." The definition of *tone* and *mood* are exactly the same for poetry as they are when you analyze a story. Just remember:

• Mood—*Your* emotional response to the poem
• Tone—*The author or poet's* attitude toward the subject and reader

Understanding the difference between these two terms is important. Also remember that your interpretation of tone and mood for a piece must coordinate with one another. Since poetry is such a sophisticated art, the poet is most likely aiming for a specific tone and therefore a specific mood on your part. If you read the poem carefully, you should grasp what the poet wants you to take away from the poem.

Theme

The word *theme* means the same thing in poetry as it does in other types of literature. To determine a theme in a poem is to formulate a statement that conveys the underlying message. You are trying to explain the deeper meaning and significance of the piece. Themes typically deal with important issues that we face, lessons we learn from our experiences, and problems that we encounter throughout life. It is vital to remember that a theme is NOT a summary.

Form

Another element of poetry that you should be familiar with is form. As you are probably well aware, visually identifying something that is a poem is usually very easy. Poems do not have to follow the same rules that books or magazines do. A poet can place the words wherever he or she desires—the words of the poem do not have to fill up an entire line of paper from left to right.

Since a poet has this unique privilege to be able to place words wherever he or she likes on the paper, form becomes a crucial element to analyze in poetry. As you read a poem, you need to ask yourself questions such as, "Why did the poet decide to break the line where he did and start a new line?" or "Why are there three lines in each stanza?" Simply asking yourself the question, "How does the form of the poem add to its impact?" is important and should enable you to get an even deeper meaning of the poem than you had previously.

Onomatopoeia

A poet will use onomatopoeia when he or she wants to imitate a sound that a person would hear. For example, if you encountered a line of poetry that read, "Splash! The cool, blue river water ran over my head," the word *splash* would be an example of onomatopoeia. The word mimics the sound someone makes when jumping into water. Other words that show onomatopoeia include moo, bang, hiss, and snort.

SAMPLE POEMS

Now that we have reviewed some basic elements of poetry, let's look at some sample poems.

Directions:	Read the following poem and then answer questions 1–5.

WEB

An early morning walk,
Shimmering drops of dew cling to sneakers
Desperately trying to hold their perfect shape.

A chickadee's song
Splits the dew laden air;
Ears shiver.

Perfect drops of dew ensnare themselves
On a spider's web, gleaming in nature's
Perfect pattern.

Concentric circles, radiating beads of perfection
Defying gravity in a quiet moment.
Approach cautiously.

Hoping for one moment
To be a part of nature's mysteries.
Creep closer and closer—inspect this delicate miracle—

CRACK!
The owner scuttles across her home
Freeing her prisoners of dew.

They fall like tears of glass, no longer superior.
Thankful for the moment,
A miracle dissolved.

1 The central subject of the poem is
  A a walk through the woods
  B a spider's web
  C early morning dew
  D the singing of a bird

2 The narrator is _____ when the spider runs across the web.
  A scared
  B excited
  C disappointed
  D surprised

3 The tone of this poem can best be defined as
   A energetic
   B reflective
   C nervous
   D appreciative

4 The line, "They fall like tears of glass," is an example of
   A personification
   B simile
   C metaphor
   D imagery

5 Another appropriate title for this poem might be
   A "Song of the Chickadee"
   B "A Quiet Moment"
   C "Attack of the Spider"
   D "Nature's Miracle"

Explanation of Correct Responses

1. **B** The focus of the poem is the spider's web. The other choices come up at some point during the poem, but the majority of the poem focuses on the beauty found in the spider's web. Do not let yourself be deterred by the other answers. The key term in this question is "focus." It is not asking for mentioned elements. Instead, it wants to know what the majority of the poem is about. Remember, the title of a poem is usually crucial to understanding the central subject. In this case, the title is "Web," which should give you an immediate clue.

2. **D** The key line that shows surprise on the part of the narrator are lines 16 and 17 when they state, "CRACK! / The owner scuttles across her home." The capitalized "CRACK" shows that the narrator has been surprised and is overdramatizing the sound the spider makes as it moves across the web. Also, remember that this question is asking you to focus on one specific occurrence in the poem. It is not asking you to evaluate how the narrator feels throughout the whole poem. So make sure you analyze that specific occurrence in order to answer that question correctly.

3. **D** While the narrator moves through the woods and inspects the spider's web there is definitely a sense of appreciation for the wonders found in nature. Also, the references to the spider's web as a "miracle" and "beads of perfection" indicate a tone of being thankful or appreciative for the things that the narrator is witnessing.

4. **B** Once again, the key term in this sentence is "like." Anytime you see a comparison using "like" you are looking at a simile. This particular simile compares the dew to tears of glass.

5. **D** Similar to other types of literature, a poem should have a title that reflects the general message or subject. For example, the chickadee does sing but only briefly. So choice A is not correct. Choice B, "A Quiet Moment," does not accurately reflect the poem. Additionally, a spider never really attacks as given in choice C. However, "Nature's Miracle" is an accurate reflection because it focuses on the spider's web, which is definitely the focus of the poem.

The poetry that you will encounter in the AIMS exam will most likely be fairly straightforward. As long as you read carefully and identify the parts of the poem that contain figurative language, you should not have too many problems identifying the central message.

Directions: Read the following poem and then answer questions 1–6.

GAME NIGHT

Retreat within—Find the focus—Hone in like an eagle.
Surrounding sounds vanish in a mist
The pound of your heartbeat echoes in your ears.

Within the soft, calm confines of your mind,
You see the net,
Hanging like a passive nest of white vipers.

Only way to get through the nest:
A secret password is required.
Rehearse the password, recite again and again—

"Swish" "Swish" "Swish"

Can't forget the password
Or the vipers will reject you.

Return to the reality of the locker room
Suck in a deep breath and charge onto the court—
Shaking the stands like a Titan with a massive stride.

Ready to show you've mastered the password—
Swish, Swish, Swish

1 The central focus of the poem is about preparing for a
   A football game
   B soccer game
   C basketball game
   D hockey game

2 The concept of the password symbolizes
   A making a basket in a game
   B getting past angry vipers
   C missing a point in a game
   D being mentally focused in a game

3 The line, "The pound of your heartbeat echoes in your ears" is an example of
   A metaphor
   B personification
   C hyperbole
   D imagery

4 The mood of this poem can best be described as
A exhausting
B inspiring
C confusing
D exciting

5 The narrator of this poem could best be described as
A focused
B nervous
C excited
D scared

6 The line, *"Swish," "Swish," "Swish"* is an example of
A personification
B onomatopoeia
C rhyme
D hyperbole

Explanation of Correct Responses

1. **C** You should realize that this poem is about a sport as soon as you read the title, "Game Night." However, figuring out what kind of game is the tricky part. There are key descriptions in this poem that let you know the narrator is preparing for a basketball game. Describing the net as "a nest of white vipers" tells you that the net is white. The description of the password as being "Swish" is crucial as well because that is the sound that a perfectly thrown basketball makes when it goes through the net, therefore allowing you to get past the "nest of vipers." The way that this particular question is written should also give you a clue in case you are totally in the dark after having read the poem. Since all of the choices focus on a sport, you have to determine that the poem is about playing some type of game. You then of course use the above-mentioned clues to figure out the particular type of game.

2. **A** Since the password is "Swish," the concept of the password is a metaphor for making a basket. Instead of simply stating, "I want to make a basket during the game," the poem provides a unique description about scoring during a game.

3. **D** Since this description focuses on hearing something, it is an example of imagery. Remember that imagery is a description that utilizes your physical senses. Anytime that you come across a description that you can imagine physically happening to you, realize that an author or poet is using imagery.

4. **D** After reading this poem, you should feel some degree of excitement. The narrator is getting pumped up for a big game. Therefore, the reader should be able to reflect that intense excitement.

5. **A** When you attempt to answer this question, you may have a hard time deciding between choices A and C. Even though the mood is a sense of excitement, the narrator is focused. Lines such as "Retreat within" and "Within the soft, calm confines of your mind" all add to the focus that the narrator possesses.

6. **B** By using the word "Swish," the author is mimicking the sound a basketball makes as it perfectly goes through the net. Since the word "Swish" is representative of a sound, it qualifies as onomatopoeia.

The two sample poems you've just read are very similar to what you can expect to encounter on the AIMS exam. They do take some careful reading. You should be discovering that the message of the poem is not extremely difficult to grasp. If you are, that is fine—just remember to keep practicing reading poetry. Like anything, the more you do it, the easier it is going to be. With that in mind, look at one more sample poem.

| Directions: | Read the following poem and then answer questions 1–5. |

INVISIBLE

Do you see me?
Do you see me in your hallways?
Do you see me in your P.E. class?

Do you see me in the cafeteria
Eating a cold sandwich
All alone?

Do you see me?
Do you see me in the last row
Of biology class?

I'm here everyday.
But no one sees me.
Like a ghost that haunts the halls, I drift from class to class.

You saw me when I tripped,
Contents of my backpack spilling everywhere.
I heard the smothered laughter behind hands.

I heard when you called me a loser
Behind my back.
How do you know I'm a loser?

Do you see me when I frown?
Do you see me when I draw little flowers on my notebook?
Or do you see me when I help someone solve a math problem?

Please see me.
If you look hard enough,
You might just see a friend.

1 The narrator of this poem is most likely a
   A senior citizen
   B college student
   C lonely ghost
   D high school student

2 The use of the pronoun "you" throughout the poem is meant to
   A show the narrator's frustration toward one individual
   B show the narrator's frustration toward a large group
   C show the narrator's frustration toward a teacher
   D show the narrator's frustration toward P.E. class

3 Which of the following themes can a reader infer from this poem?
   A It is important to respect the differences of all people.
   B It is important to realize people do not like to be alone.
   C It is important to know everyone at a particular school.
   D It is important to know someone before forming opinions.

4 Which of the following is an example of a simile?
   A "Like a ghost that haunts the halls, . . ."
   B "I heard the smothered laughter behind hands."
   C "Do you see me when I draw little flowers on my notebook?"
   D "Do you see me in your hallways?"

5 You can infer that the narrator feels that the only time she is noticed is when she
   A helps someone with math problems
   B is in her biology class
   C does something embarrassing
   D walks through the hallways

Explanation of Correct Responses

1. **D** Based on the contextual clues of this poem, you can infer that the narrator is a high school student. Details such as going to P.E. and biology class tell you right away that this student is in school. Wandering the hallways and eating in the cafeteria also add to that interpretation. You may have a difficult time deciding between the choice of high school student and college student, but keep in mind the aforementioned details. A college student probably would not be taking a P.E. class. Also, the feelings of loneliness and not belonging are common among high school students. Those feelings tend to diminish as people grow older.

2. **B** This may be a difficult question to answer for several reasons. Typically, when you encounter the pronoun "you," a statement is being directed toward one person. However, in this poem, the narrator's frustration is not focused on one specific person. Rather, her frustration seems to be focused on all of the students that ignore her and make fun of her. By using "you," the narrator effectively conveys her message to a large group, broadening her message. The poem is not directed toward one student who has hurt her feelings. Instead, it is directed toward all of the students who have hurt her. The use of "you" makes the poem personal on a certain level. After thinking about it logically, you should be able to recognize that the poet's intent is to address one large group.

3. **D** Remember that the theme is the message that you are supposed to gather after you have read the poem. Choice D is correct because it captures the important message the poem is trying to send to the reader. Through the narrator's voice, the poet wants you to understand that people end up feeling lonely and hurt when no one notices them. This narrator makes it clear that she feels she would be a great friend if someone would just take the time to get to know her. Therefore, the reader is supposed to learn not to form opinions or judgments about people before they get to know them.

If you are still unsure about how to detect theme in a poem, use the process of elimination. When you get to a multiple-choice question that asks you about theme, read over the provided choices. Immediately eliminate any that are providing a summary. Then begin to narrow down the choices that sound like they are making a statement that revolves around advice, morals, lessons learned, and so on. For example, you can avoid choices B and C because they focus more on the events of the poem and do not really focus on the issue of theme. That leaves you with choices A and D. Choice A certainly provides advice and wisdom, but it is not the central message of the poem. The narrator's intent is to get you to think about not forming opinions about people before you get to know them.

4. **A** All the things you have learned about figurative language should be paying off. Choice A has the word "like" in the statement, so you are looking at a simile. The narrator is comparing herself to a ghost, adding to the idea that no one can see her.

5. **C** The narrator states that when she trips and falls, people laugh at her. This seems to be the only time in the poem when her classmates actually look at her. She is ignored throughout the day and in all of her classes. The key word in this question is "infer." The poem never directly states that she feels embarrassed when she falls. Of course, for the majority of us, falling and spilling our things can be considered embarrassing. This question is asking you to make that jump in understanding and feel empathy for the narrator. Logically, she would be embarrassed while tripping and falling. Therefore, you can infer that choice C is correct.

POETRY REVIEW

This chapter should have helped you to understand the fundamentals of poetry. The AIMS exam will not ask you extremely complicated questions concerning poetry, but you will be expected to comprehend basic poetry. Below is a quick review of the important terms associated with poetry and tips on successfully analyzing poetry.

Always Read the Title First

Remember that the title will typically have a significant bearing on your understanding of the poem. Many times the title gives you a clue as to the poem's central message.

Read the Poem Several Times

Poetry can be difficult to understand if you do not read carefully and thoughtfully. Not understanding a poem on the first attempt is certainly OK and is very common. Simply read the poem several times or until the meaning begins to become clear.

Number the Lines of a Poem

Many times this will already be done for you. However, if you are reading a poem that does not have line numbers, take a few minutes to jot down the numbers in your test booklet. It will save you time in the long run.

Stanza

A stanza is simply a chunk of lines in a poem. It is similar to a paragraph in a story. The exam may ask you to evaluate a particular stanza, so you must be familiar with this term and its meaning.

Rhyme

Rhyme is how the poet connects words that have similar sounds. Remember that not all "good" poems have to rhyme—in fact, many great poems do not rhyme.

Rhythm

Rhythm is the flow of the words of a poem and how they connect to make a certain sound when read aloud. A poem that has good rhythm is similar to a song—you can detect a definite beat.

Tone and Mood

Tone and mood typically deal with words that relate to emotion. Tone is the emotion or emotions that the author/narrator is experiencing. Mood is the emotion or emotions that the reader is experiencing.

Theme

Theme is the important message that the poem is trying to send. Theme is NOT a summary of a poem. If a question asks you to choose the theme, avoid choices that begin with, "The poem is about . . . ."

Form

Form is the way the poem actually appears on the page. Form takes into account how the words are placed, how many lines are in each stanza, and how many stanzas are in a poem. Form is important because poetry is such an open art that the poet can structure a poem any way he or she likes. You need to ask yourself why a certain word appears on a line and why there are so many lines in a given stanza. By analyzing form, you force yourself to take a deeper look at the poem.

Chapter 4 | **Historical and Cultural Literature**

Y ou may be wondering why there is a chapter about history in a book that is supposed to help you prepare for an English test. Well, simply put, literature and history cannot be separated from one another. Memorable events and people in history such as World War II, Martin Luther King Jr., and the Holocaust manage to inspire authors to create amazing works of literature.

WHY HISTORICAL LITERATURE?

When you are able to identify the historical context surrounding a piece of literature, you are able to get a much firmer grasp on the concepts presented by the author. If you have never heard about the Civil Rights Movement and then read a book presenting characters dealing with the issue of segregation, you may not be able to understand all of the important issues and themes that the book presents.

Analyzing literature within a historical context also gives you the opportunity to see common themes that emerge among literature, poetry, and art. For example, literature about the Civil Rights Movement would deal with equality, racism, and freedom to name just a few. The more familiar you are with a historical time period or event, the more likely you will be able to anticipate the themes and issues that the novel, poem, and so on will deal with.

According to the language arts standards provided by the state of Arizona, the AIMS exam could potentially ask you questions specific to literature in history. You will not be asked to identify when a particular author lived or the date that a novel was written. Rather, you will be asked to compare stories and poems that reflect the same historical context. You may read a short story about the Civil War and then read a poem about the same war. Questions would then ask you to find similarities and differences between the two pieces. Even though the test will not ask you to name specific locations of battles, for example, having some basic knowledge of the Civil War is extremely helpful. You need to know that the Civil War was fought between the North and South of the United States, and that they were fighting over the issue of slavery. Such simple knowledge will help you understand the literature on a much more meaningful level. Let's begin by looking at some examples.

We all grow up hearing about our family stories. Grandpa was known for this, Aunt Sue was known for that. All of our families have these amazing stories to tell. These stories are what glue us together; they are what give us that comfort and solace found only in a family. One of my family's stories always manages to stand out for me. It is the story of my great-grandmother's immigration to the United States. Her story shows the amazingly strong woman that she was. Here is her story in her own words.

Land of Opportunity

We were all crammed on a boat. The boat was supposed to hold only a thousand, but somehow they managed to get two thousand bodies on that boat. You cannot imagine the stench! Many of us had not had the chance to bathe since leaving our home countries, and we had been at sea for nearly three weeks. Many people had difficulty handling the rough waters of the Atlantic. The stench of vomit mixed with sweat and grime made for quite a nauseating odor. I was seventeen years old when I left my home in Lithuania. I remember looking at young children clinging nervously to their mothers' skirts, crying to vocalize their discomfort. I remember painfully wishing that my mother was with me. I was on my trip to America alone. My parents had decided that if I was to ever have a chance at a better life, I was to find it elsewhere. I had left Lithuania filled with excitement, but now, after three weeks at sea, I felt only homesickness and regret.

As dangerous as it may sound for a girl my age to be traveling such a distance alone, it was surprisingly safe. Among all of us on the boat, there must have been at least thirty languages spoken and who knows how many nationalities. Even though we were from all parts of the world, we all shared the unspoken bond of respect and care for one another. The common goal of arriving to America to start a new life and to be able to have the opportunity to realize our dreams was enough to keep us all safe.

As chance would have it, I had the fortune to meet a girl by the name of Barbora. She, like myself, was young and traveling alone. We immediately became friends and shared many hours discussing our new lives. We envisioned our perfect homes, our handsome husbands, and our chubby-cheeked children as we reveled in the wonders of the land of possibility.

Finally, after days that felt like months, the ships crew announced that we would soon be reaching Ellis Island. From the boat, I cannot begin to describe what I saw. I felt that I was looking at a photograph—there, in the distance I could see the Statue of Liberty bearing her torch of freedom and promise. To many people today, the Statue of Liberty does not quite hold the same significance that it did for Barbora and I. Barbora let out an excited squeal and proceeded to hug me while we both jumped up and down on the deck, unable to express our joy in a mature manner. We could both feel our homesickness and regrets quickly dissipate. That statue was truly a symbol for us—in that statue we saw our new lives blazing before us, calling us to the coast of New York.

However, that joy was short-lived. As soon as people began to realize that the journey would soon come to an end, a sense of dangerous restlessness began to permeate the air on deck. People began to form lines discreetly, hoping to be the first off the boat to become American citizens. People then began to push and swear at one another, vowing that they had been in line first. The tension steadily escalated until a member of the ship's crew promptly knocked a particularly obnoxious passenger out cold. It was certainly enough to show that calm would be maintained.

Once the boat docked, we all slowly filed off the boat, gaping in wonder at the sights and bustle surrounding us. Activity was everywhere. Groups of people were being herded like cattle from one area of the dock to the next. Barbora and I gripped hands, determined not to become separated. Simply getting off the dock seemed to be the first hurdle to becoming an American citizen.

After hours of waiting in line, filling out paperwork, and speaking to translators, Barbora and I were finally free to leave and go our separate ways. We had the papers in our hands that proclaimed us citizens of the United States! We were ready to fulfill our dreams.

My first task was to locate my cousin, Elizabeta. She had left Lithuania several months ago. I planned to stay with her and help her take care of the children and clean house. Locating an apartment in New York would be no easy task. My most pressing problem was that I knew no English with the exception of "hello" and "thank you." I literally could not ask for directions. The feelings of helplessness and fright began to crowd out any logical thinking. I could not believe that I had neglected to think of this problem beforehand. I felt tears begin to bite at the backs of my eyes, trying to force themselves out. Among a mass of hundreds of people rushing up and down the city sidewalk, I could not have felt more alone in the world. I thought of Barbora—probably sitting safely at her aunt's house, treating them to stories of her journey to America. The frightened tears continued to taunt me with their eminent overflow.

After finally resigning myself to the fact that I would have to figure out something, I sat down on a park bench to try to devise a plan of attack. Out of the three dollars I had with me, I decided that maybe this problem would best be solved with a bag of hot, buttery popcorn. The treat did indeed help to calm my nervous mind, and I decided that I would have to try to find someone who spoke Lithuanian. If I could do that, maybe I could find my cousin's house. I sat on the curb, mulling over this with my popcorn, finished off the last few bites, and wiped my greasy hands on my skirt. I stood up, ready to face the next challenge that would come my way.

I began walking down the street on a mission. As fortune would have it, I encountered a man I had met earlier on the boat. He was coming to America with his two young sons in the hope of opening his own restaurant. I rushed up to him, speaking much too quickly and frantically for him to understand even remotely what I had said. He calmed me down, and I repeated my words more slowly. After he understood my problem, he gave me directions. I was so grateful finally to have a concrete location to find, that the built-up tears from several hours ago managed to find themselves running down my cheeks. He could not suppress a chuckle as he marveled at my state. However, he was a gentleman and did not make me feel any more ashamed of myself than I already was. He kindly patted my hand and said that he was sure my cousin was anxiously awaiting my arrival and that I had best be on my way. I smiled through my embarrassed sniffles and thanked him again for his help.

Now that I knew which direction I needed to go, I felt that I could admire New York instead of remain in a state of perpetual fright. I marveled at the buildings, the numerous shops, and restaurants. Most of all, I was amazed at the sheer amount of people. As I began to realize what my new life would entail, a flicker of excitement began to bubble up in my stomach. This incredible city, this wealth of energy and opportunity, was to be mine. I smiled as I gamboled down the sidewalk, thinking of my parents. The opportunity that they had given me would not go to waste—I would make them so proud.

Statue of *What?*

"Welcome to America!"
She seemed to shout across the deep blue sea.
"Here you will find wealth, opportunity, a second chance!"
Her voice was so strong, so powerful
It managed to filter into all corners of the world.
No matter how far, people heard it and thought,
"I want opportunity, a better life,
I will follow that voice."
And so they came by the thousands,
Lured by that promise that came from oceans away,
Lured by visions of wealth and success.
And then they saw her—
Standing so proud and magnificent

The bearer of the gospel they held so dear.
Off the boat they came,
Ready to realize their promised dreams.
"Where do I begin? I'm ready to work!"
"I don't hire no Irish."
"You mean you don't speak English?"
"Go back to where you came from!"
The promises have turned to angry shouts
Dreams dashed to the ground in a million pieces
Barely enough to survive,
Feed the children cabbage water.
"Welcome to the land of dreams," she still goads
Sending her message across the water.

1 What common theme do both the story and poem emphasize?
  A People always want more wealth and goods.
  B People fear going to new, undiscovered places.
  C People will always try to realize the American Dream.
  D An individual will always have conflict with society's expectations.

2 Although the story has a tone of _____ , the poem has a tone of
_____ .
  A hope, defeat
  B inspiration, neglect
  C misery, joy
  D excitement, anxiety

3 In the poem, the line "Dreams dashed to the ground in a million pieces" is an example of
  A metaphor
  B imagery
  C hyperbole
  D personification

4 In the story, the Statue of Liberty is a symbol of _____ . In the
poem, it is a symbol of _____ .
  A trust, hatred
  B opportunity, dishonesty
  C safety, danger
  D freedom, captivity

5 Both the poem and story focus on the experience of the _____ .
  A Lithuanian
  B immigrant
  C Statue of Liberty
  D worker

Explanation of Correct Responses

1. **C** Your historical knowledge is crucial in being able to identify the correct choice. If you know that throughout the early 1900s America became home to a large number of European immigrants, you would recognize that all of these people were leaving their home countries to realize the American Dream. Unfortunately, not all of the people who came to America were able to obtain what they had hoped. They were met with prejudice and disdain from other American citizens, and they soon discovered that were going to be underpaid for their labor. Although many immigrants were indeed able to make a very successful life for themselves and their families, many did not. You should know that the quest for the American Dream is a very prominent theme found in literature.

2. **A** After you have read both pieces, you should quickly be able to identify that even though they deal with the same theme, they are saying two very different things about the American Dream. While the young woman in the story is hopeful and believes that America will enable her to realize her dreams, the narrator of the poem gives us a much dimmer view on the American Dream. The people in this poem have come to America with the same hopes and dreams as the girl in the story. However, they realize that they will be unable to meet their dreams due to different reasons, such as not being able to speak English or because they belong to a particular race or nationality. This once again emphasizes how important it is to have some degree of historical knowledge when you read. In order to see the contrast between the story and the poem, you need to know that people have had very different experiences while trying to realize the American Dream.

3. **C** The idea of something breaking into a million pieces is an example of hyperbole because it is overly exaggerated. Something probably would not break into a million pieces. It might break into three, a hundred, or four, but breaking into as many pieces as a million is a little over the top. Remember that a writer typically uses hyperbole to make an important statement. In this case, the reader needs to realize how harshly the immigrants' dreams have been destroyed. They are so destroyed that the dreams have shattered into a million pieces, becoming completely irreparable.

4. **B** The story clearly shows that the Statue of Liberty represents a concept of opportunity, a new life, financial success, and so on. Everything that the Statue of Liberty represents for the young girl in the story is positive and promising. However, in the poem, the statue's symbolism changes into something much different. The Statue of Liberty has become a symbol of dishonesty and a symbol that sends people false hope and promises. The last lines of the poem state, "'Welcome to the land of dreams,' she still goads / Sending her message across the water." One of the key words in this line is "goad." To goad someone means to taunt or tease. Based on the narrator's point of view in this poem, the Statue of Liberty is teasing about America being the land of dreams. Therefore, the Statue of Liberty is sending out a false message to the immigrants and becomes a symbol of dishonesty.

5. **B** This question is once again asking you to detect similar themes and ideas that appear throughout historical literature. Both pieces focus on the experiences of immigrants. The Statue of Liberty is mentioned in both pieces. However, the focus is of course on the people who see the Statue of Liberty and are arriving in America. When you get a question that asks you to analyze the experience of a particular group, you need to select an answer that reflects a broad range of experiences. For example, all immigrants to the United States in the early 1900s probably had to learn a new language. Each group of immigrants also faced different challenges and obstacles adapting to a new country. The ability to present different perspectives on thematic issues such as the American Dream is what makes the historical context of literature so valuable.

Let's look at another sample piece taken from a different point in American history.

| Directions: | Read the following short story and then answer questions 1–4. |

Equality for All

"I have a dream." What an amazingly simplistic sentence yet how it managed to shake the country to its very foundation. There have been few people who have managed to shape our world and our views on humanity like Martin Luther King Jr. He was a man who captivated millions and a man whose voice could grab you and rattle your very soul. He was a man that led thousands on the path to equality for civil rights. I was lucky enough to know this man and be a part of his incredible journey toward freedom for the human race.

That was one of the most amazing things about Dr. King—his journey toward freedom. He did not want equal rights just for African Americans; he wanted equal rights for humans. He never believed that one race was better than or entitled to more than another. He simply saw us all as humans. I believe that his most admirable trait was that he had the amazing ability to measure a man based on his integrity and behavior, never on his appearance. Many people found a calm in Dr. King, an acceptance for who they were and how they could best benefit society. He embraced all humans: black, white, or brown.

Even to this day, I find myself hearing his words and advice echo in my mind, so many years down the road. His death was so incredibly tragic yet so expected. How can a man be safe knowing that he is forcing society to analyze its ills, forcing itself to recognize the hatred and anger that it has allowed to exist? There will always be someone who will be so frightened by those who speak the truth that he or she will feel compelled to eliminate a threat, especially through violent means. It takes such immense courage, a total abandonment of worry for one's self, to do the things that Dr. King did. He was a hero in every sense of the word. His bravery and wisdom have managed to impact even those today.

1 Martin Luther King Jr. was a leader for the
   A Suffrage Movement
   B Unionized Workers Movement
   C Civil Rights Movement
   D Affirmative Action Movement

2 Martin Luther King Jr. died because of a(n)
   A assassination
   B heart attack
   C brain tumor
   D car accident

3 According to the essay, Dr. King's greatest strength was his ability to
   A give moving speeches to large audiences
   B appreciate people based on their inner qualities
   C not worry about his own personal safety
   D have a courageous dream for the human race

4 During the time period in which Martin Luther King Jr. lived, which of the following would be a dominant subject found in literature?

A social inequality

B famous world leaders

C combating slavery

D prejudice and racism

Explanation of Correct Responses

1. **C** Martin Luther King Jr.'s name is synonymous with the Civil Rights Movement. If, for example, you had never heard of Martin Luther King Jr. before, several contextual clues throughout the essay might give you some hints. For example, the essay mentions that Dr. King did not just fight for rights for African Americans. Instead, he fought for rights for humans. However, the contextual clues may help you piece together only so much. You must have some type of historical foundation when reading this type of material. As mentioned earlier, the AIMS exam will not ask you to answer extremely detailed historical questions, but they want to know if you have basic historical knowledge. If you had never heard about Dr. King or the Civil Rights Movement before, you would have difficulty understanding the significance of the essay.

2. **A** This essay definitely contains clues that should lead you to the correct response. Of course, you may not need clues. You may simply know that Dr. King was assassinated. However, if you need help to figure that out, the following statement from the essay should assist you. "His death was so incredibly tragic yet so expected. How can a man be safe knowing that he is forcing society to analyze its ills, forcing itself to recognize the hatred and anger that it has allowed to exist?" For example, if Dr. King died of a car accident, how could that be considered expected? Also, the reference to a man being safe certainly indicates that his life could be put in danger and could be at risk of assassination.

    His death is also important historically because it shows what a brave leader Dr. King was. As mentioned in the essay, Dr. King was talking about equal rights and equality during a time when many people believed that African Americans were inferior and did not deserve the same treatment as Caucasians. Unfortunately, some people disagreed with Dr. King to the extent that they believed they should kill him so that he could no longer spread his message of equality.

3. **B** All of the choices listed certainly provide reasons why Dr. King was such a strong leader. However, the author states that Dr. King's greatest strength was his ability to judge people on character, not race. Make sure that you answer these types of questions according to what the essay or story states, not based on your own particular opinion.

4. **D** Once again, this question is asking you to see the dominant issues and themes that a particular time period had to cope with. In the time period in which Dr. King was making the greatest impact, society was battling with racism and prejudice between African Americans and Caucasians. Racism and prejudice affect many people. Therefore numerous pieces of literature, artwork, and movies have been created based on this idea. When the AIMS exam asks you these types of questions, they want to make sure that you can understand how so many famous people and works of art can come out of one time period.

WHY CULTURAL KNOWLEDGE?

The AIMS exam will not only ask you about your historical knowledge in conjunction with literature, it will also ask you about your cultural knowledge in conjunction with literature. For example, in Arizona, a lot of literature relays the experience of the Mexican American. People who live in Arizona can probably get more meaning from this type of literature than someone who is unfamiliar with Mexican culture. Mexican culture is a large part of the state, and many residents of Arizona are familiar with that influence. However, people who live in Arizona may not be as familiar with Cuban culture, for example. On the other hand, people who grow up in Florida might be much more familiar with Cuban culture.

The purpose of the AIMS exam tests this concept of culture to see how well you can understand the influences that different cultures have on the books we read, the art we see, and the food we eat. America is a blend of many different and dynamic cultures that make us the country we are today. In order to be a well-educated individual, you need to see the value of these different cultures and the experiences that we all have as American citizens partaking in the cultures that influence us every day. As you read the following short story, think about this issue of different cultures. There will be several practice questions after the story.

Directions: Read the following short story and then answer questions 1–5.

"We Shall Endure"

"*Hija*, you're going to miss the bus again!"

I fumbled with the laces of my sneakers, rushing to intertwine the limp strings.

"I'm almost ready!" I called back to my frazzled mother.

I raced through the kitchen, scooping up my backpack and hoping that I had everything I needed for the day. I quickly gave my mom and baby brother Jose, who was perfectly balanced on my mom's hip, a peck on the cheek. Then I scurried through the door, sprinting after the already receding bus.

"Wait! Stop, please stop!" I shouted at the rear red lights of the bus. My feet pounded the sidewalk, and my arms pumped through the cool morning air.

"*Hola* Isabella!" Mrs. Alvarez called from her lawn. I quickly glanced over at the warm voice and did my best to respond politely.

"*Buenos días*, Mrs. Alvarez," I managed to gasp out.

"You'd better hurry—that bus is picking up speed."

Nodding in frustrated agreement, I charged ahead, turning Mrs. Alvarez into a blur.

Two sprinted blocks later, the bus finally came to a halt. Exhausted, I put both hands on the side of the bus, choking on much needed oxygen.

"Isabella, it looks like you could use a new alarm clock. How was your morning workout?" taunted John.

I looked up in annoyance at the bus driver.

"You mean to tell me that you saw me running like a *loca* and you didn't stop!" I cried out in disbelief. John did not say anything, and I tried to maintain my scowl. However, his twinkling, joyful eyes quickly killed any previous annoyance. "I mean really, would it have killed you to stop?" I asked tiredly as I boarded the bus.

"It's not my fault you can't manage to get anywhere on time."

"Yeah, yeah, I'm working on it."

I worked my way to the middle of the bus and slid into an empty seat. Appreciating a moment devoid of raw lungs and a pounding heart, I leaned my head upon the cool window and closed my eyes. Today was certainly going to be exciting. Right after school, I had plans to go to St. Mary's Hospital for my first day as a student intern. Ever since I was a child, I knew that I wanted to be a doctor. I would conduct "surgery" on all of my dolls, analyzing their stuffing and making critical decisions. Stuffing transplants were my specialty. Now I was going to get the opportunity to shadow a nurse for several months and actually see someone working in the medical profession. I was ready to impress them and ready to learn a ton.

Several hours later, I found myself bored as a rock in biology class. Mr. Thomas was blabbering about amoebas, and I could barely force myself to stay awake. My mind began to drift. I pictured myself in a white coat ten years from now. I was giving orders to nurses, demanding high-tech surgical instruments from assistants, and driving a Mercedes. My stomach began to bubble as I pictured myself as the first doctor in my family. I was not just the first doctor in my family but the first college graduate and, most importantly, the first *female* high school graduate. My mother had given birth to me when she was seventeen and chose to drop out of school. Even though my mom never finished high school, she is one of the smartest people I know. She knows how to keep Jose from crying. She can keep our entire family in line. She is also prepared for any physical disaster, whether it may be a skinned knee or an amputated limb. If I can one day make tortillas like her, I will feel like I have mastered her cooking. She can do a million and one things simultaneously, like feed Jose, make fifty perfect tortillas, and help me with my homework. She is amazing. I hope that I can do half the things that she can do by the time I die.

As much as I want to be a doctor, my mother wants it twenty times more. She always makes sure that I do my homework and stands over my shoulder half the night while my nose is pushed in a book. She says that I am too smart to waste my days in the kitchen with a baby on my hip. I hate when she says that because I do not think she knows how much I admire her. Anyway, I know she wants the best for me and that she wants me to see things that go beyond our neighborhood.

"Miss Ruiz? Miss Ruiz!"

My daydreaming fog was soon destroyed by the nasally interruptions of Mr. Thomas. I realized that he must have been asking me an amoeba-related question, which I had neglected to hear.

"I'm sorry, Mr. Thomas. Could you please repeat the question?" A thousand faces turned in my direction, and I could feel the top of my head grow hot.

"Maybe we should pay attention next time. Maybe what I'm teaching up here is actually valuable. Maybe it'd be nice if a student would feel it worth her while to take an interest in my class."

Mr. Thomas had a tendency to be a bit dramatic. "I really am sorry. What was the question?" I asked again.

"Isabella, that ship has sailed. Morgan, perhaps you could tell me what we call the center of an amoeba."

I shrunk into my seat, feeling so embarrassed. Usually, I was on top of things in biology class. "It must be that internship," I thought to myself. I was so excited that keeping my mind on anything else was hard.

After what felt like five hundred years, the bell indicating the end of sixth period finally rang. I bolted out of my desk, maneuvering my way through the crowded hallways. I was supposed to be at the hospital at exactly 3:00. The hospital was about a fifteen-minute walk from the school, and it was now 2:30. I should have been able to make it there in time without any problems. However, I wanted to make sure that I was not a second late. Above all else, I did not want to make a bad first impression.

I walked briskly down the street, enjoying the cool air after being stuck in a hot, stuffy classroom all day. I breathed in deeply, letting the air clear out my apprehension. I was so afraid that the people at the hospital would not like me, would not think I was smart enough, or would not like the way I dressed. I could think of a million things that they would not like. I took another deep breath and realized that I had arrived at the hospital. I always marveled at hospitals. The organization, the planning, and of course the life saving that went on inside that building amazed me. The cleanliness and sterilization seemed to ooze out of the building itself, creating a bubble of sanitary air that completely enclosed the outside of the building.

"Well, here goes nothing," I thought to myself as I stepped inside the calmly lit lobby. A cool draft rose up to meet my face as soon as I stepped inside, bringing with it smells of rubbing alcohol mingling with faint odors of cafeteria food. I spotted a woman sitting at an information desk and thought that would probably be the best place to start to figure out where I needed to go. As I approached her desk, the woman smiled warmly at me and removed her glasses.

"Can I help you with something?" she asked politely.

"Yes, please. My name is Isabella Ruiz, and I am wondering where I need to go for the high school student intern program."

"Well, welcome to the program first of all. Let's see, where do you need to go?" A perfectly manicured fingernail scanned down a list of names. "Aha! Here you are. You will be reporting to Judith Drake on floor twelve, room ten. Just go up that elevator over your shoulder, and follow the signs to room ten."

"Thank you so much for your help."

"Good luck," she smiled encouragingly.

I boarded the elevator, my heart pounding in my ears. The elevator came to a gentle bouncing stop at floor twelve, and the doors opened with a soundless glide. I looked around the waiting room that was tastefully decorated with fake plants and muted, calming colors. I saw the signs pointing me toward room ten.

When I got off the elevator, finding room ten seemed to be a fairly simplistic task. However, the room was not where the sign said it was. I must have gone in circles for a good ten minutes, coming no closer to finding the room. My palms began to sweat. I realized that I was within two minutes of officially being late. I broke out into a run, frantic that I would blow this opportunity before it even began. While rounding a corner, I promptly crashed into an elderly nurse who had her nose buried in a patient's file.

"Oh no! I'm so sorry," I cried as I scrambled to collect the files that had exploded from her arms like confetti upon impact.

"That's quite all right," she replied as she began scooping up her files. "Where are you going in such a hurry?"

"Well, I'm trying to find room ten to meet with Judith Drake."

"That doesn't sound right. Who told you to go to room ten?"

"The lady at the information desk in the lobby," I replied nervously, thinking that now I was really going to be late.

"I'm certain that you're not going to Judith's office. I would go to room twenty on the sixth floor. You'll find what you need there," she answered confidently.

"Thank you so much!" I called over my shoulder as I raced down the hallway to reach the elevator. I was fuming. How could that lady give me the wrong information! This was such an important day, and it was getting off to a horrible start. Now I was going to have to explain why I was late, why I could not find the room, and so on and so on. My eyes grew hot, and I felt tears knocking at the back of my eyelids.

"Finally!" The elevator had reached floor six, and I squeezed out of the doors as soon as there was enough space to let me through. I rushed down the hallway and immediately found room twenty. I peeked through the glass in the door and could see about ten young women sitting in the room, listening to a tall, blond woman standing at the front, gesturing with her hands. I turned the doorknob slowly, trying to make as little noise as possible. I tiptoed into the room with a sheepish smile on my face.

"Can I help you?" the tall woman asked.

"I'm so sorry I'm late," I began to explain. "I had the wrong room number so I came here as quickly as I could."

"That's all right. Go ahead and take seat."

I slid into a seat, the upholstery making a squealing sound that seemed to echo through the silence of the room. I smiled to try and cover up my red face.

"Now let's continue with orientation," the woman began. "Working at any level at a health facility is an extraordinary responsibility."

I settled into my chair, soaking up every word that the woman said. However, as I expected the woman to continue, a Hispanic woman stood up and repeated what the blond woman had just said but in Spanish. I looked in confusion around the room and realized that there must have been several girls who did not speak English. The Hispanic woman finished translating and looked back at the other woman, giving her a nod to let her know it was OK to continue.

"One of the most important elements of a successful hospital is its cleanliness," she continued. "Our job here is to make people healthy again. We cannot do our job if there are germs or contaminates posing a threat to our patients."

The other woman translated appropriately, and several women nodded in agreement. I thought that this was certainly an odd way to begin an orientation for interns. However, I figured that she must be emphasizing the importance of keeping things clean and to keep the patients away from germs.

"With that in mind, your job is of extreme importance here at our facility. The success of our patient care begins with you. If you neglect to disinfect a bathroom or do not properly follow procedure to wash linens, then the doctors and nurses here cannot give their best medical service."

As the Hispanic woman was translating, I began to realize what was happening. This was not an orientation for student interns. This was an orientation for custodial staff. I looked around the room more closely and realized that every person in this room, with the exception of the woman giving instructions, was Hispanic. Then a much harsher realization set in—the woman on the twelfth floor. She had been the one who told me to come here. She did not even know what I was looking for. She just *assumed* that I belonged with the other Hispanic employees. She did not think to assume that I belonged in the student intern room. She thought I was here to learn how to scrub a toilet.

This time the hot tears were not lightly tapping at the back of my eyelids. Instead, they were pounding. I knew I had to get out of that room before the dam broke loose. I pushed myself up from my chair, kept my eyes on the floor, and hurried through the door. I needed to find a restroom.

I crashed through the bathroom door and quickly locked myself in a stall. I got there not a moment too soon because the rivers of tears were soon cascading down my face. I lightly beat my forehead against the steel of the stall, shaking my head. How was I supposed to succeed when there were people in this world who thought I was made for picking up someone else's mess? Why didn't

that woman see the next world-renowned brain surgeon instead? How could someone be so ignorant? My first thought was to hunt that woman down and give her a piece of my mind. I would just kindly correct her. I would inform her that I was currently ranked in the top 2 percent of my high school class and had already been awarded several large college scholarships. Really, in the end, did any of that even matter? Was my future boss even going to care that I had graduated at the top of my class? Would he or she just see me walk through the door and put a toilet scrubber into my hand? Giving up would be so much easier. I would have no more nights filled with homework, no more stressing over grades. However, suddenly a quote that my English teacher had written on the board appeared in my mind, "We draw our strength from the very despair in which we have been forced to live. We shall endure." My teacher told us that it was spoken by Cesar Chavez, a great Hispanic leader. I began to think that if he could fulfill his dreams and, more importantly, help others, couldn't I do the same thing? My life was what I was going to make it. I was not going to let ignorance deter me from my path of success.

I wiped my eyes dry and washed my face with a paper towel. My eyes were a little swollen. However, I gave my reflection my best smile, and my confidence began to return. I gave myself one more smile and knew what I had to do next. I had to find floor twelve, room ten—even if I was going to be a little late.

1 The elderly nurse directs Isabella to the wrong room because Isabella is _____.
   A a student
   B Hispanic
   C a female
   D American

2 Which of the following inferences can be made about Isabella's family?
   A They have not obtained a high degree of education.
   B They do not support Isabella's dreams and goals.
   C They want Isabella to work right after she graduates.
   D They want Isabella to get married after school.

3 Which of the following themes does the story most emphasize?
   A The importance of obtaining a good education
   B The rewards of accomplishing goals and dreams
   C The dangers found in racial and cultural stereotyping
   D The value of a strong and supportive family

4 According to Isabella's attitude at the end of the story, which of the following would be the next likely event to occur?

  A She would go home to her mother.

  B She would go talk to Judith Drake.

  C She would go yell at the elderly nurse.

  D She would continue to cry in the bathroom.

5 The elderly nurse makes the mistake of _____ Isabella.

  A analyzing

  B helping

  C hating

  D judging

Explanation of Correct Responses

1. **B** When the elderly nurse encounters Isabella, she sees that Isabella is Hispanic and automatically assumes that Isabella is supposed to be in training with the custodial staff. She does not take the time to ask where Isabella is supposed to be going or why she is at the hospital. Unfortunately, many people make judgments about one another as soon as they lay eyes on a person. In this story, the woman is, of course, wrong in her judgment and proceeds to hurt Isabella's feelings deeply.

2. **A** At one point in the story, Isabella mentions how excited she is that she is going to be the first female high school graduate from her family. This tells the reader that not many members of her family have had the opportunity to pursue their educations. Isabella, however, plans to continue her schooling well past high school and one day hopes to become a doctor.

3. **C** This story focuses on stereotyping individuals based on race or culture. Unfortunately, human beings have the tendency to place people into groups and to label those groups. Once those groups have been labeled, stereotypes are developed. Individuals then assume that all people from a particular group are going to behave in a certain way. For example, think of the groups that exist at your high school. How are the jocks supposed to act? How are the Goths supposed to act? How are the cheerleaders supposed to act? Once we begin assuming that a person is supposed to meet certain criteria because he or she comes from a certain group, we do not give ourselves a chance to meet or get to know that person. Imagine if the nurse had simply asked Isabella why she was trying to find Judith Drake. Instead, however, the nurse jumped to an incorrect conclusion because she fell into the trap of a stereotype. She assumed that since Isabella was Hispanic, there was no conceivable way that Isabella was supposed to be part of the student intern program.

4. **B** Even though Isabella is upset, she does not let the nurse ruin her original intent. Isabella clearly plans to find Judith Drake, explain why she was late, and proceed to be a part of the intern program. Isabella is certainly frustrated by what the nurse did to her, but she is not going to let it deter her from her goals. Isabella thinks of the importance of pressing on and exits the bathroom confident and ready to continue pursing her dreams.

5. **D** As mentioned before, the nurse simply makes the mistake of judging Isabella. She does not consider that her judgment could be wrong. Once again, this question shows how dangerous and ignorant individuals can be if they judge someone before getting to know that person.

CHAPTER REVIEW

Keep in mind the following key points when reading historical or cultural literature:

1. Use clues that you can find throughout the story, essay, poem, and so on to help you figure out the historical context (time period) in which the text is taking place.
2. Determine the theme based on the historical or cultural context. For example, if you are reading a piece focused on the Civil Rights Movement, the theme should be focused on racism, prejudice, or equality.
3. Look for clues to help you understand what specific culture a story may be focusing on. Does the story integrate words that are from another language? Does the story give details concerning cultural traditions?

REMEMBER

History and culture are deeply intertwined with literature. You cannot neglect either when reading literature. Keep in mind that great historical events are what often inspire people to write in the first place.

Chapter 5

Informational and Persuasive Text

P eople read for many reasons. We read for entertainment, for instructions, and for directions, just to name a few. However, one of the most important reasons why we read is to obtain information. Think of all the tasks that you do during the day in which you read to gather some sort of information. When your teacher writes your homework or upcoming test dates on the board, you are reading for information. When you research a topic for an English paper, you read for information. As mentioned earlier, the AIMS exam intends to measure your ability to comprehend several different types of text. The purpose is to make sure that not only can you understand a fictional story but that you can also understand an instruction manual, product warranty information, or an editorial. This chapter will cover how to answer questions specific to informational and persuasive text.

WHAT IS INFORMATIONAL TEXT?

Simply put, informational text is written material that provides you with information about a subject. Unlike fiction, informational text does not typically contain figurative language, plot, or interesting characters. The purpose is simply to give you the needed information as quickly as possible. Imagine trying to get through an instruction manual that used character dialogue to deliver instructions. That would not only confuse but would probably frustrate you. You simply want the instructions, not plot development or characters.

Questions that focus on informational text will typically be straightforward. As long as you read carefully, you should not have problems comprehending the general message behind a piece of informational text. Just remember to read carefully because the reading may get technical and somewhat dense.

The AIMS exam will ask you to evaluate several different types of informational text, ranging from business letters to license agreements. Keep in mind that these types of text tend to be a little more dense as far as the reading is concerned. To be honest, they typically do not make for very exciting reading. When was the last time you read an instruction manual for fun? However, being able to understand this type of text is important and makes everyday life much simpler. Read the following sample of a business memo.

MEMO

To: Marketing Employees of Denim Designs Inc.
From: Alex Cortez, Head of Marketing
Subject: February 6th Sales Meeting
Date: February 1, 2006

The meeting scheduled for Monday, February 6th, has been moved to Tuesday, February 14th. The location will still be in the conference room on the first floor. Please come prepared with ideas concerning the new ad campaign for "Deep Blues," our new line of denim clothing. We look forward to seeing you next week and anxiously await your ideas concerning our new products.

After an individual has read the memo, he or she will immediately know that the date of an important meeting has been changed. The reader is also told that the meeting topic will remain the same. There are no colorful descriptions or riveting plotlines. However, the memo serves an important function by telling an employee quickly and simply what is occurring at the workplace. Therefore, this type of text would be considered informational.

A good rule of thumb for informational text is to ask yourself the classic "5 W's"—who, what, where, when, and why. A good piece of informational text should answer all five of those questions within the first paragraph. For example, a good newspaper article immediately informs the reader about the most important aspects of the story or event. The sample memo effectively deals with these fundamental questions. The "what" is that the meeting has been changed. The "where" is the conference room. The "when" is February 14th and so on.

People do not read informational text for entertainment. They read it to gather important information quickly.

Directions: Read the following and then answer questions 1–2.

LICENSE AGREEMENT

This is a legal agreement between the user and Pixel Performance Software, Inc.

BY USING THE SOFTWARE, YOU ACKOWLEDGE THAT YOU HAVE READ AND ACCEPT ALL OF THE TERMS AND CONDITIONS OF THIS AGREEMENT. IF YOU DO NOT AGREE TO THE TERMS OUTLINED IN THIS AGREEMENT, PROMPTLY RETURN THE SOFTWARE.

LIMITED LICENSE: This software is to be used only for personal use. The software may not be reproduced in any way. This software may not be installed on multiple computers or networked between various computers.

COPYRIGHT: Titles, patents, and copyrights are the sole property of Pixel Performance Software. This software may not be altered in any way and any alterations will be in direct violation of California State Law 205-89715.

LIMITED WARRANTY: This software is guaranteed for ninety (90) days from the date of purchase. Pixel Performance will issue a full refund for defective merchandise; however, malfunctions caused by the user will not be issued a refund.

For questions or concerns regarding this agreement, please call 1-800-265-8570.

1 Based on the layout, what is the most important function of the agreement?

    A to warn the user of possible software defects

    B to protect Performance Pixel Software

    C to provide instructions for installation

    D to protect the user of the software

2 Which of the following may a user NOT do to the software?

    A return the software

    B reproduce the software

    C install the software

    D use the software for personal use

Explanation of Correct Responses

1. **B** Any sort of legal agreement or document almost always serves to protect the company. The agreement is not interested in protecting the buyer or user. Rather, its sole purpose is to ensure the legal rights of the company.

2. **B** Based on violations that the agreement lists, it is clearly unacceptable to reproduce the software. This answer can be found simply by carefully reading the text.

Although warranties and license agreements are not the most interesting reading, you may encounter one on the exam. Read carefully. If you are unsure of a particular answer, go back to the reading selection to locate information for correct responses.

Keep in mind that informational text aims to get a concept or idea across to a reader with as little "extra" as possible. Let's continue to analyze informational text and answer some practice questions. Explanations for correct answers will follow each piece of text.

| Directions: | Read the following and then answer questions 1–5. |

CALL FOR ACTORS, DANCERS, AND STAGEHANDS!!

The **Northwest Theater Company** is currently looking for individuals who would like to be a part of the upcoming production of William Shakespeare's *"A Midsummer Night's Dream."*

We need the following:

- 10 female actors between ages of 15–30
- 15 male actors between ages 10–50
- Numerous backstage positions to assist with set construction, lighting, costumes, and makeup

Auditions will be held **April 20th** at the **Northwest Playhouse** on 5324 Cherry St.

Please come prepared with a selected monologue. If you have questions, please contact Julian Ross at (123) 456-7890.

1 Which of the following positions does the theater company NOT need?
   A stagehands
   B directors
   C actors
   D dancers

2 Based on the design of the flyer, what information is the most important?
   A The play to be produced is *A Midsummer's Night Dream*.
   B Actors, dancers, and stagehands are needed for the production.
   C Actors must come prepared with a selected monologue.
   D The playhouse is located at 5324 Cherry St.

3 Based on the design of the flyer, the reader knows to focus their attention first on parts of the flyer that are
   A in large, bold lettering
   B arranged in lists
   C in small, italic lettering
   D are marked with an asterisk

4 The flyer states that _____ female actors are needed for the production.

   A 20

   B 30

   C 15

   D 10

5 If actors wish to audition, they should come prepared with a

   A costume

   B dance routine

   C script

   D monologue

Explanation of Correct Responses

1. **B** The flyer advertises the need for stagehands (choice A), actors (choice C), and actors (choice D). There is no mention of needing a director. Therefore, you can determine that choice B is the correct response.

2. **B** This question asks you to analyze how the layout of the flyer contributes to your understanding of the information. When information needs to get relayed quickly and efficiently, visual organization becomes very important. Just a quick glance at the flyer immediately tells you what the information is about. The heading of the flyer is in big, bold lettering, drawing your eye to that information first. Therefore, you realize that the most crucial information is that the theater company is currently looking to fill openings. The other information is important. However, by the way the flyer is organized, you know that the heading contains the most valuable information.

3. **A** This question is very similar to the last question. It is simply asking you to analyze how the visual layout of the flyer helps the reader to understand the information. As soon as your eye is drawn to a particular aspect of the flyer, your brain automatically registers that you are looking at important information. If you come across a question similar to this on test day, just ask yourself, "Logically, what part of this flyer should I notice first?"

4. **D** Once again, you are looking at a very straightforward question. All you have to do is carefully look over the flyer to locate the correct answer.

5. **D** This answer has the same rationale as question 4. Simply look over the flyer to locate the correct answer.

With informational text, the best thing you can do is simply pay attention to what you are reading. Of course, if you cannot recall the answer to a question, look over the material again to locate the correct response.

Analyzing Diagrams

Informational text can also be relayed by a diagram. This is a very effective way to get nuts-and-bolts information across to an individual. It also lets a person visually organize information. By simply looking at a diagram, a person can immediately interpret information. One of the things the exam will likely ask you to do is to complete missing segments of a particular diagram. As you analyze the following examples, several tips will be given that are specific to diagram interpretation.

When the exam asks you to analyze a diagram, you are most likely going to be asked to fill in a missing component of the diagram based on a short reading. Diagrams may include webs, flow charts, Venn diagrams, and others. Completing a missing portion of the diagram forces you to make inferences about what you have read and to think logically about what would fit based on the context of the diagram. Read the sample paragraph below.

One of the places that I feel I must visit before I die is Hawaii. I have heard so much about Hawaii and have seen such beautiful pictures that not experiencing that tropical paradise would be a tragedy. To be able to have the chance to hike in a rain forest, see a live volcano, and to go surfing sounds like the most unbelievable vacation ever. Some people may argue that there are better places to go. In my opinion, though, nothing could beat pristine beaches and crystal clear waters. I look forward to the day when I can actually make my dream a reality.

Complete the chart below:

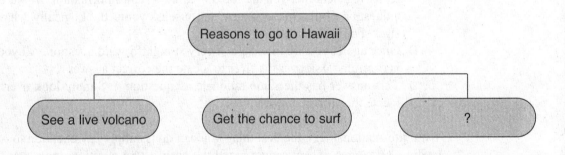

Based upon the reading, the chart should logically be completed with, "Hike in a rain forest." Read the next sample paragraph to continue practicing with diagrams.

The best movies I have ever seen would have to be "Zoolander" and "Napoleon Dyna-mite." I really enjoy a good comedy, and I think that both of these movies are absolutely hilarious. They both have great main characters that have very memorable personal-ities, and they both have great lines. However, even though both of these movies are in the comedy genre, they are distinctive in their own ways. For example, "Zoolander" focuses on the world of male models, while "Napoleon Dynamite" focuses on the world of high school. Also, although both movies have great plot lines, they are very differ-ent. "Zoolander" takes the audience through a mad caper where male models are actually trained assassins. The main character, "Zoolander," must be prevented from killing the prime minister of Malaysia. On the other hand, Napoleon needs to figure out a way to get his friend elected class president. They are both great comedic movies, but they have several elements that set them apart.

Complete the diagram below based on the reading:

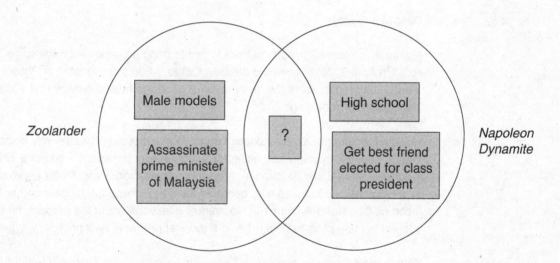

When you evaluate a Venn diagram, you are looking at the similarities and differences between two topics. In this case, you are comparing movies. The similarities between the two movies go in the middle of the diagram, or the overlapping portion of the diagram. The dif-ferences go in their own circles in those portions that do not overlap. Several of the differ-ences are provided, so you must determine what the similarities are between the two movies. Based on the reading, you could fill in the middle of the diagram with something like, "Both comedies" or "Distinctive main characters." Ultimately, the purpose of a Venn diagram is to make the similarities and differences between two concepts visually obvious.

Analyzing Letters

Another type of informational text that you will likely see on the AIMS exam is a business letter. Business letters serve many functions. They may be used to communicate between employees, between companies, or between customers and companies. As in all informational text, the purpose is to relay important information with as little "fluff" as possible. Read the sample business letter below.

Directions: Read the following and then answer questions 1–5.

2720 W. 3rd St.
Phoenix, AZ 85201
April 10, 2006

Mrs. Ella Stilles
Customer Service Manager for Outdoor Fun
1852 South Magnolia Ave.
Chatsworth, CA 91311

Dear Mrs. Stilles:

My name is Renee Torres, and I would like to bring an important issue to your attention. On April 8, 2006, I went to the new Outdoor Fun store located in Phoenix, AZ. I had heard much about the great outdoor gear and helpful service that this store was known for providing.

However, once I arrived at Outdoor Fun to do my shopping, I was sorely disappointed. I spent nearly forty minutes looking for a high-quality backpack, and not a single employee offered any assistance. After much frustration, I was finally approached by a disgruntled employee who behaved as though I was the biggest bother he had faced all day. Not only did he fail to answer questions about the product, he took no interest in attempting to help me find a more appropriate backpack for my needs.

With no help from this employee, I ultimately decided on a pack that felt the most comfortable for my frame. Willing to overlook the first employee's rudeness, I excitedly took my new pack to the cash register. However, as I approached to pay for my pack, I realized that there was no one manning the cash register. I stood around for nearly five minutes before a slow-moving employee finally decided to let me pay for my new purchase. Without any greeting, eye contact, or thank you, I left the store with my new pack and a load of resentment.

Based on the high-quality products that your store provides, I would like to shop at Outdoor Fun again in the future. However, if customer service does not improve, I will gladly take my money to a location that appreciates it.

Thank you for your time,

Renee Torres

Renee Torres

1 The purpose of this letter is to
  A express appreciation
  B issue a complaint
  C explain a purchase
  D evaluate customer service

2 The customer's biggest disappointment about her shopping experience was
  A the quality of the employees' behavior
  B the selection of products available
  C the expensive price of the backpack
  D the quality of the products available

3 The statement, "I stood around for nearly five minutes before a slow-moving employee finally decided to let me pay for my new purchase," reflects a tone of
  A desperation
  B regret
  C enthusiasm
  D sarcasm

4 Based upon the letter, you can infer that Renee will
  A purchase a tent and sleeping bag for her camping
  B never again return to shop at Outdoor Fun
  C return to shop if she receives an apology
  D return her backpack for a full refund

5 The title of the individual receiving this letter is
  A vice president
  B marketing manager
  C advertising executive
  D customer service manager

Explanation of Correct Responses

1. **B** The central purpose of this letter is to complain about the way she was treated during her shopping experience. Renee does explain the purchase of the backpack, but she integrates that detail to show how rudely she was treated.
2. **A** The focus of the letter is certainly the poor customer service she received while shopping. Renee clearly explains that she was impressed with the quality of the products. She just disliked the customer service.
3. **D** The key term in this statement that reflects sarcasm is, "Let me pay for my new purchase." Of course, paying for something is not exactly a privilege. She is angered because five minutes elapse before someone finally decides that taking her money is worth the hassle.
4. **C** Based on the concluding paragraph of this letter, the reader knows that Renee wants to continue shopping at Outdoor Fun because she likes the products they provide. However, it can be inferred that if she does not receive some sort of apology or explanation, she will no longer shop at Outdoor Fun. To answer this question correctly, you must weigh choices B and C. In this case, C is the best answer because the reader knows if the situation is resolved, Renee will continue to be an Outdoor Fun customer.
5. **D** This answer can be found if you pay attention to the heading of the letter. In any business letter, the name of the person receiving the letter, any formal title he or she may have, and the individual's address is always provided at the top.

Directions:	Read the following and then answer questions 1–3.

16581 Running Springs Drive
Flagstaff, AZ 86004
December 20, 2006

Mr. William Nelson
Vice President of Marketing
20368 North West St.
Tucson, AZ 86045

Dear Mr. Nelson:

I wanted to take an opportunity to thank you for the job interview on December 18th. I enjoyed hearing more about the position. Based on the information you gave me, I think that I would fit the position of assistant design manager very well.

The guided tour of the facilities was very impressive, and I would be honored to work at such a fabulous establishment. The newest innovations that your company currently utilizes are not only far ahead of similar companies but enable your company to be a leader in business industry.

Based on my organizational and communication skills, I feel that I would be a perfect fit for your company. I also think my previous experience as a design employee would transfer nicely to a management position. Based on our interview, I feel that we would work well together and my skills and abilities would be of great value. Thank you again for the interview. I hope to hear about your decision in the near future.

Sincerely,

John Waterstreet

John Waterstreet

1 The writer of this letter is applying for the position of
   A vice president of marketing
   B design employee
   C assistant design manager
   D assistant marketing manager

2 The purpose of this letter is to
   A issue a complaint
   B express appreciation
   C provide information
   D describe his job skills

3 The writer of the letter feels he would be good at this job because
   A he has taken a guided tour of the facilities
   B he liked the person interviewing him
   C he has strong organizational and communication skills
   D he likes the current innovations used by the company

Explanation of Correct Responses

1. **C** At one point in the letter, the employee refers to the job for which he has been interviewing. Do not let yourself get confused by choice A—that is the current job title of the person to whom the letter is being written.
2. **B** This letter is clearly written with the intent of expressing thanks. He starts the letter off with, "I wanted to take an opportunity to thank you . . . ." This should leave no doubt in your mind as to the purpose of this letter.
3. **C** John reminds the reader about his qualifications and what would make him a good candidate for the job. He does mention getting a tour and how he admires the company's innovations, but those are not reasons why he would be successful at the job.

KEY POINTS REVIEW

Now that you have seen a sampling of different types of informational text, let's review some key points.

- Read carefully and slowly. Informational text tends to be very dense, so make sure you take your time when reading it.
- Go back over the reading. If you encounter a question that asks you to recall a small detail or concept from the reading, make sure you go back to the text to locate the correct response.
- Always select the *best* response. When you are answering multiple-choice questions, you may come across two answers that could work. Remember to choose the response that best answers the question. Two choices may technically be correct, but you are looking for the best response.

Another type of text that the AIMS exam will ask you to evaluate is persuasive text.

WHAT IS PERSUASIVE TEXT?

Persuasive text is written with the intent of persuading someone to change his or her idea about a particular topic. Persuasive text typically deals with an issue that has two opposing sides, for example, school dress code issues or on-campus cell phone use. When you write persuasively, you are trying to convince your reader to think like you. When you read persuasive text, the author is trying to get you to think like him or her. You would not read a persuasive piece about how to bake a pie. However, you may read a persuasive piece about why apple pie is clearly better than peach pie. The essential component of persuasive text is that it has two arguable sides. When you read persuasive text, your job is to locate the central argument and identify the supporting details and elements.

Directions: Read the following and then answer questions 1–5.

How many times during the day does the average sixteen year old hear the word, "No!"? My rough estimate would be about a million. It seems that young adults today are constantly being told that they are not responsible enough, not mature enough, or not intelligent enough to handle more freedom. Contrary to popular belief, I know that I, as well as many other teenagers, are mature enough to handle more freedom.

The first freedom that teenagers need to be given is to be able to decide their own curfew. It is ridiculous that our city feels that it is their responsibility to tell teenagers when they should be home. Shouldn't that be the decision of the teenager and his or her parents? By forcing every teenager to be home by a certain hour, the city is telling all teens under seventeen years old that they are not to be trusted past 11:00 P.M. I know that many of my friends work after-school jobs and have to stay at work until 11:30 P.M. Can they help it if they are out past 11:00 P.M.? It is absurd to punish people for working. If the city and the police are worried that teens are going to cause trouble when they are out past 11:00, they need to drive by fast-food restaurants to see how many of us are actually working.

Another freedom that teens should be given is to be able to decide how they want to dress. Our school has a ridiculous dress code in place that dictates all students wear a school uniform. This dress code robs each student of his or her individuality and enforces society's notion that it is best to look the same. If they were given the opportunity to wear what they chose, most students would make the right choices. They would not come dressed to school in provocative, inappropriate, or offensive clothing. The trouble is that adults are just too afraid to give teens a chance to show that they can be responsible.

The last and most important right that should be given to teens is the right to vote at the age of sixteen. Everybody knows that the current voting age is eighteen, but I believe that we should be able to vote earlier. If teenagers took an active interest in the world, adults could see just how mature and responsible we can be. Adults certainly understand politics. If we were able to show them that we are interested in politics too, we may find a common ground. I think adults need to see that teens can behave responsibly if they are just given the chance.

I believe teenagers across the country would be much happier if adults gave them more freedom. Doing away with curfews and school dress codes, and lowering the voting age would help teens prove how responsible we can be.

1 Which of the following would be an appropriate title for this essay?
   A "Teens Need More Freedoms!"
   B "Lower the Voting Age"
   C "Teenagers Rule!"
   D "Why There Should Be No Curfew"

2 The purpose of this essay is to convince the reader that
   A teenagers should be treated the same as adults
   B the majority of teenagers are immature
   C teenagers deserve several more freedoms
   D curfews are very important

3 To make the argument more convincing, the author should use
   A factual research
   B personal experience
   C school surveys
   D parental advice

4 Which of the following statements supports the author's stance on a later curfew?
   A "Many of my friends work after-school jobs and have to stay at work until 11:30 P.M."
   B "Can they help it if they are out past 11:00 P.M.?"
   C "Contrary to popular belief, I know that I, as well as many other teenagers, are mature enough to handle more freedom."
   D "Doing away with curfews and school dress codes, and lowering the voting age would help teens prove how responsible we can be."

5 Which of the following is NOT a freedom mentioned in the essay?
   A curfew
   B dress code
   C driving
   D voting

Explanation of Correct Responses

1. **A** After you have read this essay, you should realize that the essay focuses on different freedoms that teenagers think they deserve. Therefore, an appropriate title would summarize the main idea of the essay. The other choices are not as effective titles. Several of the choices do touch on issues that are covered in the essay, but they are not the sole focus. You want to choose a title that reflects the overall concept of the piece.

2. **C** When you get a question like this one, you want to make sure that you understand the focus of the essay. This will help you to understand what the author most wants you to get from the essay. For example, several of the choices mention topics that arise in the essay, but they are not the most vital components. As you go through the answer choices, you may have difficulty deciding between choice A and choice C. Keep in mind, though, that you are looking for the *best* response. Choice A may be tempting, but the essay does not explicitly state that teenagers deserve to be treated the same as adults.

3. **A** Persuasive text is always opinion based. However, how can an author make his or her opinion more convincing and valid in the eyes of a reader? The answer is to use documented, factual research. If you have facts to back up your opinion, arguing with you will be much more difficult. Personal experience takes an argument only so far. Student surveys and parent input may be valuable but not as impressive as documented facts.

4. **A** By showing that many of his or her friends work at night, the author is presenting a case that validates getting rid of a curfew. If the author had just simply stated that teenagers should be allowed to stay out later, the argument would not be nearly as effective. By integrating examples, the author provides support and evidence for the claims. The statement provided in choice A most clearly supports the author's stance because it gives a valid reason.

5. **C** This question is making sure that you have understood this essay. The issue of driving is never mentioned within the essay.

Another popular type of persuasive text that you may encounter on the AIMS exam is an editorial. Editorials are typically found in newspapers and are called, Letters to the Editor. Editorials are usually written by people who live within the community. They focus on issues that the community currently faces, such as public transportation and school issues. Editorials may also address national issues such as presidential races, social programs, and so on. Whatever the topic may be, editorials are always opinion based. They give people the opportunity to share their ideas with the community or the country.

Directions:	Read the following and then answer questions 1–5.

Dear Editor:

It has come to my attention that the traffic situation in our fine city has quickly escalated out of control. Even though our city spans only fifteen miles, I have to budget at least forty minutes to get across town at noon. I do not understand how there can be so many vehicles on the road. It seems to be that our city is growing and that we need to make some changes to accommodate the growth.

In order to ease the daily traffic situation, I propose that the city organizes a public transportation system. Buses would help to decrease the amount of cars. Another potential solution would be a train system. Perhaps the city could initiate some type of low-cost carpool <u>incentive</u> program as well. Nearly every car I pass has one person in it. If the city could possibly provide an incentive to carpool, imagine how many fewer cars there would be.

I realize that one of the most appealing features of our city is that it has maintained its small-town feel. However, we have come to a point where we have to face reality. Something must be done to ease the traffic situation we all face everyday.

Sincerely,

Shawna Johnson

Shawna Johnson

1 Which of the following is NOT a suggestion for traffic improvement?
  A public transportation
  B ride a bicycle to work
  C carpool incentives
  D public train system

2 Based on the writer's opinion, which of the following ideas would she likely support?
  A expanding the roadways
  B a high-cost subway system
  C people walking to work
  D maintaining a small-town feel

3 Within the sentence, "Perhaps the city could initiate some type of low-cost carpool <u>incentive</u> program," the word <u>incentive</u> means
  A privilege
  B temptation
  C responsibility
  D reward

4 According to the letter, the city has not dealt with its traffic problem due to
   A lack of financial and community resources
   B wanting to keep a small-town image
   C little community support and backing
   D a decreasing driving population

5 The arguments given in this letter could be made more effective by
   A providing more ideas for potential traffic solutions
   B citing successful examples from other cities that utilize public transportation
   C outlining how the city could budget the financial resources for a train system
   D describing more problems and issues that drivers in this city face

Explanation of Correct Responses

1. **B** This letter discusses choices A, B, and D but not choice C—riding a bike to work.

2. **A** When you evaluate the other arguments that the editorial provides, you can logically infer that the author would support expanding the roadways. Something that is high cost, as provided in choice B, would not be something she would support because she specifically mentions supporting low-cost programs. The focus of the letter is certainly how to ease the traffic so that people can still drive to work and not have to walk as suggested by choice C. As far as maintaining a small-town feel, the author seems more in favor of improving traffic than being concerned with the city's image.

3. **D** Keep in mind that when you are asked to define words, use context clues. You may have a good idea of what <u>incentive</u> means without having to use context clues. If you are unsure, though, make sure to utilize the context.

4. **B** In order to answer this question correctly, you have to pick up on the times that the author mentions the importance of the "small-town feel" that the city desires to maintain. That issue is clearly in opposition to improving the traffic situation. For example, if the town were suddenly to have public buses or larger roadways, people may grow to dislike the town because it would no longer feel like a small town.

5. **B** As with any argument, if you can integrate documented facts or details, your argument will greatly improve. Imagine if the writer was able to provide an example of a town that faced the same problem and managed to solve it without losing the appeal of the town. People would then see that the problem can be dealt with while barely sacrificng the city's image. Choice C might appear appealing because it focuses on integrating facts into the argument. However, what kind of qualifications does this writer have to draw up a budget for a public transportation system? Once again, remember you are looking for the best choice. In this case, the best choice is definitely choice B.

CHAPTER REVIEW

When you encounter informational or persuasive text on the exam, keep these key points in mind:

- Informational text can be dense, so read it carefully and thoroughly
- If you cannot recall the answer to a detailed question, go back through the reading to locate the correct response.
- When reading persuasive text, locate the central argument and the key supporting points or ideas.
- As with all multiple-choice questions, always keep in mind that you are looking for the best response. Another choice may seem tempting, but find the best answer within the text itself.

Part Three | Mastering the AIMS Writing Exam

| Chapter 6 | **The Writing Process** |

The writing exam requires you to write an essay. Since the AIMS writing exam is written in class, it is crucial that you go through all steps of the writing process. This chapter will guide you through each step of the writing process so that on test day, you can use each step to produce a fantastic essay.

STEPS OF THE WRITING PROCESS

Whenever you write, you must proceed through each of the following five steps.

1. Prewriting
2. Rough draft
3. Revising
4. Editing
5. Final draft

> **REMEMBER**
> The AIMS writing exam is not a timed test, so you should have ample time to go through each step carefully.

STEP 1: PREWRITING

The first and most important step of the writing process is certainly prewriting. What does it mean to prewrite? Essentially, prewriting is a way for you to brainstorm your ideas before you actually begin putting them onto paper in an organized essay. Even though you may not realize it, you utilize prewriting techniques every day. Think about getting ready for school in the morning. You probably brainstorm different outfits that you want to wear, thinking about what shoes, jeans, or shirt would look best together. Based on your brainstorming, you pick an outfit and head out the door. If you simply throw on whatever you picked out of your closet, you would not have a matching, organized outfit. By brainstorming first and trying out different combinations, you create the best-looking outfit possible. Writing is the same. The more you put into your prewriting, the better the final product will be.

> **HINT**
> If you put the time and effort into prewriting, your essay will much better than if you just start writing your final draft.

75

When you are prewriting, there is not one "right" way to do it. In order to make it useful for you, you need to think about how your brain organizes thoughts and ideas. You should experiment with different prewriting techniques before test day so that you know which method will be the most beneficial and efficient for you. The following are some examples of how to prewrite. However, if you use a technique that is not listed below, feel free to continue using it. Remember, prewriting is very individualized, so use a method that you like.

Web Diagram

You have probably been familiar with this technique since elementary school. You simply write your topic in a bubble in the middle of the page and extend out with other bubbles. This technique can be very successful if you feel that you organize your thoughts best in a visual format or if you need to be able to "see" your ideas first. All of the extending bubbles represent key aspects of the essay that you are going to write. The web diagram shows how the secondary ideas connect to the main topic. Look at the example of a web diagram below:

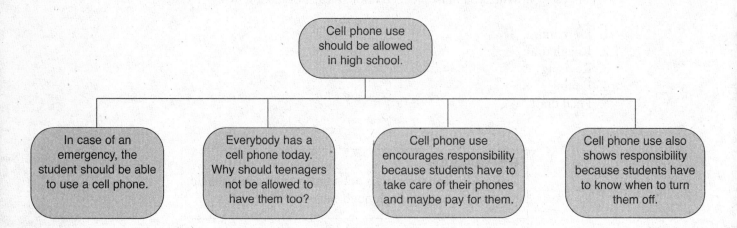

By simply looking at this diagram, you can see that this essay is going to be about the use of cell phones in public schools. All of the extending bubbles represent reasons why cell phones should be permitted in public schools. Once this student has brainstormed all the reasons why cell phones should be permitted, all she or he has to do is begin writing the rough draft while looking at the prewriting to remember all the great points already brainstormed.

Free Writing

If you feel that a visual representation of your ideas is not what you need, something like free writing may be the best prewriting option for you. Free writing is simply what is says—you freely write down and brainstorm your ideas with no structure or clear organization. This technique can be successful if you feel like you simply need to get your ideas out before you begin writing. Look at the example of free writing below:

Cell phones should not be allowed. Causes lots of distractions. Annoying to teachers and students. Disrespectful. Makes social life seem more important than class. Causes embarrassment for students.

Free writing does not give the clear sense of organization that a web diagram does, but that is OK. It still clearly shows that this student is against the use of cell phones at school for the listed reasons. Remember, prewriting is for only you. No one else will see it. It will not be graded or evaluated, so do what works best for you. If that simply means writing down your ideas, that is fine.

Outline

Outlining does take more time than web diagramming or free writing, but it is well worth the effort. Outlining works well if you like a highly visual, organized structure to get your ideas in place. If you decide to use an outline for your prewriting, make sure you are brainstorming and organizing your ideas at the same time. Look at the example of an outline below:

Cell phone use at school should be acceptable

I. Necessary in case of emergency
  A. Parents may need to contact student
  B. School is not always reliable when it comes to messages

II. Encourages student responsibility
  A. Students have to take care of their phones
  B. Some parents make kids pay for their phone

After looking at this student's outline, telling how the rest of the essay is going to fall into place is very easy. Each heading becomes its own paragraph. Each supporting detail is listed and promotes the issue of cell phone use at school.

> **REMEMBER**
> Regardless of which prewriting method you choose, you must go through this step. It will help you to create an organized, detailed essay.

STEP 2: ROUGH DRAFT

Once you feel that you have spent sufficient time prewriting, the time has come to create the rough draft. Keep in mind that a rough draft is exactly that—rough. Too many students make the mistake of believing that the first draft of an essay is a perfect essay and that no improvements need to be made. This is far from the truth. Typically, you can make vast improvements on your rough draft. Once again, the AIMS writing exam is *not timed*, so you have the opportunity to write a rough draft. Let's look at how you should begin putting a rough draft together.

Review Your Prewriting

Look at all the great ideas you brainstormed. Begin putting them into fully developed sentences.

Organize Ideas into Full Paragraphs

Organizing ideas into full paragraphs can be a tricky part of writing, making the rough draft even more important. The purpose of a rough draft is to *begin* to organize your thoughts. If you do not like how they come out the first time, you have the opportunity to change them. Remember to refer to your prewriting constantly while you are writing your rough draft. Your prewriting is there to help you, so make sure you use it.

Skip Lines While You Write

This sounds very simple, but it will really help you when it comes to writing the final draft. Since a rough draft is meant to be fixed, skipping lines gives you space to write additional ideas, make corrections, and so on.

REMEMBER
- Do your prewriting before you begin writing.
- Skip lines when you write.
- Use this as an opportunity to *begin* to organize your ideas.

Cellular phones are everywhere today. Everyone seems to have a cell phone. Cell phones have become a vital form of how people communicate. Of course, lots of teenagers have cell phones, too. This seems to be causing problems for high schools across the country. Some schools have banned cell phone use on campus, while others request that phones simply be turned off during class time. In an essay, persuade your school principal of what your school cell phone policy should be.

| Directions: | Use the space below to prepare a rough draft of your response writing on alternate lines. |

_____

_____

_____

_____

_____

_____

_____

_____

_____

_____

_____

_____

_____

_____

_____

_____

_____

_____

_____

_____

_____

_____

_____

_____

_____

_____

_____

_____

_____

_____

_____

_____

_____

_____

_____

_____

STEP 3: REVISING

Now is time to reflect on your rough draft and decide how it needs to be improved. The purpose of revision is to focus on the larger problems of the rough draft. Do not worry about little things like correcting your spelling when you are revising. When you revise, you are rewriting sentences, making your ideas clearer, and reworking entire paragraphs. You should ask yourself three key questions during the revision process:

1. Are my ideas clear?
2. Are my ideas logical and organized?
3. Have I included enough information and details?

Are My Ideas Clear?

Imagine a complete stranger is reading your essay. Would he or she be able to understand your ideas without any further explanation from you? Or, would that person have lots of questions in order to understand what you are saying?

Are My Ideas Logical and Organized?

Think of your essay almost like a road map. The ideas you present should go down a road that your reader can easily follow. There should be clear indications of when you are turning or changing ideas. There should also be a clear indication of when the road is ending or when you have come to the conclusion of your essay. Do not expect your reader simply to be able to follow your train of thought. As the writer, you must guide your reader along, making his or her job of understanding the essay as easy as possible. No one should have to make leaps to understand what you are trying to say.

Have I Included Information and Details?

If you are going to write about an issue or topic, make sure you have enough to say about it. You must explain the topic to your reader, giving him or her plenty of information to support your ideas. Do not make your reader fill in the blanks. Provide ample support and information.

Once you have thought about these questions in relationship to your rough draft, start revising. Keep in mind that the purpose of revising is to make sure that the bigger issues concerning your rough draft are addressed. Before you begin revising your own rough draft, look at the sample rough draft below. Read over the rough draft first. Then try to revise the draft to make it a stronger essay by rewriting sentences and moving around ideas.

Cell phones cause way too many disruptions on our campus. Students constantly use them as an excuse to not pay atention in class. Is their social life that much more important than class? There phones are always ringing during class. This is major disrespect to teacher's and students. And how am I expected to pay attention in class when cell phones are ringing all the time? We need to bann cell phones on campus because they are totally disttracting and they cause way too many interruptions.

Most importantly, we need to ban cell phones because they are distracting. Why should I care if someone's boyfriend needs to talk to them? I need to focus on the class, not someones dating crisis or where they need to go to for lunch.

And cell phones are really disrespectful to teachers and students. Class time needs to be respected. And cell phones don't.

Lastly, cell phones just cause too many disruptions. I just don't get why people need to bring them to class anyways. If a phone rings for only a few seconds, it's still really distracting and the teacher has to bring everybody's attention back and I feel like half the class is wasted just trying to get people to focus again and it gets really annoying and I just wish they would turn them off.

So, we need to ban cell phones. If students didn't have cell phones, there wouldn't be as many distractions or interruptions. And teachers and students would get a lot more respect. Make a phone call on your own time, not on class time.

Directions: Use the space below to revise the essay on page 81. Try to make the ideas clearer and try to integrate more details into the essay. Rework sentences and entire paragraphs if you feel that it will improve the essay.

_____

_____

_____

_____

_____

_____

_____

_____

_____

_____

_____

_____

_____

_____

_____

_____

_____

_____

_____

_____

_____

_____

Now read an example of a revised version of the same essay. Pay attention to how details are added and how sentences are restructured. Also, think of ways that this essay could continue to be improved.

Every day I go to school with the intention of learning and paying attention in my classes. However, this intention is quickly shot. I find myself being constantly distracted by the obnoxious noise of ringing cell phones. How am I expected to pay attention in class when apparently a student's social life takes priority over academics? If class time is to be taken seriously, cell phones need to be banned from our campus because they distract students from learning, they are disrespectful to teachers and fellow students, and they cause constant disruptions.

Most importantly, cell phones need to be banned because they are a distraction. Students should not be concerned with whether or not their boyfriend or girlfriend is trying to get a hold of them. For one thing, the focus should be on what's going on in class. If you're constantly worried about what your plans for lunch are, how are you going to learn anything?

Cell phones are also very disrespectful to teachers and other students. It's hard for a teacher to ignore the obnoxious ringing of a cell phone just like it's hard for students to ignore it, too. It seems that are enough interruptions throughout the day as it is. Ringing cell phones should not be one of them. Permitting a phone to ring during class sends the teachers and students the message that classroom time is not something to respect or value.

Last but not least, cell phones simply cause constant disruptions. Even if a phone rings for only a couple seconds, everyone's attention is on the phone. No one is paying attention anymore, and everybody has to refocus their attention on the class.

A simple fix to the issue of cell phones is simply to ban them on campus. There would be fewer distractions and interruptions, and a tone of respect for teachers and students would exist across our campus. If students need to make or get a call, they should do it on their own time, not on everyone else's.

Does this version look different than the first version? Your answer should be yes! When you revise, you do major work on the draft. Revising is not simply putting a comma in somewhere or changing one word of a sentence. Many times, paragraphs will change into totally different paragraphs. That is OK. It is the purpose of making revisions. You need to realize that writing is meant to be altered. Just because something has been written a particular way before does not mean it has to stay that way.

| Directions: | Use the space below to revise the rough draft that you started on pages 79–80. Put your own ideas into your own words. |

STEP 4: EDITING

This step is when you fine-tune the revised version of your essay. Now is the time to make sure your words are spelled correctly, that your grammar is correct, and that you have used the correct punctuation. The most important thing to keep in mind when editing is to read over your essay *slowly and carefully*! You will catch many simple mistakes if you just take the time. If you are unsure about how a particular word should be spelled, look it up in the dictionary. Make sure all of your sentences have some kind of end punctuation, such as a period or a question mark. Here are some tips for editing certain aspects of your essay.

Spelling

Read your essay backward. If you read your essay backward, you will force your brain to focus on each word out of context. You will catch many more errors this way. When we read the correct way (from beginning to end), we do not catch as many errors because our brains have a way of glossing over mistakes and seeing what should be there. If you make yourself focus on each individual word, you will find those that are misspelled.

Punctuation

Apply what rules you already know about punctuation. The following chapter discusses punctuation in detail. Simple rules such as ending every sentence with the correct punctuation mark (period, exclamation mark, or question mark) may sound very simplistic. However, you must be very aware of how you are ending your sentences. Be sure to read over your essay again, this time paying attention only to your punctuation. If you focus on one element of editing at a time, you are much more likely to catch errors than if you try to find all of them at once. As you correct punctuation, make sure that you are also looking for fragments and run-on sentences. If you find an incomplete sentence or a run-on, include the proper punctuation mark to make each sentence grammatically correct.

STEP 5: FINAL DRAFT

This is the version of your essay that should be perfect if you havve gone through each step of the writing process. Your ideas should be well organized and well developed. The essay should contain a minimal amount of grammatical errors. Your work should also be *legible*. Even though the quality of your handwriting is not stressed much past elementary school, you must write your final draft in neat, legible handwriting. You may have the most outstanding essay in the world, but if no one can read your writing, how can anyone know? Do not make someone guess what a word in your paper is just because he or she cannot read your writing. Keep in mind that when you write the final draft of your AIMS essay, your grader is going to have no patience to try and figure out your handwriting after he or she has already graded a hundred essays.

REMEMBER
- Have minimal errors in spelling and grammar
- Write as legibly as possible!

Directions:	Use the space provided below to write your final draft about cell phones on campus.

_____

_____

_____

_____

_____

_____

_____

_____

_____

_____

_____

_____

_____

_____

_____

_____

_____

_____

_____

_____

_____

_____

_____

MORE WRITING PRACTICE

You must understand that the day you sit down to take the AIMS exam should not be your first attempt at using the writing process. Just like anything else, whether sports, dancing, or driving, the more you write, the better you are going to write. The more you use the steps of the writing process, the more comfortable you will be using them on test day. Use the following activities to help practice the steps of the writing process.

Practicing Prewriting Techniques

The most important thing you can do to ensure successful prewriting is not to worry about how the prewriting looks! You are the only one who is going to see your prewriting. Whether it is sloppy or does not make any sense to anyone but you does not matter. The purpose of prewriting is simply to generate as many ideas as possible. Let's practice exhausting ideas for particular topics. Prewrite for each of the following topics. Use whatever prewriting method you prefer, such as a web diagram or an outline. Try to use a variety of methods in order to discover which method you like best. Use the space provided to prewrite. Brainstorm until you absolutely cannot think of another idea for a particular topic.

Topic #1: Should there be mandatory drug testing for student athletes?

Topic #2: Should high schools still have proms even though some principals and teachers believe they give students an opportunity to cause trouble?

Topic #3: Name important qualities that adult role models should have.

Topic #4: Should high schools have mandatory random backpack searches to help reduce drug abuse on campus?

Topic #5: Should high schools be allowed to require students to have a personal computer at home so that students always have access to the internet and a way to type assignments?

Once you have exhausted all possible ideas for the above topics, you should feel fairly comfortable prewriting. Even if you do not use all of the ideas from your prewriting in your final draft, you now have the option of choosing from the very best of your ideas to include in your essay.

Practicing Revision Techniques

The revision step is the step that most students seem to have problems with. You absolutely must understand that the first draft of any essay is not going to be as good as it could be and that there are always areas in a piece of writing that need improvement. Even famous writers revise—that is one of the reasons why their writing is famous. Do you think an author submits the first version of a book and expects it to be perfect? Of course not. Authors continuously revise their work, looking for a better way to express their ideas. Just like a professional writer, you need to spend time revising your sentences, reorganizing your ideas, and replacing dull, boring words with words that really make an impact. Spending time revising will really pay off on test day, helping you to create a fantastic, passing essay. So let's practice revising.

Read the following sample essays. Revise each essay, focusing on making the ideas and organization clearer. Add and subtract details that you feel are necessary or unnecessary. Imagine that you are reading over these essays for a friend and that he or she needs your advice on how to improve them. Keep the central ideas and messages the same, but offer plenty of constructive criticism. Keep in mind that several of these essays need *major* work. Do not be afraid to move entire paragraphs or rewrite entire paragraphs so that they make more sense.

HINT
When you revise an essay, read the entire essay first before you begin revising. Do not revise sentence by sentence. You need to get across the general message or idea first. Your revision will be much more successful this way, and the revised essay will be better organized.

Sample Essay #1: *Many high schools have adopted drug-testing policies for student athletes. In an essay, express your opinion as to whether or not schools should have mandatory drug-testing policies for student athletes.*

Many schools have problems with students using drugs. Especially with athletes using drugs. I think that schools should drug test student athletes. It's important because they represent our school. And because they could hurt themselves or somebody else. And also because it could cause major trouble for the school if they get caught.

Our school athletes represent our school. It's not good for bad students to be the ones that everybody outside our school sees. If we want our school to have a good image, the student athletes are part of that image. If they show up to a game high, what is the audience going to think of our school? There going to think that our school is full of a bunch of stoners.

And people do dangerous things on drugs. Someone playing football might really hurt someone if their all high. Its to dangerous for people to have to compete against someone on drugs. You never know what might happen to them.

The last reason why we should drug test athletes, is because they cause trouble. Someone who's high isn't going too care about what their coach says. And their going to do whatever what they want. Because there high. And someone who doesn't listen to their coach causes a bad image for the school. That's not right. Not all the student's do drugs and everybody's going to think that they do. If athletes are causing trouble at other schools.

So in conclusion, students should have to be drug tested if they want to play sports. It will give the school a good image and keep everybody out of trouble. And it will make sports less dangerous.

After you have carefully read over this essay, revise the introductory paragraph in the space below. Make sure that the revised introduction makes the author's opinion clear and contains a thesis statement.

_____

_____

_____

_____

_____

_____

_____

_____

_____

_____

_____

_____

_____

Now compare your revised introduction to the following sample. This revision is a good representation of a strongly written introduction:

Unfortunately, drugs are very popular among teenagers. In my school alone, I know plenty of students who use drugs regularly. All groups of students use drugs, including student athletes. In order to help our school, student athletes should have to undergo random drug testing. If student athletes are drug tested, it will ensure that our school has a good reputation because our athletes represent our school, it could prevent injuries, and it would keep the school out of trouble.

Several elements of this introduction should stand out to you. For example, the statement, "In order to help our school, student athletes should have to undergo random drug testing," immediately informs the reader about the author's opinion. The statements that follow also list reasons why student athlete drug testing would be a positive decision. When you are supporting an opinion, you want to make sure to provide your reasons in the introductory paragraph.

Sample Essay #2: *A hot issue on lots of high school campuses right now is if they should still have prom. Schools are beginning to argue that prom is becoming an excuse for students to break the dress code and to drink dangerous amounts of alcohol. In an essay, express your viewpoint on whether or not high schools should still have a prom.*

Prom is a high school tradition. For many students, its what they look forward to all year long. Although there are some kids who goof off and ruin it for others, most students look at prom as a fun opportunity. To meet with friends and get dressed up. And to make great memories.

Most importantly prom is a tradition. I can remember my mom talking about her high school prom and how much fun she had. Shouldn't I get those memories too? I don't plan on getting drunk. And I don't plan on dressing in a dress that shows off things it shouldn't. I can be responsible and I think most students can.

And is it really fair to let a few bad students ruin things for everybody else? Why should I get punished because some idiot cant behave like an adult? It's just not right to make everybody suffer because some students abuse the privilege. Me and my friends don't want to be robbed of an important high school event because of those students. Instead of punishing us good students, the school should just tell the bad kids they can't come to prom.

Most importantly, prom is a chance to make really good memories. With best friends, boyfriends and girlfriends, and to have a totally safe blast. I know if I didn't have these memories I would regret it for the rest of my life.

Prom is a high school tradition and I think students are entitled to have memories with their friends and dates. It's not right for the school to make such an important decision based on some jerky, stupid kids. I don't plan on getting wasted at prom and I know my friends don't either. Why punish us?

You may be wondering how you could make this essay better. The essay is fairly strong. It does present some logical, valid reasons for the author's opinion. However, the essay could be improved in several areas. In some places, sentences could be combined. There are several fragments that must be fixed. Additionally, some of the author's choices or words need improvement. With that in mind, begin to revise this essay using the space below.

_____

_____

_____

_____

_____

_____

_____

_____

_____

_____

_____

_____

_____

_____

_____

_____

_____

_____

_____

Now look at a sample paragraph that has been revised and compare this paragraph with your revisions. The sample revision is based on the third paragraph of the essay:

To punish all students because some students cannot behave themselves is unfair treatment. I do not think it is right to make everybody suffer because a select few students cannot value the importance of prom. The majority of students deserve the privilege and they have worked hard to be good students. My friends and I do not want to be robbed of important high school memories because of other students' behavior. A good solution to this issue is to simply not allow the badly behaving students to come to prom."

Several improvements were made in this paragraph.

- Sentences have been combined.
- There are no more fragments
- The words have been altered to have a more mature tone. For example, "some idiot" has been changed to "a select few students."

Just by making small changes, you can see a substantial improvement in the quality of the writing.

Sample Essay #3: *Many young people tend to look up to adults as their role models. Think about the kind of qualities that are important for an adult role model to have. In an essay, describe the kind of qualities an adult should have in order to be considered a good role model."*

Role models can be tough to find these days. It seems like most kids my age don't really have anybody to look up to. There is just too much violence and drugs in our world for people to worry about being a role model for somebody else. But sometimes you get lucky and find someone who you think can make a good role model. I think that a good role model has to be trustworthy and caring. I think that they also have to be a hardworker.

I always look to find a role model who is a hard worker, like my mom for example. She works too jobs just so that we kids can be taken care of. I think that's a good example of someone who works really hard. She's tired a lot, but I guess she thinks its worth all her hard work because her kids are taken care of. I respect my mom a lot for the work she does. And she always finds ways to make us laugh which is really important to.

A good role model also has to be really caring. Why would I look up to someone who was mean or rude to me? I wouldn't. So a role model has to be nice to other people and not always be worrying about themselves first. If they show you that they care about you first, then that's being a good role model to somebody.

And a role model has to be caring. That's really important too.

My mom is definetly my role model. She works really hard and I respect that. Its hard to find a good role model these days, so I guess I'm pretty lucky.

Several issues should grab your attention as you begin to think about how to revise this essay. There are several grammatical and spelling errors, the ideas are not fully developed, and more supporting details must be included. The essay begins by mentioning that the author's role model is his mother. In the next few paragraphs, the focus changes to general qualities of a role model. However, in the conclusion, the author's mother is mentioned again. As you revise this essay, decide what you want the focus of the essay to be. Should it be the author's mother or should it be general qualities found in a role model? Also make sure to correct spelling and grammatical errors.

Revise this essay using the space below.

_____

_____

_____

_____

_____

_____

_____

_____

_____

_____

_____

_____

_____

_____

_____

_____

For example, let's pretend that you choose to stick with the mother as the focus of your revision. The body of the essay should then continue linking the mother with qualities that are found in a role model. The sample revision focuses on the fourth and fifth paragraphs. The most important issue concerning the revision of the fourth paragraph is that as it stands, it is not a paragraph. Remember that a paragraph should typically have three to five sentences. This paragraph has only one full sentence and one sentence fragment, so you need to add more information into that paragraph. Now look at the sample revision.

"The last quality that a role model should have is that he or she should be caring. My mother shows this quality very well. Since she does work so hard and sacrifices so much for me and my brothers, I know that she really cares about us. I see my mother being such a caring person, which makes me want to be a caring person too. Maybe one day I can be someone's role model.

In our world today, finding someone that you can look up to is hard. I am really lucky because I have my mom and I respect her so much. She is my role model because she works hard, she is respectful, and she is a caring person. I hope that I can have the same qualities when I am an adult."

One of the key elements that you should notice about the revision is that the fourth paragraph was expanded to include more details and information. The concluding paragraph also restated the author's ideas, summarizing why his mother was such a good role model.

Sample Essay #4: *In order to combat drug use on high school campuses, many schools have started using mandatory backpack searches. Students are not told ahead of time of when these searches will take place. These searches are conducted at random, meaning that no specific students are targeted. In an essay, state your opinion on whether or not schools should use mandatory drug searches.*

Having drug searches on campus is totally pointless. For one thing, students will still figure out a way to still have drugs at school, even if they know they might be searched. And as bad as adults seem to think high schools are, there are not enough students around abusing drugs to need these kinds of searches. Most importantly having random searches inflicts upon student's rights. Don't we have a right to privacy just like adults? I know I don't want to come to a school where I feel like the teachers and the principal are constantly breathing down my neck, waiting for me to bring drugs to school so they can bust me.

The biggest reason why we shouldn't have backpack searches is because it goes against our rights. I'm pretty sure that it says in the constitution that we have a right to privacy and that we're protected against searches. Just because we're teenagers, people think that we don't deserve the same rights. Well, how would a grownup feel if someone just came barging into their house saying that they needed to search it because there might be drugs in it? They probably would have a fit and say get out of my house. I think teenagers deserve to feel the same way. Just because you're a kid doesn't give someone the right to not trust you.

It's important for kids to feel safe at school. And having adults just search your backpack because of the few students who do use drugs on school would make everybody feel very unsafe. Why do adults always assume that teenagers are doing bad things? I for one have never brought bad stuff to school so why should I be treated as if I do bring bad stuff? I think I deserve to be treated like I behave. If I act like a good student, that's how I should be treated. Don't lump all students into one catergory because it's not fair and it makes students feel untrusted and unsafe at school.

In conclusion, I don't think it's fair at all to have random backpack searches. I think the school should go after the kids that are bringing drugs to school and don't act like we're all bringing drugs to school. Cause remember, not all teenagers are trying to do bad things.

This essay presents several strong ideas, and there is a lot of support for the author's opinion. However, once again, this essay could be improved by revising sentences and improving word choice. Revise this essay with the intent of making it sound more mature by replacing words such as "bad stuff" with "illegal substances." Then have a study partner, parent, or teacher give you feedback on your changes.

_____

_____

_____

_____

_____

_____

_____

_____

_____

_____

Sample Essay #5: *Since technology has become such a large part of daily life, schools are finding ways to use it on their campuses, making it a large component of many classes. Several schools have caused quite a stir because they are requiring that students have computers at home so they can utilize the Internet, type, and do other homework assignments that require a computer. Write an essay stating whether or not schools should be able to require students to have a computer at home.*

In today's world it is a fact of life that you need a computer to get by. Computers are now how we communicate through email and blogging and I know that all my school papers have to typed. I also have to use the internet at home to do research for school assignments. If I didn't have a computer at home, my school life would be made very difficult. I think it's ok for schools to require that students have computers at home because it's reality that they need one, it cuts down on student excuses for not having the work done, and it pretty much makes life a lot easier.

Like I said earlier, it's just simple reality that you need a computer. I know at my school, the teachers pretty much assume that all students have a computer anyway, so you might as well require it. Our world is run by technology—we all have cell phones and IPods and stuff like that. I would bet that in 20 years, all students would be required to have personal laptops too. That's not a bad thing, it's just the reality that our lives are all about technology.

Also if your teacher knows that you're required to have a computer at home, there's no excuse for not having a paper typed and ready to hand in when it's due. You can't say something like, "I couldn't find a computer" because you're supposed to have one at home. I think it would make a lot more students responsible for their work and they wouldn't have to waste time coming up with lame excuses.

And if everybody had a computer at home, they wouldn't have to worry about finding a ride to the library or trying to use a friend's computer. They wouldn't have to bother their parents or anybody because the computer would be right in their house. It would just make life easier on everybody involved.

In conclusion, I think the school has the right to tell students that they need to have a computer at home. students could get more work done on time, it would make life easier, and it's just the plain and simple reality of our world today that you need a computer to get by.

Revise this essay in the space below, making improvements that you feel are necessary. Ask a study partner, parent, or teacher to review your changes with you.

_____

_____

_____

_____

_____

_____

_____

_____

_____

_____

_____

_____

_____

_____

_____

_____

_____

_____

_____

_____

_____

All of this practice with revision should help you see how beneficial it can be. Typically, you can make massive improvements on a first draft if you simply commit to revising it. Remember that good revision takes time. It is not something that you can simply blast through. Do not expect to be able to revise a paper adequately in five minutes. Be prepared to spend ample time getting your essay to say exactly what you want it to say. Your hard work will be well worth your efforts when you are told that you passed the AIMS writing exam. Let's review some of the key elements of the writing process.

WRITING PROCESS REVIEW

Prewriting:

- Use as a brainstorming device to generate ideas about the topic
- Use web diagrams
- Use free writing
- Use outlining
- Use any other forms that work for you

Rough Draft:

- The rough draft is supposed to be ROUGH!!
- Get your ideas organized into an essay format
- Be prepared to do major construction on this version of your essay

Revising:

- Fix all of the weaknesses in your rough draft
- Use this step to improve the quality of your ideas, organization, and word choice
- Be prepared to spend quality time on this step—do not rush through it!
- Writing is supposed to be changed and altered—that is how it gets better
- Check for run-on sentences and fragments

Editing:

- Focus on the little mistakes in the draft
- Fix spelling, punctuation, and grammar

Final draft:

- The perfect, error-free version of your essay
- Pay close attention to the legibility of your handwriting—take the time to write clearly and nicely
- Do a final proofread check to find any errors that might have escaped you the first time through
- Do not let your essay exceed two pages

Now that you are familiar with all the steps of the writing process, let's look at writing traits specific to the AIMS writing exam.

Chapter 7 | The Six Traits of Successful Writing

For the writing portion of the test, you will be expected to produce a neat, organized, and developed essay. The purpose of this chapter is to explain in detail what the state of Arizona is looking for when they grade your essay.

THE SIX TRAITS

The state of Arizona uses a grading system known as the six traits to determine whether or not an essay is considered passing:

1. Ideas and Content
2. Organization
3. Voice
4. Word Choice
5. Sentence Fluency
6. Conventions

Each trait is graded on a scale from 1 to 6, where 1 means incompetent and 6 means outstanding. Scoring a 4 on a particular trait is considered meeting the standard. However, each trait is scored equally, so that a high score on one trait will help to counteract a low score on another trait. The scores from each trait are then averaged together to determine if your writing meets the standard.

Another important issue is that you are provided two pages on which to write your essay. Any writing beyond two pages will not be graded. Make sure you have enough information in your essay, but do not exceed the two-page limit. So let's take a look at each trait to understand how they come together to form a great piece of writing!

TRAIT 1: IDEAS AND CONTENT

The most important part of a piece of writing is the ideas that are expressed in it. Without a good idea, you do not have anything to say. When your AIMS essay is graded, examiners look for several things when assessing ideas and content:

1. How well-developed are your ideas?
2. How well-supported are your ideas?
3. Do you have interesting details?
4. Do your ideas all connect to form a clear message?

The best thing you can do to make sure that you get a high score for ideas and content is to BRAINSTORM or PREWRITE, which is of course the first step of the writing process. It is crucial to brainstorm or prewrite before you begin to write your essay. Let's practice brainstorming ideas about the following essay question:

Your school principal has decided that next year, students will be required to wear school uniforms. This has caused quite a stir on campus. Write an essay convincing your fellow students why school uniforms are a good or a bad idea.

> **NOTE**
> The AIMS exam has used persuasive prompts for their writing assessments, so that's what we'll focus on throughout this chapter. Other forms of writing will also be mentioned at the end of the chapter.

There are many ways you can begin to brainstorm ideas for this kind of question. Recall that in the last chapter, we discussed some brainstorming methods. They are mentioned again below for review purposes.

Freewrite

If you opt for this type of brainstorming, it means you simply like to jot down your ideas before you begin writing. An example of freewriting may look like this:

School uniforms = BAD
—no expression/individuality
—no freedom to choose own clothes
—not school's decision

Now use the space provided to jot down your own ideas about why school uniforms would be a good or a bad idea.

Outline

If you feel you brainstorm best with a more organized, structured approach, an outline could benefit you best. Outlines can be a little more time consuming than other forms of brainstorming, but they can be extremely useful when you begin to write your essay. Fill in the blanks for the following example outline, explaining why school uniforms would be a bad idea.

School uniforms are a BAD idea

I.   No individuality
     A. All people look the same
     B.

II. Uniforms are expensive
     A.
     B.

III.
     A.
     B.

Web Diagram

A third form of brainstorming is a web diagram. A web diagram uses bubbles that center around the main topic to generate ideas and support for that particular topic. Look at the sample web diagram below:

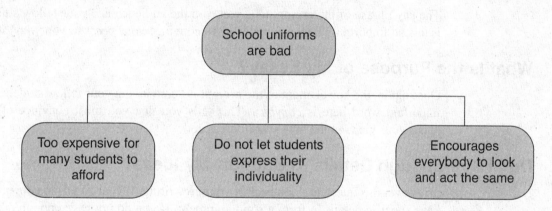

Now complete the web diagram below based on why school uniforms are a good idea:

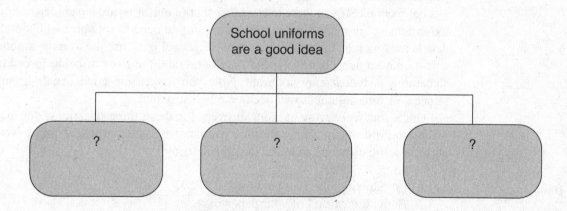

REMEMBER

These are not the only ways to prewrite; they are simply examples. However you want to prewrite is fine, but make sure you do it. Prewriting will help you develop your ideas in an organized fashion. Since the AIMS exam is an *untimed* test, there is no excuse not to prewrite.

TRAIT 2: ORGANIZATION

Now that you have brainstormed all of your great ideas, it is time to organize them. First, ask yourself the following questions:

1. Who is my audience, or who is my paper being written for?
2. What is the purpose of my essay?
3. Do I have enough details to support my ideas?

In order to answer the questions, let's stick with the issue of school uniforms. If you recall, the question was:

Your school principal has decided that next year, students will be required to wear school uniforms. This has caused quite a stir on campus. Write an essay convincing your fellow students why school uniforms are a good or a bad idea.

Who Is My Audience?

The key phrase of the prompt tells you who the audience is: "your fellow students." Why is this so important? Because you have to convince your *peers* to your way of thinking.

What Is the Purpose of My Essay?

Once again, the key element of the prompt is "convincing your fellow students." The most important word here is *convince*. This tells you that you must convince other students about your view on the new school dress code.

Do I Have Enough Details to Support My Ideas?

To answer this question, look back at your prewriting. If your goal is to convince, you must have specific details to form a solid argument. If you do not have enough details to form a solid argument, you need to brainstorm some more. Determining what exactly makes up "enough" details may be difficult. For each point that you mention to support your stance, you should have a minimum of three supporting details for each body paragraph.

For example, if you were to state that school uniforms are a bad idea because they are too expensive for many students, you are going to need to support that claim. Supporting details may include the price of an average school uniform, the average amount of available money students have to spend on clothes, and the issue of being forced to purchase something a student may not want. Now you have some good details to support your stance and your argument will become much stronger.

Once you feel secure in your answers for these three questions, you need to start organizing your ideas, always keeping your audience and purpose in mind. Now let's look at the specific elements of a well-organized essay:

1. Introduction: the first paragraph
2. Body: the "meat" of your paper
3. Conclusion: the last paragraph

Introduction

One of the most important parts of a successful essay is the introduction. The introduction needs to catch your reader immediately, sparking his or her interest. The introduction should have:

1. Several opening sentences that grab your reader
2. A smooth transition into the thesis statement
3. A clear, logical thesis statement

Since the introduction is so important, let's go over each of these items.

Attention Grabber

Would you want to read a paper that started with, "My paper is about the dress code. The dress code is a good idea"? Would you want to read a paper that started with, "Imagine trying to find your best friend for lunch. The hallways are packed, and you're searching among faces to find your friend. However, you don't stand a chance because everybody in your school looks exactly the same"? Which one of those opening statements grabs your attention? It should be the second one.

What makes the second statement more interesting than the first one? First of all, it is much more creative. Secondly, it lets readers become a part of the experience in the paper. They are able to imagine themselves in that hallway, looking for their friend. Therefore, they want to read more about the topic. You can use several different techniques to grab the reader:

• A quote
• An anecdote/story
• A rhetorical question

The author could have used a quote in the introduction. For example, he or she could have written,

"I've grown certain that the root of all fear is that we've been forced to deny who we are." These words by Francis Moore Lapp could not hold more truth than they do today as our school discusses robbing us of our identity.

In the second attention-grabbing statement, the author actually used an anecdote/story. He or she described the packed hallway, which is an anecdote. Finally, the author could have used a rhetorical question. This is a question that is asked merely for effect. No one expects to receive an answer. For example, the author could have written, "How would you feel if someone started telling you what to wear and you did not have a choice?"

Transition

Once you have a good attention grabber, you need to transition into a thesis. Transitions are extremely important. You do not want to jolt your reader with sentences and ideas that do not seem to join together smoothly. Transitions provide that smooth bridge from your attention grabber to your thesis. Let's pretend that you wrote the rhetorical question above. You plan to write a thesis stating that school uniforms should not be required. How could you transition from one to the other? Here's one possibility:

How would you feel if someone started telling you what to wear and you did not have a choice? [Attention grabber] Well, that is exactly what the school board is trying to do. Board members are trying to take away our choices—and they should not be able to do that. [Transition]

Thesis

A thesis is a one- or two-sentence statement found in the introduction of your paper. It clearly states your opinion and what you plan to cover in your essay.

A thesis statement is very important, especially in persuasive writing. In fact, a good thesis statement is the foundation of a good persuasive paper. The AIMS exam gives writing prompts that focus on persuasive writing techniques. Therefore, you should spend some time practicing and understanding good thesis statements. For example, if you needed to write a persuasive paper discussing violent video games a strong thesis statement would be:

Modern-day video games are far too dangerous because they contribute to violence among teenagers and society.

By simply looking at this thesis statement, you know what the writer's opinion is. The author believes that violent video games harm society and teenagers.

A thesis statement for the opposite side of the argument may be:

Violent video games are forms of entertainment and should not be blamed for violence among teens.

Once again, you can read this statement and understand exactly what the paper is about.

Let's practice writing thesis statements with some different topics. For each topic, write two thesis statements—one that is for the issue and one that is against the issue.

Example Topic: Keeping Animals in Zoos

For: Keeping animals in zoos is important because animals provide education and entertainment.

Against: Keeping animals in zoos is wrong because it is inhumane and deprives animals of their natural habitats.

Your turn!

Topic: Allowing prayer in public schools

For: _____

_____

_____

Against: _____

_____

_____

Topic: Mandatory drug testing for professional athletes

For: _____

_____

_____

Against: _____

_____

_____

Topic: Taking all soda vending machines off school campuses

For: _____

_____

_____

Against: _____

_____

_____

Topic: School dress code

For: _____

_____

_____

Against: _____

_____

_____

As you write thesis statements, you should begin to notice a pattern:

1. A thesis makes your opinion immediately clear.
2. A thesis states the reasons for your opinion.

Once you have a strong thesis, you need to put it into the introductory paragraph. For an effective introduction, combine the following elements:

- Attention grabber
- Transition
- Thesis

Read the following sample of an introductory paragraph. The focus of this essay is whether or not animals should be kept in zoos.

Imagine yourself in a cage, surrounded by metal bars. You have no route for escape. Every day is a battle due to the taunts that come from the people outside your cage. They poke their fingers in at you, laughing at how ridiculous you look. (Attention grabber) This may sound like a description from a science fiction movie, but animals in zoos are subjected to this treatment everyday. They are kept in the name of education. However, zoos only provide humans with the opportunity to disgrace animals. (Transition) Keeping animals in zoos is unacceptable because it is inhumane and deprives animals of their natural habitats. (Thesis)

From this example, you should begin to see how the elements of a successful introduction come together. The first step is to grab your reader, in this case with an anecdote. Then you provide either one or two sentences as a transition to your thesis statement.

Now you practice writing an introduction. Think back to the dress code prompt, and put all of introductory elements together.

Attention grabber: _____

_____

_____

_____

_____

Transition: _____

_____

_____

Thesis: _____

_____

_____

A strong thesis statement will naturally help you write a strong essay as long as you stick to your topic and refer back to your prewriting. If you are writing an essay about the benefits of a school dress code, your thesis may read:

A school dress code would be beneficial to have on campus because it would discourage cliques and students would be inclined to be less judgmental of one another.

When looking at the second part of this thesis, "because it would discourage cliques and students would be inclined to be less judgmental of one another," we know the paper will talk about cliques and judgmental behavior. Naturally, those items should be the focus of the body.

Body of an Essay

The body of an essay is essentially the meat of your paper. This is where all of your brainstormed ideas and details come into play. Typically, the body of an essay consists of three paragraphs.

REMEMBER
All ideas in the body should connect to your thesis. It is your job to *convince* a reader why your viewpoint is correct. You will need to provide plenty of support to make a strong argument.

The following outline will help you organize the body portion of your essay

PARAGRAPH 1: Introduction.

PARAGRAPH 2: Discuss first subtopic from thesis.

Example: Explain how the dress code will discourage cliques

PARAGRAPH 3: Discuss second subtopic from thesis.

Example: Explain how the dress code will discourage judgmental behavior among students

PARAGRAPH 4: Mention any counterarguments and why they are wrong

Example: People who oppose the dress code due to ruining student freedom are incorrect because . . .

PARAGRAPH 5: Conclusion—use this paragraph to summarize your main points and to restate your thesis. If you used some type of anecdote in your introduction, reference it again. End on a powerful and passionate note—inspire your reader to action. You want to remind your reader again about why you have been right this whole time!

Example: Numerous examples show that having a dress code on our school campus will greatly improve student behavior.

Further on in this section, we will discuss how to construct effective sentences within your paragraphs. For now, you should understand how to form your ideas and organize them effectively.

REVIEW

- Identify key words that indicate who your audience is and what the purpose of your writing should be.
- Always prewrite or brainstorm before writing your essay.
- Construct a strong thesis statement that clearly explains your opinion and reasons for your opinion.
- Expand on your thesis throughout the body of your essay.
- Your conclusion should restate your thesis and should once again inspire your reader to change his or her thinking.

TRAIT 3: VOICE

The next crucial piece of good writing is the voice. When discussing voice, we are talking about your unique way of expressing yourself. No one else can say something just like you do. Voice is the way you choose to say something. It is unique to you.

One of the biggest factors that determines your voice is who you are speaking or writing to. Would you talk the same way to your best friend as you would to your English teacher? Probably not. The same is true with writing. A note you write to your best friend and an essay you turn in for a grade are going to have very different voices.

In order to have the proper voice, you have got to understand who your audience is. For the dress code prompt, who is your audience? Remember, it is your fellow students. However, your essay is going to be published in a newspaper, so your writing cannot be like a note to your best friend.

Let's do a couple of practice activities to get the hang of how audience and voice connect. Read the following scenario:

It's several weeks after your sixteenth birthday, and you are now an official, licensed driver. You do not have your own car yet, but your parents have been generous enough to let you use one of their cars. However, you can use the car only with their permission. It is Friday night, and your parents are out to dinner. You are at home trying to get ahead on your homework. Your stomach starts to growl, and you search the refrigerator for something to eat. To your disappointment, the refrigerator contains a carton of orange juice and some questionable-looking leftovers. Your stomach continues to growl, and you decide to take action. You hop in your parent's car, heading for the nearest fast-food restaurant. You get your dinner and are happily cruising along, heading back toward home. However, as you are making a left-hand turn onto your street, another car comes out of nowhere and hits the passenger side of your parent's car. The passenger side door is smashed, and the windshield is cracked.

Write a note to your parents explaining what happened.

_____

_____

_____

_____

_____

_____

_____

_____

_____

_____

_____

_____

_____

Write a note to your best friend explaining what happened.

_____

_____

_____

_____

_____

_____

_____

_____

_____

_____

_____

_____

_____

Write a note to your insurance agent explaining what happened.

_____

_____

_____

_____

_____

_____

_____

_____

_____

_____

_____

_____

Once you have completed all three activities, you should be able to see the differences among them. What makes them different? The audience.

Now think back to the prompt about the student dress code and try to decide which voice would be the most appropriate. Your audience is your fellow students, so you need to write your essay appropriately.

Look at the following sentences:

1. *We totally don't need a dress code because it totally takes away our freedoms.*

2. *We as students of our high school don't need a dress code because it infringes upon our rights of expression.*

3. *A dress code is a preposterous idea, encouraging society's ideals of conformity and mob mentality.*

Looking at these three sentences, which one would seem the most appropriate in a student newspaper?

Sentence #1 is too informal, sounding too much like a conversation between friends.

Sentence #3 contains several words that many high school students may not be familiar with and it could be deemed as somewhat offensive. People do not want to hear that an idea that they believe is preposterous.

That leaves sentence #2 and hopefully that was the sentence you chose. What makes sentence #2 the most appropriate? It addresses the correct audience (your fellow students) and contains words that most high school students would be familiar with. It sounds like a student, yet still maintains a mature, serious tone.

When thinking of voice REMEMBER:
- Identify your audience
- Write appropriately for your audience.

Another key element of voice is the commitment or enthusiasm you show in your writing. Particularly when you are writing on a persuasive issue, your voice needs to show dedication to your topic. When asked to write persuasively, take a firm stance on the issue and do not back down. Your job is to convince people that you are right! Read the following sentences:

I think that a dress code is a great idea because I think it would help prevent cliques on campus.

This sentence has a fairly strong voice. Unfortunately, it has one major downfall, using "I think." In fact, it even uses the phrase twice. Now read the same sentence over, simply omitting "I think."

A dress code is a good idea because it would help prevent cliques on campus.

By removing "I think" from the sentence, there is more dedication to the topic. Additionally, the impact of the sentence becomes much stronger. Including "I think" in a persuasive paper diminishes the impact of your statements for several reasons:

1. It states the obvious. Of course you are doing the thinking—you are the writer.
2. It is unnecessary and makes your writing redundant.
3. It diminishes the strength of your argument.

REVIEW
- Your voice is unique. Don't be afraid to express your true feelings.
- Let your passion and enthusiasm shine through with your choice of words.

TRAIT 4: WORD CHOICE

Word choice is a very important trait because the words you use are the tools to express your ideas. The stronger the words you use, the more effective your writing will become. When your essay is graded, they will be looking to see if you have a lot of variety in your vocabulary and that your words make an impact.

Let's briefly look at the power of word choice. Rewrite the following sentences by replacing the underlined words with more meaningful, vivid words.

Example: Dinner last night was <u>good.</u>

Dinner last night was delicious.

1. The chocolate cake was <u>good</u>.

_____

2. He walked by with an <u>angry</u> look on his face.

_____

3. The small child began to <u>cry</u>.

_____

If you replace these words with much more meaningful and descriptive words, your sentence becomes much more interesting.

For example, when you change, "The small child began to cry" to "The small child began to wail," a much more meaningful image is created. You are able to picture a much more concise image. Think of word choice as a way to show off the extent of your vocabulary. The better, more descriptive words you use, the higher the score you will receive. Never forget that the AIMS exam allows you to use a thesaurus. This can be an incredibly useful tool to help you find a better word if you cannot think of one on your own.

TRAIT 5: SENTENCE FLUENCY

This particular trait focuses on the construction of your sentences. When you demonstrate strong sentence fluency in a piece of writing, your sentences vary in structure, rhythm, and flow.

Structure

When you put together a sentence, you can use several structures. Good sentence fluency uses all of the following structures to create variety in a piece of writing.

Simple Sentence

A simple sentence is a just that: simple. All it needs is a subject and a predicate or, more simply, a noun and verb.

Example: She went to the store yesterday.

A simple sentence is immediately recognizable by its simplicity. There is not a lot of distinct variety in this type of sentence. It simply gives you information without adding a lot of extras. You will not be marked down for using this type of sentence. However, you will be marked down if you use only simple sentences in your writing. Simple sentences can be powerful when used sparingly because they can express ideas clearly and concisely—just be sure not to overuse them.

Compound Sentence

A compound sentence is made of two independent clauses, which means two separate sentences. A compound sentence is typically joined by a coordinating conjunction. The best way to tell if something is a compound sentence is if you can find two complete sentences within it.

Example: He was excited about the party, but he had to go to work first.

When you look at this sentence, you should be able to identify two separate, complete sentences.

"He was excited about the party" and "He had to go to work first" are two separate, complete sentences that come together to form one sentence. Compound sentences can be especially effective when contrasting or balancing between two equally important pieces of information. When you can connect your ideas into a compound sentence, do it. Using compound sentences breaks up the boring tones of simple sentences and makes your writing more advanced. However, just like any other sentence structures, do not overuse it.

Complex Sentence

A complex sentence contains one independent clause and one dependent clause. That means that when you read this type of sentence, you should be able to identify one complete sentence and one incomplete sentence. A complex sentence always contains a subordinating conjunction, showing that one piece of information is more important, or subordinate, to the other piece of information.

Example: Although my friend invited me to a party, I did not want to go.

"Although my friend invited me to a party" is the incomplete sentence, and "I did not want to go" is the complete sentence. The subordinating conjunction in this sentence is "Although," showing that "I did not want to go" is the more important issue in the sentence. Complex sentences can be very powerful. They show contrast and the importance of ideas.

Compound-Complex Sentence

This type of sentence joins a simple sentence and a complex sentence.

Example: The package arrived in the morning, but the mail carrier left before I could check the contents.

A compound-complex sentence is joined together by a coordinating conjunction, in this case "but." The simple sentence is "the package arrived in the morning." The complex sentence is "the mailman left before I could check the contents."

Compound-complex sentences can help you connect multiple related ideas into one smooth sentence. However, remember that compound-complex sentences can get lengthy, so do not overuse them.

Rhythm and Flow

If all of these technical names for sentence structures have you worried, stop. When your essay is graded, remember the AIMS evaluators are not looking to see if you can spot the differences between a simple sentence and a complex sentence. They are trying to see if you integrate all of these sentence types into your writing to create a flowing, natural piece of writing.

You may be asking yourself, how does a piece of writing flow? The best way to test to see if your sentence fluency flows is to read it out loud. An essay that flows well is a pleasure to read aloud and sounds very natural. Obviously you cannot start reading your essay aloud during the testing period, but you can practice until that point. Once you get the hang of how a good piece of writing should sound when read aloud, you should be able to do it quietly in your head. This technique will help you on test day and should contribute to a higher sentence fluency score.

Now that you know you need to integrate several types of sentence structures into your essay, let's practice with sentence fluency. Look at the groups of sentences below. Combine these groups of sentences into one or two effective sentences, trying to use a variety of simple, complex, and compound sentences.

Example: **I had to go to the store. I needed to buy apples. I needed to buy bananas. I also needed paper towels.**

I had to go to the store because I needed to buy apples, bananas, and paper towels.

1. She exercises in the gym every morning because she wants to maintain good fitness and a healthy lifestyle so that when she gets older she'll be able to maintain good fitness and a healthy lifestyle.

_____

_____

_____

_____

2. I love coming to high school because I get to see all of my friends. And we get to hang out between classes. My friends make me laugh. They are really funny.

_____

_____

_____

_____

3. Summer break is great because I get to go swimming and hiking and hang out with my friends and sleep in late and relax. Sometimes I get bored. And I miss my friends sometimes.

_____

_____

_____

_____

Once you compare the old sentences with their improvements, you should be able to see how a piece of writing flows. The original examples are cumbersome to read aloud and seem confusing and muddled at times. When you read your revised sentences aloud, they should connect the ideas within the sentences clearly, giving the writing more meaning and impact.

Fragments

Simply stated, a fragment is an incomplete sentence. A complete sentence must have both a subject (noun) and a predicate (verb). Without these two elements, a sentence quickly becomes a fragment. Look at the example below:

I always look forward to the weekends because I get to sleep in. Really late.

Which part of the above example is a fragment? The phrase "really late" is an incomplete sentence because there is no subject or verb. It is also visually identifiable because it is so short in comparison to the complete sentence that precedes it. Read the revision below:

I always look forward to the weekends because I get to sleep in really late.

This revision has combined the two parts of the example into one complete sentence. You could revise the same sentence to read:

I always look forward to the weekends because I get to sleep in. I enjoy sleeping in really late.

The last revision has become two sentences. Unlike the original, both sentences are complete and contain the necessary verbs and nouns. As you write your essay, make sure to avoid fragments. If you know you have a tendency to use fragments in your writing, the revision step is even more crucial. If you read over your essay carefully, you will be able to identify fragments and correct them for your final draft. Just remember that in order to be a complete sentence, there must be a noun (a subject of the sentence, what or whom the sentence is about) and a verb (some type of action must be occurring). For example, the sentence, "The table is beautiful" is a complete sentence because the table is the noun component and the word "is" is the verb component. Remember that "is" is a form of "to be" and is therefore a verb.

Run-on Sentences

Although avoiding fragments can be difficult, run-ons tend to give many more students trouble. Run-on sentences go on and on and do not follow the rules of proper punctuation. Read the example of a run-on below:

My favorite place to vacation is in Santa Barbara, California because it is beautiful and I love the ocean and the salty air and my family always finds delicious places to eat.

The first thing that should strike you about this sentence is that a lot of information is crammed into one sentence. Run-ons do not give the reader any time to breathe; they simply throw out a bunch of information all at once. Read the revised version of the same sentence below:

My favorite place to vacation is in Santa Barbara, California because it is beautiful. I also love the ocean and the salty air. Another great benefit is that my family always finds delicious places to eat.

What was once one sentence has now become three sentences. Simply placing two periods within the original sentence has greatly improved it. In order to identify run-ons, you need to read your essay objectively. Try to put yourself into your reader's shoes. Are you bombarding readers with tons of information, giving them no time digest it all? Break up your information, giving each piece the full sentence that it deserves.

REVIEW
- Use a variety of sentence structures.
- Do not overuse a particular type of structure.
- Read your writing aloud to detect if it flows.

TRAIT 6: CONVENTIONS

This is the last and final trait that will be evaluated in your essay. Simply put, conventions measure your ability to use proper spelling, grammar, and punctuation. This particular trait makes many students uneasy because they feel they lack the ability to spell a word correctly or to use a comma appropriately. Conventions is a trait that takes practice to master. However, if you prepare yourself properly, you should have no trouble landing a high score for conventions.

The most important thing you can do to help your conventions score is to PROOFREAD your essay. Do not assume that the essay you write in your test booklet is error free. Chances are that several errors can be caught and corrected by just reading over your work. Simple errors such as using the wrong "there" instead of "their" or missing a capital letter should all be things that you catch when you proofread.

Spelling

The AIMS writing exam permits the use of dictionaries during the exam, so there should be no excuse for having a misspelled word. Also remember that the AIMS exam is not a timed test. You literally have the time to look up every word in your essay if you like. Since you are allowed the use of a dictionary and there is no time limit placed on your exam, misspelled words have the potential to impact your conventions score dramatically. Your AIMS essay grader will have no sympathy for misspellings, knowing that you had the use of a dictionary.

Grammar

Grammar is one of those topics that many students seem to dislike. It is hard. It is confusing. It is boring. Additionally, sometimes the rules of the English language just do not make sense. The good news is that you do not need to know what a verb clause is or what a modifier is specifically. The bad news is that you do need to know how to use proper grammar in your essay. However, if you have spoken English all your life, you already know the fundamental rules that govern the English language. Let's look at a few of the most common grammatical errors that show up in students' writing.

Subject/Verb Agreement

This concept may sound technical, but it is really very simple. Remember that any proper sentence contains a subject and a verb. For example, read the following sentence:

The dog ran down the street.

What is the subject of this sentence? Who is the sentence about? You should answer "dog" with questions. What is the verb of this sentence? The verb is the action word of the sentence or what is creating the activity. The only word in this sentence that creates action is the word "ran"—the verb.

In the English language, we have to make sure our subjects and verbs agree with one another. We would never say, "The dog run down the street." In this particular sentence, the subject and verb do not agree with one another. There is one dog and we cannot say that one dog run. However, you can say, "The dog is running down the street," or "The dog runs down the street," Now you have subject/verb agreement.

Another tip to keep in mind pertaining to subject/verb agreement is to make sure that you use the same verb tense throughout your essay. If you start writing in the present tense, you need to stick to the present tense. If you start writing in the past tense, you need to stick to the past tense. Read the following sentence:

The Grapes of Wrath is a story about a family traveling to California. They travel with few belongings, and they suffered for much of the journey.

Can you identify where the verb tense changes? This sentence starts out in present tense by using the verb "is." It then continues in the present by using "travel." Then we suddenly encounter a verb that puts us in the past tense. The word "suffered" does not agree with the rest of the verbs in present tense. This is an easy error to fix. Simply change "suffered" to "suffers," and you are back on track. However, you need to catch the error before you can fix it, so once again, PROOFREAD! Practice subject/verb agreement by fixing the following sentences below. Make sure the tense remains the same throughout the sentence.

1. People may say that professional sports had lost their appeal due to superficial requests that are made by players and the outrageous salaries that they demanded.

   _____

   _____

   _____

2. In order to overcome obstacles, one must be willing to tests themselves to the limit, pushes fear aside.

   _____

   _____

   _____

3. In order to have a healthy existence, it is recommend that humans drink at least eight glasses of water every day.

_____

_____

_____

4. Of all the chores that I am expecting to complete after school, vacuuming the living room is my least favorite.

_____

_____

_____

5. Football is my favorite sport because I enjoyed watching the talents of the players. It is amazing to me how fast they could run and how hard they could hit.

_____

_____

_____

Read the sample revisions of the practice sentences below.
1. People may say that professional sports *have* lost their appeal due to superficial requests that are made by players and the outrageous salaries that they *demand.*
2. In order to overcome obstacles, one must be willing to *test* themselves to the limit, *pushing* fear aside.
3. In order to have a healthy existence, it is *recommended* that humans drink at least eight glasses of water every day.
4. Of all of the chores that I am *expected* to complete after school, vacuuming the living room is my least favorite.
5. Football is my favorite sport because I *enjoy* watching the talents of the players. It is amazing to me how fast they *can* run and how hard they *can* hit.

Capital Letters

Several types of words in the English language are always written with capital letters. It is your responsibility to know which words receive capital letters and to write them properly The following is a short list of types of words that receive capital letters.

- The first word of a sentence
- Names of people, both first and last names
- Names of cities, states, and towns
- Names of famous monuments and parks
- Months of the year
- Days of the week
- Works of art and literature

A proper noun is a word that usually deals with names. Think of your own name. Do you capitalize your name when you write it on a paper you are going to hand in for school? Of course you do. When you address an envelope do you capitalize the name of the city that the letter is going to? Yes. In the list above, every entry except the first is an example of proper nouns.

Look at the following sentences. While using the above list as a reference, fix the errors in capitalization and subject/verb agreement.

1. My friends and i are discussing if we should go to the movies on Friday or Saturday night. We decide that Friday night is probably the best night to go.

_____

_____

_____

_____

2. when I went on vacation last Summer, I got to see the washington monument and it is absolutely amazing. I hoped that I could go back in the fall again.

_____

_____

_____

_____

3. I meet jamie and steven at the Library to get help on my math homework. They is both really smart, and I hoped that they could help me.

_____

_____

_____

_____

4. One of my favorite books is "the power of one" by bryce courtenay. It was the amazing story of a young boy who is growing up in Africa.

_____

_____

_____

_____

_____

Read the sample revisions of the practice sentences below.
1. My friends and I were discussing if we should go to the movies on Friday or Saturday night. We decided that Friday night was probably the best night to go.
2. When I went on vacation last summer, I got to see the Washington Monument and it was absolutely amazing. I hope that I can go back in the fall again.
3. I met Jamie and Steven at the library to get help on my math homework. They are both really smart, and I hoped that they could help me.
4. One of my favorite books is *The Power of One* by Bryce Courtenay. It is the amazing story of a young boy who is growing up in Africa.

As you continue to practice with capital letters, identifying which words get capital letters and which do not will become more and more natural. However, capital letters can sometimes be tricky. For instance, in practice sentence 4, the book title, *The Power of One,* has one word that is not capitalized. That word is "of." You may be thinking to yourself, "Why doesn't that word get a capital letter?" The answer is simply that when you capitalize book titles, little words like "of," or "to," or "and" do not get capital letters. You should capitalize the big, important words of the title. In addition, you should always capitalize both the first and last words of a title, no matter how short they are. If you did not know that only certain words in book titles get capital letters, you would capitalize it incorrectly. However, as you read, write, and practice more, you will become familiar with those little rules.

Punctuation

The way that place your commas, periods, and exclamation points can either enhance or hinder your writing. Punctuation can be a very powerful tool. If used correctly, it can increase the flow and rhythm of your writing. When your essay is graded, several types of punctuation will be looked at. Let's look at each type individually.

End-of-Sentence Punctuation

Ever since you learned how to write, you've been told to put a period at the end of all your sentences. The period's main function is to tell a reader that a sentence is finished and complete. However, remember that you can also use exclamation points and question marks at the end of a sentence as well.

- Period: Simply indicates the end of a sentence

   Example: I am looking forward to summer vacation.

- Exclamation point: Used to express excitement or enthusiasm

   Example: I cannot wait for the weekend!

- Question mark: Used to show that a sentence is a question.

   Example: Would you like to go to the store with me?

Even though you have been writing for a large part of your educational career and reviewing end punctuation may seem like a waste of time, it is something useful to keep in mind. Many students do not carefully proofread their writing. They end up making silly mistakes, such as neglecting to put a period at the end of a sentence.

Commas

Commas can be tricky. Figuring out where a comma should go and where it should not go can sometimes be confusing. However, you can follow some basic guidelines to master the use of commas.

- Commas separate items in a list or group.
- Commas precede a coordinating or subordinating conjunction.
- Commas are placed after a dependent clause.

Commas separate items in a list or group. For example, "I had to go to the store to buy apples, pears, and chicken." In this example you can see that the comma is used between "apples," "pears," and "chicken." In this instance, the comma helps connect similar things without making the sentence too wordy.

Commas precede a coordinating or subordinating conjunction. This means that commas are used in compound sentences. For example, "I wanted to go to the party, but I had too much homework." The comma here comes before "but." The purpose of this particular comma is to show how two separate ideas connect. This person had too much homework and, as a result, could not go to a party.

Commas are placed after a dependent clause. For example, "When he was thinking about last night's game, he began recounting the things he did wrong." Remember, a dependent clause in an incomplete sentence. The first part of this sentence is a dependent clause because "When he was thinking about last night's game" is not a complete sentence by itself. A comma connects a dependent clause to another clause, which then forms a complete sentence.

1. I went to the movies with Sara Katie and Rose.

_____

_____

_____

2. We had a great time on Saturday but I wish we had gotten home earlier.

_____

_____

_____

3. As she walked down the street she thought about her day at school

_____

_____

_____

The correct revisions for the above sentences are below.
1. I went to the movies with Sara, Katie, and Rose.
2. We had a great time on Saturday, but I wish we had gotten home earlier.
3. As she walked down the street, she thought about her day at school.

To increase your conventions score, the best thing that you can do is PROOFREAD! Lots of mistakes can be corrected if you simply read over your essay before handing it in. Read over your essay slowly and carefully, trying to read it "aloud." Since you will be in a testing situation, you will not really be able to read your paper aloud. However, knowing how a proper sentence should sound will greatly improve your conventions.

REVIEW
• Proofread your paper for easy-to-correct errors.
• Pay attention to spelling, grammar, and punctuation.
• Use a dictionary if you are unsure.

PUTTING IT ALL TOGETHER

Now that we have reviewed all six traits, it is time to write a practice essay. Keep in mind the six traits:

1. Ideas and content
2. Organization
3. Voice
4. Word choice
5. Sentence fluency
6. Conventions

Before you begin writing, always remember to:

• Brainstorm your ideas
• Recognize your writing purpose and audience

Directions: While focusing on using all six traits, answer the following prompt in a well-developed essay.

Parents and school administrators often complain about the amount of junk food sold through vending machines on school campuses. Your school is currently in the process of trying to eliminate all soda vending machines. Write an essay explaining why the removal of soda machines on campus is a good or a bad idea.

Directions: Use the prewriting space below for outlines, webs, freewriting, or any other method that might hep you to plan your writing.

Directions: Use the following space to create a rough draft of your essay.

Directions: Look over your rough draft, making sure to revise, edit, and proofread. Write your final draft in the space below.

_____

_____

_____

_____

_____

_____

_____

_____

_____

_____

_____

_____

_____

_____

_____

_____

_____

_____

_____

EXPOSITORY AND DESCRIPTIVE WRITING

After all of this practice, you should feel very comfortable producing a persuasive essay. As mentioned earlier in this chapter, the AIMS exam has typically used writing prompts that are persuasive. However, that is not a guarantee that you are going to get a persuasive writing prompt. In order to make sure that you are as well prepared as possible on test day, the following information will point out some key elements of different types of writing.

Expository Writing

This type of writing typically aims to inform the reader. It may also explain, describe, or give information. Persuasive writing does inform the reader as well as persuade, but expository writing does not focus on a debatable issue. For example, if you were to write in response to the question, "Describe the qualities that you look for in someone who you consider a role model," you should notice that the key word in this prompt is "describe." You immediately know that you are being asked to describe qualities that you view as important. Your essay would follow in the same standard five-paragraph structure used for a persuasive essay. However, the focus would be on descriptive details, not examples to prove a persuasive stance. For instance, if you were asked to describe the qualities that you find admirable in a role model, you would list those qualities and then describe them. If you do get an expository prompt, your grader will be interested in the way you integrate descriptive details into your writing.

The following are key phrases that will help you identify an expository prompt:

- **Tell** what happened when . . .
- **Write a report** on . . .
- **Explain** how to . . .
- **Describe** how to . . .

This type of writing is typically much more personal and would be acceptable if written in the first person. For instance, if you get a prompt that asks you to describe how to have the best family vacation, you are going to refer to yourself throughout the essay, using "I" and "my." If you do not get a persuasive writing prompt on the exam, you will likely be given an expository prompt.

The nice thing about expository writing is that you are the expert on the subject. The person grading your essay probably has not been on one of your family vacations and is relying on you for an accurate description of your vacation. Just remember to include as many important details as possible in an expository essay. Look at the following sample of an expository essay below.

"Explain what steps a teenager can take to promote academic success during his or her years as a high school student."

Throughout high school, there are a million things to be worried about. You worry about making it on the varsity team. You worry about whether or not she likes you. You worry about who will ask you to prom. Among all of these things that cause a high school student to worry, obtaining good grades tends to be at the bottom of the list. Grades fall by the wayside due to social obligations and much more pressing matters, such as note writing during your chemistry class. However, if a student takes the proper steps and manages to view grades as important, he will have a successful academic year.

The first step to academic success in high school is to adopt good time management skills. It is obviously much more fun to go out with a group of friends than to read your history book. If you neglect to read your history homework, though, you will not do well on your next test. Students need to learn that they do not necessarily need to become bookworms to do well in school. They just need to manage their time and to prioritize their obligations. For example, if you want to go out with friends but you know you have a history test tomorrow, make yourself study first. After you feel that you have prepared for the test, then go out with your friends. It can be difficult to deny yourself the fun things for a few hours, but getting a good grade on a test will make it all worthwhile.

The next step to academic success is to get extra help when you are confused in a class. It is difficult for a lot of people to grasp a concept firmly within one class period. If you feel at a loss after leaving your biology class, you should consider getting extra help from your teacher. This step directly relates to step one because you have to take time out of fun in order to spend time getting help from a teacher. For example, you probably want to spend your lunch hour with your friends, not your teacher. However, most problems can be solved within just a few meetings with a teacher. When you go in for extra help, the teacher is able to focus on your question alone and does not have to worry about answering thirty other questions from other students.

The last step to academic success in high school is to surround yourself with friends who share your goals. It will be much easier to stay focused on obtaining good grades if all of your friends are trying to do the same thing. It becomes difficult to be the only person in your group to care about grades if all of your friends are going out every night. Having friends that will help you stay focused is not only academically beneficial, but it also helps you make some supportive friendships.

Staying focused in high school takes a lot of dedication and perseverance. There are distractions at every turn, and there always seems to be something to do that is much more fun than studying. However, academic success in high school is extremely valuable for your future. Good grades can earn you scholarships and financial rewards for all of your hard work. So next time your friends call wanting to go out, think about what you have to accomplish first. After you have met you obligations, go have fun!

There are several key points that need to be mentioned concerning expository writing. First of all, there are several similarities between the above sample essay and a persuasive essay. The sample essay follows the same standard five-paragraph format, and the introduction and conclusion mirror one another. The introduction also informs the reader what the essay will be about and then proceeds to present one step for academic success in each body paragraph. The organization that you see here is very similar to that in a persuasive essay. Obviously the author is not trying to argue a specific idea in this essay. Rather, the focus of the essay is to provide suggestions for success. Readers certainly may disagree with the steps for academic success that this author recommends, but the subject matter of the essay is not a hotly contested topic.

The voice that an author would adopt for an expository piece is different than that for a persuasive piece. For example, in a persuasive essay, an author tends to have a voice that is passionate about the topic and approaches the topic with a certain level of seriousness. Imagine if you were asked to write about an emotional issue such as whether or not the death penalty should be legal. The topic itself is extremely serious and therefore demands a serious voice. However, in expository writing, the writer's voice can range from serious to humorous. Authors will use a range of voices to create an interesting expository piece of writing.

If you do get an expository prompt on the exam, make sure to follow all steps of the writing process just like you would for a persuasive prompt. Do your prewriting to brainstorm ample information for your topic. A drawback of expository writing prompts is that they may seem like they do not provide enough material for five paragraphs. Do your prewriting to make sure that you can think of enough information and details to constitute a five-paragraph essay. Remember that one of the six traits is idea development. If you do not develop your ideas in enough detail, you will get marked down on this particular trait.

Descriptive Writing

Descriptive writing is exactly that. You are describing something so clearly that the reader can picture it in his or her mind while reading. If you get this type of prompt, your grader is going to want to see details that relate to the five senses: how does something taste, look, feel, or smell? For example, if you were asked to describe a place where you like to go to be alone, you would have to describe it to your reader. What makes this place special? What does it feel like to be there? A good rule to thumb is to integrate as many sense details as possible. Let your reader imagine what it is actually like to be there. Read the following sample of a descriptive essay below.

Describe the best vacation that you have been on. What did you do? Where did you go? What made this vacation so memorable and special?

People dream of having the opportunity to one day travel to a different country. Many people are never even given the chance to leave the state in which they were born. However, I was lucky enough to be able to travel to Japan when I was thirteen years old. I went to Japan to visit my uncle, and it was a dream vacation. I believe that vacations to new places where you can see different cultures and traditions make for a truly memorable experience.

The best part of my Japanese vacation was going to see all of the Buddhist temples. I will never forget when I first saw an outdoor temple that consisted of a statue of Buddha that was at least ten stories tall. The sheer size and artistry of the statue was enough to invoke awe in all those who stood in its presence. I remember the fragrance of incense wafting through the breeze and the quiet murmurings of those who had come to worship. The very air exuded reverence and mystery. This experience has remained so strong because it was my first time being in a place of worship that was not a Christian church. As a young teenager, it made a deep impression and helped me begin to understand the diversity that exists in our world.

Another memorable element of this vacation was the food! I recall ordering a pizza from Domino's from my uncle's apartment and a topping choice was corn. Corn certainly is not an exotic topping, but it was something that I had never had on a pizza before. Needless to say, our corn pizza was delicious, and not a single kernel went unconsumed. One night we had an exquisite meal that was composed of a specially bred beef known as kobe beef, which was served with various vegetables. The beef came to our table raw and arranged in the shape of a rose. Now you may be wondering how a customer is expected to consume raw beef. In the middle of the table was a large pot of steaming broth that was seasoned with several different spices and vegetables. With our chopsticks, we placed a thin piece of the beef into the broth and let it cook. Within minutes, we were eating savory, buttery pieces of moist beef. The servers were also dressed in authentic Japanese attire, making for a memorable cultural experience. The women wore beautiful silk kimonos and had their hair styled in intricate, gravity-defying fashions. The beautiful costumes and the impeccable service of the waitresses made the dinner alone worth every penny.

The last strong memory that I recall from our vacation was the power of the city itself. My uncle's home was in the middle of Tokyo, and we had the opportunity to walk the city streets on a daily basis. Being raised in a small town, I had never been in a real city. Tokyo was breathtaking. I remember feeling like I was caught in a river of never-ending people who knew exactly where they were going and I was just along for the ride. The energy of so many people made the streets seem alive. I remember noticing that for so many people to be in one, small place, the city was immaculate. There was no litter on the streets or sidewalks, taxi drivers wore white gloves, and people took a genuine pride in their city. Even at thirteen I recall wishing that some American cities would adopt such an attitude.

Even though I was in Japan for only one week, the memories and experiences have made that trip my most memorable vacation. Being exposed to a completely new culture and having the opportunity to experience it on so many levels was an eye-opening adventure. I hope that every individual is given the opportunity to witness what I did and have such a broadening experience.

Several features in the sample essay should grab your attention. The essay is focused on describing events and details to the reader that explain why the trip to Japan was the author's most memorable vacation. Integrating descriptions that relay what the author smelled, saw, and felt all make this essay a descriptive piece of writing. This essay is different from the expository example because it is much more personal and focuses on smaller, descriptive details. Descriptive writing is more personal because it is asking you to describe something that you have done. Therefore, it is coming from your experience.

Unlike in persuasive writing, using the pronoun "I" throughout a descriptive essay is perfectly acceptable. Persuasive writing tends to discourage using "I" because it is not an appropriate word for the type of serious, professional voice that you want to use.

Expository and descriptive writing are likely going to be the other modes of writing that you will encounter on the exam if you do not get a persuasive writing prompt. Just remember to integrate specific, supporting details—that is what your grader is looking for! Another tip to keep in mind with either descriptive or expository writing is to make sure that you stick to the prompt! Especially with descriptive writing, students have the tendency to go off topic very quickly. If a prompt is asking you to describe your most memorable vacation, it is asking you to focus on *one* vacation. Do not end up describing five of your favorite vacations. Make sure to go through the writing process and brainstorm your ideas, eliminating any that go off topic.

Review of Expository and Descriptive Writing

- Using the pronoun "I" for both types of writing is acceptable.
- Integrate details that focus on sight, smell, sight, touch, and taste for descriptive writing.
- Stick to the prompt, and do not go off topic.
- Brainstorm to ensure that you have enough information for a five-paragraph essay.

Part Four

AIMS Practice Tests

PRACTICE TEST A ANSWER SHEET

Fill in the bubble completely.
Erase carefully if answer is changed.

1. Ⓐ Ⓑ Ⓒ Ⓓ	21. Ⓐ Ⓑ Ⓒ Ⓓ	41. Ⓐ Ⓑ Ⓒ Ⓓ
2. Ⓐ Ⓑ Ⓒ Ⓓ	22. Ⓐ Ⓑ Ⓒ Ⓓ	42. Ⓐ Ⓑ Ⓒ Ⓓ
3. Ⓐ Ⓑ Ⓒ Ⓓ	23. Ⓐ Ⓑ Ⓒ Ⓓ	43. Ⓐ Ⓑ Ⓒ Ⓓ
4. Ⓐ Ⓑ Ⓒ Ⓓ	24. Ⓐ Ⓑ Ⓒ Ⓓ	44. Ⓐ Ⓑ Ⓒ Ⓓ
5. Ⓐ Ⓑ Ⓒ Ⓓ	25. Ⓐ Ⓑ Ⓒ Ⓓ	45. Ⓐ Ⓑ Ⓒ Ⓓ
6. Ⓐ Ⓑ Ⓒ Ⓓ	26. Ⓐ Ⓑ Ⓒ Ⓓ	46. Ⓐ Ⓑ Ⓒ Ⓓ
7. Ⓐ Ⓑ Ⓒ Ⓓ	27. Ⓐ Ⓑ Ⓒ Ⓓ	47. Ⓐ Ⓑ Ⓒ Ⓓ
8. Ⓐ Ⓑ Ⓒ Ⓓ	28. Ⓐ Ⓑ Ⓒ Ⓓ	48. Ⓐ Ⓑ Ⓒ Ⓓ
9. Ⓐ Ⓑ Ⓒ Ⓓ	29. Ⓐ Ⓑ Ⓒ Ⓓ	49. Ⓐ Ⓑ Ⓒ Ⓓ
10. Ⓐ Ⓑ Ⓒ Ⓓ	30. Ⓐ Ⓑ Ⓒ Ⓓ	50. Ⓐ Ⓑ Ⓒ Ⓓ
11. Ⓐ Ⓑ Ⓒ Ⓓ	31. Ⓐ Ⓑ Ⓒ Ⓓ	51. Ⓐ Ⓑ Ⓒ Ⓓ
12. Ⓐ Ⓑ Ⓒ Ⓓ	32. Ⓐ Ⓑ Ⓒ Ⓓ	52. Ⓐ Ⓑ Ⓒ Ⓓ
13. Ⓐ Ⓑ Ⓒ Ⓓ	33. Ⓐ Ⓑ Ⓒ Ⓓ	53. Ⓐ Ⓑ Ⓒ Ⓓ
14. Ⓐ Ⓑ Ⓒ Ⓓ	34. Ⓐ Ⓑ Ⓒ Ⓓ	54. Ⓐ Ⓑ Ⓒ Ⓓ
15. Ⓐ Ⓑ Ⓒ Ⓓ	35. Ⓐ Ⓑ Ⓒ Ⓓ	55. Ⓐ Ⓑ Ⓒ Ⓓ
16. Ⓐ Ⓑ Ⓒ Ⓓ	36. Ⓐ Ⓑ Ⓒ Ⓓ	56. Ⓐ Ⓑ Ⓒ Ⓓ
17. Ⓐ Ⓑ Ⓒ Ⓓ	37. Ⓐ Ⓑ Ⓒ Ⓓ	57. Ⓐ Ⓑ Ⓒ Ⓓ
18. Ⓐ Ⓑ Ⓒ Ⓓ	38. Ⓐ Ⓑ Ⓒ Ⓓ	58. Ⓐ Ⓑ Ⓒ Ⓓ
19. Ⓐ Ⓑ Ⓒ Ⓓ	39. Ⓐ Ⓑ Ⓒ Ⓓ	59. Ⓐ Ⓑ Ⓒ Ⓓ
20. Ⓐ Ⓑ Ⓒ Ⓓ	40. Ⓐ Ⓑ Ⓒ Ⓓ	60. Ⓐ Ⓑ Ⓒ Ⓓ

Chapter 8

Reading Practice Test A

1548 S. Birch St.
Flagstaff, AZ 86001
(928) 779-3785

November 20, 2006

Veronica Thomas
Vice President
2358 N. 3rd St.
Phoenix, AZ 85051

Dear Mrs. Thomas:

My name is Dylan Banks, and I am currently the head of the "Combating Cancer Walk" committee. I was wondering if your company would be interested in making a financial contribution to this year's Cancer Walk, taking place in January of 2007. Our program raises thousands of dollars for cancer research, with all of the walkers raising the money through pledges they have collected. Last year, we obtained a record goal of $350,000.

However, as much money as we raise for cancer research, it is still somewhat expensive to fund the walk. If you choose to make a financial contribution, your money will go toward water and snack stations that are placed on the course for the walkers, commemorative T-shirts, and necessary police and traffic staff. This walk is gaining popularity every year, and in turn, the resources needed by the walk committee continue to grow.

If you choose to contribute, please send your donation in the enclosed envelope. I cannot express the gratitude we on the walk committee have for those companies and individuals that have contributed throughout the years. Without business contributions, we would be unable to organize this successful fund-raiser. An added benefit of donating to the walk is that all businesses receive an advertising banner placed at the end of the walk. If you have any questions concerning donations, please feel free to call me.

Sincerely,

Dylan Banks

Dylan Banks
Committee Chair of Combating Cancer Walk

1 All of the money raised by the walkers is
  A donated to cancer research
  B saved for funding next year's walk
  C given back to the donating companies
  D spent on T-shirts and snacks

2 The walk committee needs financial contributions for all of the following *except*
  A police staff
  B pledges
  C T-shirts
  D snacks

3 If Mrs. Thomas chooses to make a contribution, she should
  A write a letter to Dylan Banks
  B personally telephone Dylan Banks
  C buy refreshments for the walkers
  D mail money to the walk committee

4 The walkers raise money for cancer research by
  A selling commemorative T-shirts
  B getting individual pledges
  C donating their own money
  D asking for business donations

5 The walk committee needs more financial contributions because
  A they are not getting enough pledges
  B fewer companies are donating
  C fewer people are participating
  D the walk is gaining popularity

6 What benefit do businesses receive if they make a donation?
  A A discounted walk fee for all of their employees
  B An advertising banner placed at the end of the walk
  C Free commemorative T-shirts for all employees
  D A public thank you from the walk committee

7 Which of the following people would be a likely participant in the walk?
  A A young mother
  B A financial banker
  C A cancer survivor
  D A teenager

8 What is the purpose of this letter?
  A to express appreciation
  B to request financial assistance
  C to offer professional advice
  D to request information

9 Which of the following types of businesses would **not** be likely to donate to the walk?
  A doctor's office
  B financial bank
  C the Red Cross
  D hospice centers

Directions: Read the following essay excerpt and then answer questions 10–18.

This short excerpt is taken from *Walden; Or, Life in the Woods* by Henry David Thoreau. Thoreau wrote this book during the two years that he lived at Walden Pond. It contains his reflections on nature, politics, and human nature.

Walden
by Henry David Thoreau
(Reprinted with permission from Dover Publications)

The change from storm and winter to serene and mild weather from dark and sluggish hours to bright and elastic ones, is a memorable crisis which all things proclaim. It is seemingly instantaneous at last. Suddenly an influx of light filled my house, though the evening was at hand, and the clouds of winter still overhung it, and the eaves were dripping with sleety rain. I looked out the window, and lo! where yesterday was cold gray ice there lay the transparent pond already calm and full of hope as in a summer evening, reflecting a summer evening sky in its bosom, though none was visible overhead, as if it had intelligence with some remote horizon. I heard a robin in the distance, the first I had heard for many a thousand years, methought, whose note I shall not forget for many a thousand more—the same sweet and powerful song as of yore. O the evening robin, at the end of a New England summer day! If I could ever find the twig he sits upon! I mean *he;* I mean *the twig.* The pitch-pines and shrub-oaks about my house, which had so long drooped, suddenly resumed their several characters, looked brighter, greener, and more erect and alive, as if effectually cleansed and restored by the rain. I knew that it would not rain anymore. You may tell by looking at any twig of the forest, ay, at your very wood-pile, whether its winter is past or not. As it grew darker, I was startled by the *honking* of geese from southern lakes, and indulging at last in unrestrained complaint and mutual consolation. Standing at my door, I could hear the rush of their wings; when, driving toward my house, they suddenly spied my light, and with hushed clamor wheeled and settled in the pond. So I came in, and shut the door, and passed my first spring night in the woods.

In the morning I watched the geese from the door through the mist, sailing in the middle of the pond, fifty rods off, so large and *tumultuous* that Walden appeared like an artificial pond for their amusement. But when I stood on the shore they at once rose up with a great flapping of wings at the signal of their commander, and when they had got into rank and circled about over my head, twenty-nine of them, and steered straight to Canada, with a regular *honk* from the leader at intervals, trusting to break their fast in muddier pools. A "plump" of ducks rose at the same time and took the route to the north in the wake of their noisier cousins.

For a week I heard the circling groping clangor of some solitary goose in the foggy mountains, seeking its companion, and still peopling the woods with sound of a larger life than they could sustain. In April the pigeons were seen again flying express in small flocks, and in due time I heard the martins twittering over my clearing, though it had not seemed that the township contained so many that it could afford me any, and I fancied that they were peculiarly of the ancient race that dwelt in hollow trees ere white men came. In almost all climes the tortoise and the frog are among the precursors and heralds of this season, and birds fly with song and glancing plumage, and plants spring and bloom, and winds blow, to correct this slight oscillation of the poles and preserve the equilibrium of Nature.

10 This passage is mainly about

A the migration of geese and other birds

B the transition from winter to spring

C the peacefulness found in nature

D the pleasure of living by a pond

11 The statement, "I heard a robin in the distance, the first I had heard for many a thousand years," is an example of which type of figurative language?
A simile
B metaphor
C imagery
D hyperbole

12 When Thoreau says that the geese are "trusting to break their fast in muddier pools," he is saying that the geese will
A find food in another location
B fly quickly to another pond
C find a pond with more mud
D remain at Walden pond

13 The dominating tone that is found throughout this essay is one of
A fascination
B confusion
C observation
D humbleness

14 At the end of the essay, the reader can conclude that Thoreau
A will shortly leave his home at Walden Pond
B will follow the geese and other birds into Canada
C will remain at Walden Pond and enjoy nature
D observe the behavior of the frogs and turtles

15 The statement, "It is seemingly instantaneous at last," means that
A the arrival of the geese and other birds comes without warning
B the transition from winter to spring happens all at once
C his house is suddenly filled with an unexplainable light
D the rain suddenly stops and air is filled with bright sunshine

16 Within the sentence, "So large and tumultuous that Walden appeared like an artificial pond for their amusement," the word tumultuous most likely means
A confusing
B loudly
C messy
D agitated

17 In the statement, "I fancied that they were peculiarly of the ancient race that dwelt in hollow trees," Thoreau is comparing the _____ to an ancient race.
A pigeons
B martins
C geese
D ducks

18 After reading the essay, the reader can infer that Thoreau
A takes pleasure being in nature
B is a scientist who studies birds
C does not enjoy the change of seasons
D wants to hunt the geese and ducks

Directions:	Read the following story and answer questions 19–27.

The following excerpt is from Bram Stoker's famous gothic horror novel, *Dracula*. This excerpt occurs at the end of the novel when the characters are hunting down Dracula in order to kill him before the sun sets. This particular excerpt is told from Mina's point of view, who is one of the central characters of the story. She relates the events as they unfold, watching her friends and her husband, Jonathon, hunt down the count.

Dracula
by Bram Stoker
(Reprinted with permission from Dover Publications)

Every instant seemed an age whilst we waited. The wind came now in fierce bursts, and the snow was driven with a fury as it swept upon us in circling eddies, at times we could not see an arm's length before us; but at others, as the hollow-sounding wind swept by us, I seemed to clear the air-space around us so that we could see afar. We had of late been so accustomed to watch for sunrise and sunset, that we knew with fair accuracy when it would be; and we knew that before long the sun would set. It was hard to believe that by our watches it was less than an hour that we waited in that rocky shelter before the various bodies began to converge upon us. The wind came now with fiercer and more bitter weeps, and more steadily from the north. It seemingly had driven the snow clouds from us, for, with only occasional bursts, the snow fell. We could distinguish clearly the individuals of each party, the pursued and the pursuers. Strangely enough those pursued did not seem to realize, or at least to care, that they were being pursued; they seemed, however, to hasten with redoubled speed as the sun dropped lower and lower on the mountain tops.

Closer and closer they drew. The Professor and I crouched down behind our rock, and held our weapons ready; I could see that he was determined that they should not pass. One and all were quite unaware of our presence.

All at once two voices shouted out to: "Halt!" One was my Jonathon's, raised in a high key of passion; the other Mr. Morris' strong resolute tone of quiet command. The gypsies may not have known the language, but there was no mistaking the tone, in whatever tongue the words were spoken. Instinctively they reined in, and at the instant Lord Godalming and Jonathon dashed up at one side and Dr. Seward and Mr. Morris on the other. The leader of the gypsies, a splendid-looking fellow who sat his horse like a centaur, waved them back, and in a fierce voice gave his companions some word to proceed. They lashed the horses which sprang forward; but the four men raised their Winchester rifles, and in an unmistakable way commanded them to stop. At the same moment Dr. Van Helsing and I rose behind the rock and pointed our weapons at them. Seeing that they were surrounded the men tightened their reins and drew up. The leader turned to them and gave a word at which every man of the gypsy party drew what weapon he carried, knife or pistol, and held himself in readiness to attack. Issue was joined in an instant.

The leader, with a quick movement of his rein, threw his horse out in front, and pointing first to the sun—now close down on the hill tops—and then to the castle, said something which I did not understand. For answer, all four men of our party threw themselves from their horses and dashed towards the cart. I should have felt terrible fear at seeing Jonathon in such danger, but that the ardour of battle must have been upon me as well as the rest of them; I felt no fear, but only a wild, surging desire to do something. Seeing the quick movement of our parties, the leader of the gypsies gave a command; his men instantly formed round the cart in a sort of undisciplined endeavor, each one shouldering and pushing the other in his eagerness to carry out the order.

In the midst of this I could see that Jonathon on one side of the ring of men, and Quincey on the other, were forcing their way to the cart; it was evident that they were bent on finishing their task before the sun should set. Nothing seemed to stop or even to hinder them. Neither the leveled weapons nor the flashing knives of the gypsies in front, nor the howling of wolves behind, appeared to even attract their attention. Jonathon's <u>impetuosity</u>, and the manifest singleness of his purpose, seemed to overawe those in front of him; instinctively they cowered aside and let him pass. In an instant he had jumped upon the cart, and with a strength which seemed incredible, raised the great box, and flung it over the wheel to the ground. In the meantime, Mr. Morris had had to force to pass through his side of the ring of the gypsies. All the time I had been breathing breathlessly watching Jonathon I had, with the tail of my eye, seen him pressing desperately forward, and had seen the knives of the gypsies flash as he won a way through them, and they cut at him. He had parried with his great bowie knife, and at first I thought that he too had come through in safety; but as he sprang beside Jonathon, who had by now jumped from the cart, I could see that with his left hand he was clutching at his side, and that the blood was spurting through his fingers. He did not delay notwithstanding this, for as Jonathon, with desperate energy, attacked one end of the chest, attempting to prize off the lid with his great Kukri knife, he attacked the other frantically with his bowie. Under the efforts of both men the lid began to yield; the nails drew with a quick screeching sound, and the top of the box was thrown back.

By this time the gypsies, seeing themselves covered by the Winchesters, and at the mercy of the Lord Godalming and Dr. Seward, had given in and made not further resistance. The sun was almost down on the mountain tops, and the shadows of the whole group fell upon the snow. I saw the Count lying within the box upon the earth, some of which the rude falling from the cart had scattered over him. He was deathly pale, just like a waxen image, and the red eyes glared with the horrible <u>vindictive</u> look which I knew so well.

As I looked, the eyes saw the sinking sun, and the look of hate in them turned to triumph.

But, on the instant, came the sweep and flash of Jonathon's great knife. I shrieked as I saw it shear through the throat; whilst at the same moment Mr. Morris's bowie knife plunged into the heart.

It was like a miracle; but before our very eyes, and almost in the drawing of a breath, the whole body crumbled into dust and passed from our sight.

I shall be glad as long as I live that even in that moment of final dissolution, there was in the face a look of peace, such as I never could have imagined might have rested there.

19 The most important problem the characters are facing in their hunt for Dracula is the
  A resistance of the gypsies
  B setting of the sun
  C oncoming snowstorm
  D danger of the Count himself

20 Which of the following statements best reflects Mina's (the narrator) emotions as she watches the other characters charge the gypsies?
  A "At the same moment Dr. Van Helsing and I rose behind the rock and pointed our weapons at them."
  B "But, on the instant, came the sweep and flash of Jonathon's great knife. I shrieked as I saw it shear through the throat"
  C "The ardour of battle must have been upon me as well as the rest of them; I felt no fear, but only a wild, surging desire to do something."
  D "We could distinguish clearly the individuals of each party, the pursued and the pursuers."

21 Within the sentence "And the red eyes glared with the horrible <u>vindictive</u> look which I knew so well," the word <u>vindictive</u> most likely means
   A desire to cause harm
   B naturally evil
   C wanting revenge
   D looking for an escape

22 The gypsies fail to protect the cart after they realize that
   A the snowstorm is steadily getting worse
   B Dracula does not need their help to live
   C the sun has set behind the mountains
   D they are surrounded and held at gunpoint

23 Which of the following details contribute to the sense of suspense found in this passage?
   A In order to kill the count, the characters must act before sunset.
   B The gypsies surround the cart, attempting to protect the count.
   C Jonathon and Mr. Morris manage to kill the count with their knives.
   D The snowstorm makes it difficult for other characters to see.

24 What is the climax of this excerpt?
   A the gypsies protect the count in his cart
   B the sun starts to set behind the mountains
   C Jonathon and Mr. Morris kill the count
   D they see the evil, red eyes of the count

25 In the description, "He was deathly pale, just like a waxen image," the two things being compared are
   A Dracula's face to wax
   B paleness to Dracula's face
   C Jonathon's face to paleness
   D paleness to something waxen

26 The quote, "As I looked, the eyes saw the sinking sun, and the look of hate in them turned to triumph," shows that the count
   A believes that he cannot be harmed by the pursuing characters
   B thinks he has defeated the characters in their attempt to kill him
   C believes that the gypsies have successfully protected him
   D thinks that he can now bring physical harm to the characters

27 Within the sentence, "Jonathon's <u>impetuosity</u>, and the manifest singleness of his purpose, seemed to overawe those in front of him;" the word <u>impetuosity</u> most likely means
   A rapid movement
   B dominating voice
   C amazing strength
   D forceful energy

| Directions: | Read the following advertisement and answer questions 28–36. |

Do you feel like you've come to a dead end?
Are you just sitting there, wondering what to do with your life?
We've got your answer!!!

The University of Chicago

We are now accepting applications for the 2006–2007 academic school year!
We offer many different programs—here are just a few of the exciting degrees
we provide:

Advertising	Construction Management
Nursing	Teacher Certification
Communications	Web Design and Development
Photography	Restaurant Management
Interior Design	Public Relations

Interested????

- Applications are being accepted right now up until August 7th.
- Take a campus tour and see our great facilities and faculty in person.
- Our admissions and advisory staff are on-site to help you prepare for your future!
- Admission requirements and answers to commonly asked questions can be found
  on our web site at **www.uofc.com**

Hope to see you in the fall!

---

28 The university offers degrees in all of the following **except**

   A interior design

   B communications

   C creative writing

   D public relations

29 The advertisement uses the pronoun "you" throughout to

   A personalize their message for each individual reader

   B personalize their message for a large audience

   C make their message non-gender-specific

   D emphasize the importance of the individual

30 The purpose of this advertisement is to
- **A** inform students about the university's programs
- **B** provide information about campus tours
- **C** ask students personal questions about their life
- **D** encourage indviduals to apply to the university

31 What is the purpose of the questions asked at the top of the flyer?
- **A** To immediately engage and interest all readers
- **B** To get the reader to reflect on his or her own situation
- **C** To provide a concrete answer to the given questions
- **D** To distract the reader as to the ad's true purpose

32 The intended audience for this advertisement is likely
- **A** college students
- **B** high school students
- **C** students' parents
- **D** high school principals

33 If someone has questions regarding the ad or the university, they should
- **A** call the admission's office
- **B** take a guided campus tour
- **C** go to the university web site
- **D** ask a member of the advisory staff

34 An individual interested in applying to the University of Chicago might also be interested in
- **A** scholarship application information
- **B** a brochure about a technical college
- **C** year-long travel abroad programs
- **D** jobs that require a high school diploma

35 This ad is specific to students who wish to
- **A** take part in the photography program
- **B** enroll for the 2006–2007 school year
- **C** want to take a guided campus tour
- **D** have questions regarding admissions

36 The ad uses multiple question marks or exclamation points to
- **A** confuse the reader
- **B** dramatize information
- **C** improve the visual appeal
- **D** emphasize certain aspects

Directions: Read the following letter to the editor and answer questions 37–46.

Dear Editor:

I am a parent of a student who is currently attending West Valley High School. As many of the community members are aware, our neighborhood high school is facing several significant challenges. Before I begin listing the problems that face our children's school, I would like to make it clear that I respect the staff at West Valley High and appreciate the numerous sacrifices that they make on behalf of our students.

The first problem that West Valley faces is dropping enrollment numbers. In the year 2001, the school reported that its current student body consisted of over one thousand students. Today, however, the current student population stands at a pathetic five hundred students. How can our student population have decreased by fifty percent? I believe the answer to that is that the school has decided to drop popular student electives and athletic programs, the quality of instruction has decreased, and the school no longer has any school spirit. I have had several of my children graduate from West Valley and to see the state of our school today is absolutely shameful.

It may seem that dropping enrollment is not a pressing issue. It certainly means smaller class sizes for our students and more one-on-one instruction from teachers. However, as many of you realize, dropping enrollment means less money for the school. Without money coming in from the state government, the school can no longer afford fine arts and athletics programs. So what can we do as community members to save West Valley? I believe that we can do more than we realize.

The first hurdle is obviously to figure out how to increase student enrollment. Once we get more students attending West Valley, the more programs we can afford to offer to our students. If we can offer dynamic, interesting electives, then students will not want to leave. In order to increase enrollment, parents, administrators, and students need to organize recruitment efforts. Even though our school has diminished in quality compared with previous years, we still have several strong points, such as a state champion cross-country team, nationally recognized science department, and several award-winning teachers. If we want students to attend West Valley, we need to be sure to stress the positive aspects of our school. Students will receive a great education and will be prepared to tackle future challenges. I suggest that we publicly advertise the school in the newspapers, on TV, and on the radio. Once people know what West Valley has to offer, they may be more inclined to send their students to our campus.

Once recruitment has been successful and the high school sees an increase in student numbers, we can begin to reinstate electives, enabling students to personalize their education. If students feel that they have several choices when it comes to their education, they will be pleased with the education that they receive. Once the school has the financial resources, we can bring back previous programs such as creative writing, photography, and the swim team.

The last issue that the school needs to address is the quality of instruction that it is providing. The majority of the teachers at West Valley do an absolutely commendable job; however, there are several teachers that need to be let go. These teachers do not take the weight of their job seriously, hand out grades that require no work from the student, and most importantly, create a bad image for our school. As the saying goes, "It only takes one bad apple to ruin the bunch." Even though we have many wonderful teachers at our school, the community seems to hear about only the teachers who are not doing their jobs. We need to make sure that every teacher that works at West Valley is doing his or her best to educate our students and projecting a favorable image of the school.

I believe that if we take the time to initiate some changes at West Valley High School, we will see rapid improvement. As parents and community members, it is our job to ensure that our children get a quality education.

Sincerely,

Barbara Harris

Barbara Harris

37 Complete the web below.

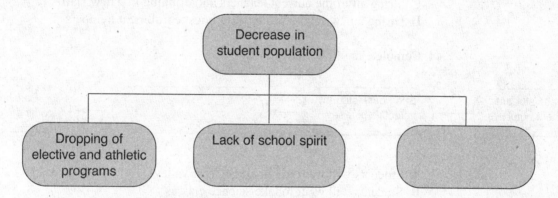

A Decrease in quality of instruction
B Dropping of the swim team
C Advertise for the school
D Negative image of the school

38 The decrease in student enrollment is a significant issue because
A it gives the school a bad image and numbers continue to drop
B quality teachers do not want to work at a school with a bad image
C the school loses money and cannot fund elective programs
D the school loses school spirit and more students leave the campus

39 The author of this letter believes that by stressing the _____
aspects of the school, student enrollment will increase.
A athletic
B positive
C educational
D elective

40 The author uses the phrase, "It only takes one bad apple to ruin the bunch" to
show that
A one bad teacher makes all teachers become bad teachers
B one bad teacher gives the whole school a bad image
C with enough good teachers, the bad teachers will not matter
D the bad teachers are beginning to outnumber good teachers

41 The value of having student electives is to

A enable the students to personalize their education

B give the teachers a variety in the courses they teach

C continue to promote growing enrollment numbers

D academically prepare students for future challenges

42 What details could this author integrate into her letter to make a more convincing argument?

A student quotes about why they are unhappy at West Valley High School

B teacher interviews about what they are doing to give quality education

C sample examples from other schools that have increased their enrollment

D parent suggestions on how they could boost student enrollment

43 Which of the following solutions would the author of this letter most likely agree to?

A Transporting students to a different neighborhood high school

B Providing after-school clubs that require minimal finances

C Firing all of the current teachers and bringing in a new staff

D Hiring a new school principal to boost enrollment numbers

44 Complete the flow chart below.

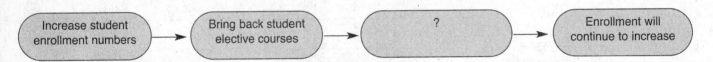

A Students will want to remain at West Valley

B Students will want to take science classes

C Quality teachers will come to West Valley

D Athletic programs will be reinstated

45 The author of this letter believes she is qualified to discuss this topic because she

A is a teacher at the school

B is on the school board

C is a parent of a student

D lives in the community

46 Which of the following is an accurate summary of this letter?

A Parents and community members are upset at West Valley because it keeps losing students to schools that offer higher-quality and more diverse athletic programs.

B Students do not like to attend West Valley because there is no longer any school spirit. This problem could be solved if the school brought back some of its athletic programs.

C The quality of instruction at West Valley has diminished and students are seeking high schools that will provide them with a high-quality, academic education.

D West Valley currently faces the problem of dropping enrollment. However, this can be solved by recruiting students, offering electives, and providing quality instruction.

Directions: Read the following poem and answer questions 47–53.

HERO

I see you marching down the hallway,
The sea of people clear before you:
Like Moses and the Red Sea.
Your football jersey number
Is scrawled in bathroom stalls
A high school monument to the gods.
Giving out high fives
That are as valuable as hundred dollar bills;
Those that are denied
Stare on in burning envy.
Many think you're a stuck-up jock
Too good for anybody
Not sharing grunts and hits
With you on the field.
They call you "roid rager" "meathead"
But I know different.
They call me "geek" or "retard"
Just to name a few.
But you told them to stop
To back off and leave me alone
I call you "Hero."

47 This poem focuses on
   A a geeky student
   B student bullies
   C a football player
   D a snotty student

48 The description, "The sea of people clear before you: / Like Moses and the Red
   Sea," means that
   A the school hallways are crowded and difficult to get through
   B the subject of the poem is similar to the biblical figure of Moses
   C the narrator of the poem tries to clear a path for the poem's subject
   D people move out of the subject's way with little effort from him

49 The narrator views this individual as a hero because
   A he stands up for the narrator
   B he is a popular football player
   C he is envied by other students
   D he gives students high fives

50 Which of the following descriptions is a simile?

  A Giving out high fives / That are as valuable as hundred dollar bills;

  B I see you marching down the hallway, / The sea of people clear before you:

  C Your football jersey number / Is scrawled in bathroom stalls

  D Those that are denied / Stare on in burning envy.

51 The phrase, "A high school monument to the gods," contributes to a(n)
_____ tone.

  A reverent

  B sincere

  C ecstatic

  D sarcastic

52 According to the poem, both the narrator and the subject of the poem are battling

  A bullies

  B stereotypes

  C coaches

  D conformity

53 The narrator emphasizes the value of

  A standing up for yourself

  B breaking stereotypes

  C the kind action of another

  D fitting in with a group

| **Directions:** | Read the following story and answer questions 54–60. |

The Race

"Hey, man. You wanna go to a movie tomorrow night?"

"I would but I've gotta do my run. I don't think I'll be done in time to go see a movie with you guys."

"Well what do you know? Mr. Ironman is too busy training again to have any fun. Dude, when is this gonna stop?"

"Pete, the race is in a month and a half. And don't call me Mr. Ironman. I'm doing a marathon, not an Ironman."

"It's your loss without a doubt. Besides, I think Andrea said she was going to go. Does that change your decision?"

"No."

"You're hopeless. You'd rather go running through the dark streets of Topeka, Kansas, than go to the movies with Andrea Ross. I give up."

I couldn't help but smile at the phone as Pete continued to rant. To his credit, skipping a movie opportunity with Andrea Ross was probably the stupidest thing I had ever done. I needed to log a ten-mile run tomorrow, though. With my classes and working my after-school job at a downtown deli, night was really the only time I had to train.

"Dude? Are you still there? Last chance, man. And if you don't go, I'm going to take Andrea to the movies myself."

"Pete, you know I have to get this run in. I haven't come this far to slack off now. And don't bother trying to take Andrea to the movies. Besides, she told me she thinks you're ugly."

"You're lucky you can outrun me, Thomas, otherwise I'd beat your head into the ground."

"Sure. Hey, have fun. When this is all over, we'll go the movies like four times a week."

I heard a frustrated grunt followed by the tone of a dead phone. I knew Pete was aggravated with me for now. I knew that on Sunday, though, he would wake up at the crack of dawn with me, riding his bike along as I slogged out mile after mile.

I was down to exactly forty days before my race—twenty-six miles designed to brutalize you both mentally and physically. I had already logged two months of training, and now I was in the home stretch. Every workout, every mile counted toward my successful finish. This was the first marathon I ever trained for, and it turned out to be way more of a commitment than I had ever anticipated. Running six days a week and lifting weights three days a week had paid off, though. I had taken up admiring my newly blossoming muscles in the bathroom, pretending to catch Andrea Ross as she fainted, shocked by my chiseled manliness. However, the fact that I had not interacted with my friends for the last two months prevented me from seeing if my Andrea fainting theory would prove correct. I just kept telling myself that all of these sacrifices would pay off. Finishing a marathon was going to be the biggest accomplishment of my entire life. I felt that finishing my first marathon at seventeen years old was something that I could be proud of.

Just as I predicted, Pete was promptly on my front porch at 6:30 A.M., Sunday morning. "Morning." I slurred through a yawn.

"Well if it isn't Mr. Ironman himself. You look like you're ready to take on the world!" he said with mock enthusiasm.

"Thanks for showing up. How was the movie?"

"Well, the movie was a waste of eight bucks, but the way Andrea was into me, made it all worth it."

I looked at Pete out of the corner of my eye as I began lacing up my running shoes. "Is that a fact?" I asked <u>nonchalantly</u>. "That sounds like quite a night. I mean, to take the most beautiful girl in school to the movies with you?" I inquired with dramatic interest, looking at him with eyes wide enough to resemble a praying mantis.

"You're lucky I'm such a good friend," Pete replied, a little hurt that I didn't believe his story. "Because I totally could have taken her to the movies if I wanted to."

"I have never doubted that for a single second."

"You ready to get this show on the road? My mom said she'd make waffles for us after we're finished. I told her since you're doing your twenty today, she should probably plan on making about three dozen waffles."

"That sounds great. Although after twenty miles, I might need four dozen." I groaned as I stretched my quads.

"Seriously, I'm starving."

"How can you possibly be hungry?" I asked, amazed. "You've been up for about fifteen minutes, not even enough time to consume the calories from the five frozen pizzas you probably ate last night."

"That's really not the issue here. Besides, blame it on the tapeworm."

I smiled and shook my head, heading down the porch steps. Pete followed behind, letting the rear tire of his bike loudly smack every step.

This was going to be the first time I had ever attempted to run twenty miles. Last Sunday I ran sixteen miles, and I hoped that I had it in me to be able to complete four more without too much agony. Pete had proven to be a truly valuable resource on my Sunday runs. His endless banter managed to distract me from any physical pain for at least the first two hours of the run. I never really needed to add anything to the conversation. Pete was a one-man TV miniseries.

We started down the street, the cool air immediately driving away any remaining sleepiness. My muscles began to warm, my heart efficiently pumped blood through my veins. I could feel that today's run was going to be a success. I felt strong, felt confident, and had a great companion. Pete and I took a right out of our neighborhood—if only we had gone down a different street.

As the sun began to peek over the horizon, bathing the air in a pinky glow, Pete jabbered about who he thought the prettiest girl at school was. As he continued to talk, it seemed that his standards for determining "beautiful" were simply anyone who did not fall into the male category. "Courtney is gorgeous and she plays soccer, hence she's a great athlete. Lisette is pretty cute too, and she tells the best jokes ever. But I think that Renee probably takes it. I would give anything to have that girl just look at me for a split second."

"So she can what? Run away screaming?" I asked between breaths.

"Maybe you should pick up the pace if you have enough energy to make lame jokes," Pete replied, pedaling ahead of me.

I pumped my legs faster, trying to catch up with Pete. "Dude, slow down!" I tried to shout, gasping for air. Pete's bike reflected the sunlight at me in reply.

Pete began pedaling faster, forcing me to pump my arms harder and harder. I rounded the corner of Smith Street and saw Pete stopped at the intersection at the top of the street. He was leaning coolly on his bike, right in front Mrs. Germund's house, apparently analyzing the impressive flowers she had growing in her front yard. "Geez, thanks for waiting. I'm glad you have time to stop and smell the flowers," I managed to gasp, putting my hands on my knees.

"Dude, something bad happened," whispered Pete. Now that I had oxygen flowing clearly to my brain, I looked at Pete's face for the first time. He was pale and his face was drenched in sweat. He also seemed to be slightly trembling. "What happened? Are you OK?" I asked apprehensively. "I got stung by a bee," Pete managed to get out. Before I knew what I was doing, I exploded with laughter. "You got stung by a bee?" I teased. "Well, we better call an ambulance for your bee sting. Dude, suck it up. It's just a bee," I continued to chuckle.

"You don't understand. I'm allergic to bees. If I don't get to a hospital within twenty minutes, I could stop breathing. I'm not being a wimp, I swear."

Before I even realized what Pete had said, he crumpled into a heap on the sidewalk.

* * *

Still in my running gear, I rapidly flipped through the pages of a magazine in the hospital waiting room. My foot continuously tapped the floor, marching out a nervous beat. Pete's mother, my parents, and I had been in the waiting room for over three hours. Pete had been unconscious when the ambulance came to revive him. All I remembered was screaming for help, sobbing for anyone to save my best friend. After five minutes of trying to deliver CPR through my tears and screams, a driver stopped and immediately called the hospital on her cell phone. Now we were waiting. And waiting.

"Ms. Monroe?" The doctor had finally emerged. Pete's mother stood up, bracing herself for the worst. Her eyes were shiny with tears of dreadful anticipation.

"Would you like to come into my office?" the doctor inquired politely.

"Doctor, please just tell me now. Thomas and his parents are part of our family."

"Well, in that case, please have a seat."

Pete's mom didn't move. She simply stared at the doctor, leaning forward, waiting.

"OK. Here's the situation," he began softly. "Pete survived the bee sting." He let these words soak in, tears of relief spilling from Ms. Monroe's eyes. She put her head onto my mother's shoulder, my mother calmly stroking her hair, like she would do to comfort my little sister.

"I'm assuming you have more to tell us, Doctor," my mother asked, still comforting Ms. Monroe.

"Yes. Even though Pete survived the bee sting, the damage to his lungs was so severe that he will never to be able to use them at a hundred percent capacity again. He will be lucky to receive an oxygen intake of about sixty percent." Just as he had announced the good news, he let these words soak in as well.

Ms. Monroe slowly lifted her head off my mother's shoulder. "I've heard of people regaining lung capacity with medical training and physical therapy. Couldn't he do something like that?"

"I'm afraid not, Ms. Monroe. A portion of the lungs has been permanently damaged. Even with many painful procedures, Pete would not be able to regain full lung capacity. I'm so sorry. You may see him now if you like."

The doctor left the waiting room in a heavy silence. To know that Pete was alive, that he had survived the most horrible thing I had ever witnessed, was joy beyond imagining. His lungs had been destroyed, though. He would not play basketball for the school this season. Or next year. Or the year after that. The enormity of the word *forever* had taken on a completely new meaning. We were all in our private thoughts when Ms. Monroe interrupted with, "Well, I want to see my son. And I need you all to come with me."

As we approached Pete's room, I tried to prepare myself. I knew that Pete had been through a terrifying experience, and I wanted to be the strong friend that he could count on.

"There's my boy," Ms. Monroe cooed as she ran her fingers tenderly through Pete's hair. "You have no idea how happy I am," his mother managed to whisper between tears that fell upon Pete's cheeks, still swollen with his reaction to the bee's poison.

"Mom," Pete began tiredly.

"What do you need?"

"Is Thomas here?"

"He's standing right behind me. Would you like to talk to him?"

Pete managed a slow, painful nod.

I had been standing in the corner of the room, unsure of myself. I had never been uncomfortable around Pete, and now I felt like a complete stranger. I did not know what to say, how to hold back my <u>impending</u> tears, or how to look at him.

"Can you please bring him closer?" Pete asked dryly.

Ms. Monroe guided me by the arm to Pete's bed. As hard as I tried, I could not keep the tears back any longer. Seeing my best friend, my invincible best friend, reduced to a swollen mass was more than I could take. I turned away, the back of my hand covering my mouth.

"Thomas, come here please."

I sniffed my runny nose, taking a deep breath. I managed to look Pete in the eye.

"I have to tell you something important."

I nodded quickly, needing him to know that I would do anything for him.

"Andrea hates crybabies," he whispered hoarsely.

At that point, the dam broke. Even at a time like this, Pete managed to make a joke. I could not keep my tears restrained any longer, and I dropped to my knees beside his bed.

"Dude . . . ." I tried to begin.

"Thomas, I'm good, man. After all, like you said, it was just a bee sting. Imagine if you hadn't called me ugly," he smiled through his puffy face

"Pete, I'm so sorry. If I hadn't been joking around, you would never have gotten stung by that stupid bee. Your lungs would be fine," I wailed.

"Will you please be quiet?"

I looked up in surprise at the harshness in Pete's voice.

"Excuse me?"

"Be quiet! I'm just happy to be alive. I don't need you acting like a little girl crying over my lungs."

"OK," I began, unsure of how to interpret this kind of reaction.

"The last thing I need from my best friend is tears and sympathy. What I need is for you to treat me like you always have. I'm still the same person. Please treat me the same."

"Sure. Anything." I nodded confidently, wiping away the damp tracks on my cheeks.

After several more days of staying at the hospital, Pete got the OK to return to school. I do not think he was nervous at all. However, I felt like my insides had been turned into Jell-O salad. In order to help his lungs recover, he had to carry around an oxygen tank for three more weeks. The doctors were afraid that as they were, Pete's lungs were not strong enough to get enough air to his brain on a consistent basis. I imagined all the teasing, all the jokes, all the stares. Pete did not seem to imagine any of that. He was pretty confident that every single girl in school was going to feel so badly for him that they would eventually be begging him to explain how the oxygen tank worked. I certainly hoped that was going to be the case. I sighed, praying that Pete's first day back would be uneventful. I entered my algebra class, which of course I had with Pete, and saw the whole class surrounded around Pete's gleaming oxygen tank.

"Man, I can't believe how lucky you are. Someone was looking out for you, no doubt."

"Pete, I just wanted to cry when I heard what had happened to you."

My mouth hung open. I guess I had completely underestimated the quality of character of my fellow classmates.

"Hey Pete," I said coolly, joining Pete's new fan club.

"There's Thomas!" Pete cheered.

Everyone cleared a path for me, letting me be the closest to Pete. All the nervousness I had from earlier quickly dissipated as I realized that Pete really was going to be able to continue his life just like usual. I felt tears at the backs of my eyes again (I felt like I had cried more in the last month than in my entire life) and smiled at Pete.

"Hey, let's go out into the hall. I need to talk to you," Pete said as he pulled his tank toward the door.

"Sure," I replied, intrigued as to what sort of conversational topic needed some privacy.

"So, how's the training going?" Pete asked, looking straight into my eyes.

"Well," I said, letting out an exasperated sigh, "It hasn't been going all that great. I've tried to stay focused, but it's been really hard since, well, since, you know." I trailed off, looking at the carpet.

"As bad as this is going to sound, I'm glad," Pete stated bluntly.

"Excuse me? I thought you were rooting for me the whole way on this," I replied, taken aback.

"I am rooting for you. But I have a favor to ask."

"What is it?" I asked tentatively, unsure where this conversation was going.

"Well, since you haven't been training as consistently as you probably should be, you're probably not going to be ready for the race, or at least you won't be in good enough shape to finish."

"Your confidence is overwhelming." I could not believe that Pete was doubting me now, after all that we had been through.

"Just let me finish," he said with traces of annoyance in his voice. "What I'm getting at is this. There's another marathon coming up in two months." He paused, taking in a deep breath. "Do you think we could do that race together?" He seemed to freeze, waiting for my answer.

I thought I was going to cry again. This whole thing had really turned me into a baby. "Dude," I began, trying to sound unmoved. "That would be really cool," I managed to croak. "But how are you going to do that, Pete? According to the doctor, your lungs will never be able to handle that kind of stress. I mean, no offense, but I don't think the race will let you take a tank along. Besides, I don't think it would be very safe and your mom would flip."

"Great. I'll be by tomorrow to start our training."

I stared at Pete's back as he walked back into the classroom, apparently unfazed by any of my apprehensions. So that was that.

* * *

After our two months of training together, Pete and I were both ready to tackle the marathon course. Against all medical predictions, Pete had managed to train successfully. He would have to stop and walk every twenty minutes, but his lungs had managed to get him through his first twenty-mile run just two weeks ago. We had become quite a team. When I did not feel like pushing myself, Pete was always there to cheer me on and vice versa. And now the day had finally come. We were lined up among an enormous crowd of people, and the energy was almost overwhelming. Race officials were running around, making sure that everything was in order before one thousand runners charged down Center Street. People were hugging, giving each other high fives, literally jumping up and down. They were already celebrating that they had managed to get this far. As Pete and I soaked up our soon-to-be victory, we locked eyes.

"I could never have done this without you, Pete," I said quietly.

"Thomas," Pete began. He seemed to be searching for words, looking at the crowd surrounding us. "Thank you. For everything."

I nodded. "You ready for this?" I asked, smiling.

"As ready as I'll ever be," Pete replied, placing his hands level with his hips.

"Don't smoke me. Remember, we're in this together," I reminded Pete.

"Like I could even if I wanted to."

We both grinned. I crouched down, arms up. Pete stared straight ahead, focused on the path that lay before us. The sound of the starting gun split the morning air. The race had begun.

54 Pete's character can best be defined as
   A aggressive
   B dedicated
   C humorous
   D practical

55 Within the sentence, "How to hold back my <u>impending</u> tears," the word impending means
   A never ending
   B embarrassing
   C approaching
   D babyish

56 Which of the following statements best expresses the theme of this story?
   A Best friends can help each other get through any sort of problem.
   B Even if people have physical problems, they can still reach their goals.
   C Throughout life, people must make difficult, complicated decisions.
   D With dedication and perseverance, any goal can be accomplished.

57 Which statement best describes the relationship between Pete and Thomas?
   A Pete is the leader of the pair, and Thomas always listens to him.
   B They trade roles as leader, letting the stronger one help the weaker.
   C Thomas counts on Pete for motivation, inspiration, and advice.
   D They support and care for one another, helping each to reach his goals.

58 Within the sentence, "'Is that a fact?' I asked <u>nonchalantly</u>," the word <u>nonchalantly</u> means
   A excitedly
   B passively
   C uninterestedly
   D energetically

59 Which of the following statements is an example of foreshadowing?
   A "If only we had turned down another street."
   B "The sound of the starting gun split the morning air."
   C "I sighed, praying that Pete's first day back would be uneventful."
   D "I looked up in surprise at the harshness in Pete's voice."

60 The author uses asterisks (*) to indicate
   A change of location or setting
   B change of perspective
   C forward time progression
   D shifts in character dialogue

ANSWER KEY TO PRACTICE TEST A

1.	**A**	13.	**A**	25.	**A**	37.	**A**	49.	**A**
2.	**B**	14.	**C**	26.	**B**	38.	**C**	50.	**A**
3.	**D**	15.	**B**	27.	**D**	39.	**B**	51.	**A**
4.	**B**	16.	**D**	28.	**C**	40.	**B**	52.	**B**
5.	**D**	17.	**B**	29.	**B**	41.	**A**	53.	**C**
6.	**B**	18.	**A**	30.	**D**	42.	**C**	54.	**C**
7.	**C**	19.	**B**	31.	**B**	43.	**B**	55.	**C**
8.	**B**	20.	**C**	32.	**B**	44.	**A**	56.	**D**
9.	**B**	21.	**A**	33.	**C**	45.	**C**	57.	**D**
10.	**B**	22.	**D**	34.	**A**	46.	**D**	58.	**C**
11.	**D**	23.	**A**	35.	**B**	47.	**C**	59.	**A**
12.	**A**	24.	**C**	36.	**D**	48.	**D**	60.	**C**

EXPLANATION OF CORRECT ANSWERS

1. **A**   As with the majority of informational text that you will encounter on the AIMS exam, careful reading will help you to determine the correct response. The letter states that the whole purpose of the walk is to raise money for cancer research; therefore, all of the money raised would, of course, be donated.

2. **B**   The walk does not need donations for pledges. The letter is asking businesses to contribute money so that the committee can afford to buy water, buy snacks, and employ police staff. The walkers are the ones responsible for obtaining pledges, and the donating businesses have nothing to do with pledges.

3. **D**   The letter provides instructions saying that if a business wishes to contribute, it should mail a check to the walk committee. A business can call if it has questions concerning making a donation. Otherwise, the business should simply mail in a check to the committee.

4. **B**   Once again, you need to make sure that you understand that the walkers raise the money by getting individual pledges. They are not the ones asking businesses for help; that is the job of the walk committee.

5. **D**   It may seem like a logical response to say that the walk committee needs money because there has not been enough interest or support, but in truth, the answer is exactly the opposite. The walk committee needs money because more walkers are participating. Therefore, the committee needs to supply more snacks and water stations, which of course cost more money.

6. **B**   The very end of the letter states that all donating businesses receive a banner placed at the end of the walk. The purpose of the banner is, of course, to give the businesses free advertising. Choice D may seem tempting because a banner may appear as if the committee is thanking the businesses, but the banners are really just giving the businesses a chance to advertise.

7. **C**   All of the people listed could certainly participate in this walk. However, the question is asking you to choose which one would be the most likely to participate. Since the walk raises money for cancer research, a cancer survivor would most likely take part in the walk to help raise money for a sickness that he or she had personally experienced.

8. **B**   This letter has no purpose other than to ask businesses to donate money. The letter is not expressing appreciation.

9. **B**   This question is similar to question 8. All of the businesses listed may certainly make a contribution. Once again, you are being asked to decide which would be the least likely to contribute. As you look at the answer choices, you should notice that three of the choices share a similarity—they are all health related. The bank is the only one that is not concerned with someone's health. Since the walk is focused on cancer, a business concerned with health would be likely to donate. Therefore, out of the choices provided, the bank would be the least likely to make a contribution.

10. **B**   *Walden* is an older text and may pose a few challenges in comprehension. If you do come across an older text on the exam, make sure to take your time reading. This material may seem more challenging than contemporary literature, but it can be figured out if you just take the time and focus on the wording. After you have read this essay, you should be able to realize that the focus is the transition from winter to spring. Thoreau mentions the multiple birds that come to the pond, but the birds are there because it is springtime. Since the arrival of the birds relies on that fact, the focus is still the winter-to-spring transition.

11. **D** This statement is an exaggeration because, of course, Thoreau could not have lived for a thousand years without hearing the song of the robin. This statement is made to dramatize the length of winter. It may have seemed like winter lasted a thousand years, which makes the song of the robin all that much more beautiful. Remember, hyperbole is used to overemphasize a statement, making a dramatic impact for the reader.

12. **A** Within this particular statement, you have to realize that the word "fast" means to not eat. If the geese are trying to "break their fast," they are trying to find food. The last part of that statement, "In muddier pools," means that they will go to another pond, or "muddy pool," to find food to "break their fast."

13. **A** Thoreau is obviously fascinated with the birds, the change of seasons, the pond, and all of the elements of nature that surround his small cabin. He takes the time to record his observations in his journal, letting the reader know that he is intrigued by nature.

14. **C** Thoreau makes it very obvious that he loves living at the pond, observing nature. He does not give the reader any indication that he plans on leaving anytime soon or that he is going to follow the birds to observe them further. Since Thoreau does not make these statements, the reader can infer that he will remain at the pond, happily observing nature and recording things in his journal.

15. **B** Within that statement, the word "instantaneous" means to happen all at once. The event that he is referring to is the transition from winter to spring. He notes that all of a sudden the birds arrive, the air warms, and the clouds lift. The other choices are certainly components of the changing season, but remember you are looking for the best answer. The particular statement that the question refers to is specific to Thoreau discussing the change of season.

16. **D** Context clues can be of use to determine the definition of "tumultuous." He uses this word when describing the geese flying out of the pond. While the geese are leaving the pond, they of course are going to be kicking up the water with their feet and wings. This action will agitate the water. "Agitated" in this sense does not mean to be annoyed, rather it means to have rapid movement. The pond water would certainly be given rapid movement after a flock of geese all fly away at once.

17. **B** The "ancient race" that he is referring to is the martins. The martins are a type of bird that is quite large in number in town. Thoreau is surprised to see that there even more in the woods. In order to answer this question correctly, make sure you go back to the essay and locate this statement. Read the surrounding context to locate the subject of the statement. Answering the question out of context may be more difficult.

18. **A** Remember that when a question asks you to make an inference, you are being asked to make a logical conclusion based on the provided information. In this case, it is logical to assume that Thoreau takes pleasure from being in nature. His observations certainly support that inference. He seems to take a somewhat scientific approach to recording his observations. However, there is not enough evidence to support the inference that he is a scientist who studies birds.

19. **B** The characters' biggest problem is, of course, the setting of the sun. The gypsies and the current weather conditions are certainly problems. However, they are minimal compared with the importance of getting to Dracula before the sun sets.

20. **C** This statement clearly expresses Mina's emotions as she watches the other characters charge at the ring of gypsies. She states that she is not afraid. Rather, Mina wants to help and attack the gypsies as well. Also, make sure that you pay attention to the question itself. It is specifically asking you about when the characters charge the gypsies. Choice B could potentially be an answer, but it occurs at a different part of the story.

21. **A** Once again, use context clues to determine potentially unfamiliar words. Dracula thinks that he has beaten the other characters, and his eyes reflect the desire to harm them.

22. **D** The gypsies ultimately forfeit the battle because they see that they have no chance for escape. They are surrounded by the other characters, and most importantly, the other characters have guns pointed at the gypsies. The setting of the sun is an important issue for them as well as for Dracula, but being surrounded at gunpoint is a much more pressing issue.

23. **A** Once again, the primary battle that the characters are fighting is that they have to kill Dracula before the sun sets. All of the other elements do contribute to a sense of suspense, but the biggest is the race against the setting sun. Keep in mind that suspense is successful only if it is allowed to build. The characters are in a race against time, and that contributes to the building of suspense.

24. **C** Remember that the climax is the peak of the story. If the suspense (rising action) has been building up to the characters getting Dracula, their triumph is certainly the climax. Throughout the whole excerpt, the characters have been trying to kill Dracula. When they finally do, the climax of the story has been reached.

25. **A** The simile in this statement is implying that Dracula is so pale that he looks like wax. Make sure to read the statement carefully so that you understand the comparison correctly.

26. **B** The key term in this answer is "defeated." Keep in mind that the goal of the pursuing characters is to kill Dracula. Once the sun has set, Dracula believes that he has defeated the characters in that attempt. Choice A may seem tempting, but Dracula can still be harmed even though the sun has now set. Another clue to point you to the correct response is that the quote uses the word "triumph" to describe the look in Dracula's eyes. Typically, if you are triumphant, that means that you have defeated something or someone. This should once again point you to choice B.

27. **D** To determine the answer, you should return to the essay and reread both this sentence and several sentences surrounding it. Although Jonathon did exhibit amazing strength, his forceful energy was the overwhelming impression given by the passage.

28. **C** Simply look at the list of programs the school offers. All of the choices are listed except creative writing.

29. **B** The word "you" is used to personalize this message. If the author wanted it to be more formalized, the word "you" would not have appeared. Choice B is better than choice A because this is an advertisement. It is obviously meant to appeal to a large audience, not to each individual reader.

30. **D** Although choice A might seem like a good response, choice D is better. Choice A infers that students are already studying at the University of Chicago. However, the advertisement uses phrases like "applications are being accepted," "take a campus tour," and "admission requirements." These statements are geared toward encouraging individuals to apply to the school—not to students already attending the university.

31. **B** The questions at the top encourage the reader to take stock of his or her life and situation. They do not provide a concrete answer or distract the reader. Instead, they get the reader to reflect on his or her situation.

32. **B** Logically, the majority of people receiving information about colleges are going to be high school students. Current college students probably would not be the bulk of the audience. Parents might be interested, but the wording of the flyer is certainly geared toward a student audience. Once again, remember that you are looking for the best answer. Although the other choices could potentially work, the majority of the flyer's audience is going to be high school students.

33. **C**   The answer to this question can be located at the bottom of the flyer where it tells the reader what to do if he or she has questions concerning the university.

34. **A**   This question is asking you to think about what other type of information a reader of this flyer might be interested in. If a person has decided to apply to the university, he or she is probably not going to be interested in going to a technical school or traveling abroad. However, the person would be interested in information regarding college expenses. Scholarships are, of course, a great way to get money for college.

35. **B**   This flyer is only temporary. Its audience is specific to students who are interested in applying for the 2006–2007 school year. If students are interested in applying next year, this flyer would not be able to provide them with adequate information.

36. **D**   Using multiple punctuation marks serves the purpose of emphasizing important points. Think about when someone is really excited. If you wrote down what they said and followed it with multiple exclamation points, a reader would understand that someone was really excited. Following the statement, "We've got your answer" with several exclamation points makes it seem like they really do have an answer for you.

37. **A**   You need to fill in the other portion of the web with a reason why the student population has decreased. According to the editorial, enrollment has decreased because of lack of school spirit, dropping of elective programs, and decrease in the quality of instruction. The editorial clearly lists those reasons at the beginning to provide explanations as to why student enrollment has dropped.

38. **C**   The author of the editorial explains that dropping enrollment is an important issue because the school loses money and can no longer afford elective programs. This in turn creates a cycle where more students leave the school because they are not interested in what little programs the school has to offer.

39. **B**   The author of the editorial believes that if the positive aspects of the school are emphasized, such as the great science department, more students will want to attend the school, which will help to boost enrollment. Always remember to look back at a piece of text if you cannot recall an answer. You have the time to do it, and chances are you will find the correct answer if you just reread a portion of the text.

40. **B**   The phrase "It only takes one bad apple to ruin the bunch" means that one bad thing can ruin a great thing. In this case, the author is using this expression when discussing the quality of instruction at the school. Even though the school has many good teachers, the bad teachers create a bad image for the school, hence ruining "the bunch." The author believes that these bad teachers have to go if the school wants to project a favorable image.

41. **A**   The author states that electives are valuable because they give students the opportunity to "personalize their education." This phrase means that students can take classes that interest them and that they can feel a certain degree of autonomy in their education. If students can personalize their educations, they will be happy at the school and will not contribute to dropping enrollment numbers.

42. **C**   Since this author is trying to propose a solution to the school's problem, providing examples from other schools that have managed to defeat the same problem be very effective. This shows that the author's proposed solutions are feasible and logical. The other choices could possibly work, but integrating examples of successful solutions would best improve the editorial.

43. **B**   This particular choice focuses on providing a solution that "require[s] minimal finances." That is certainly an important issue because currently, the school does not have extra money to spend. The author would most likely agree with this solution because it requires little money and gives students the opportunity to personalize their educations to a certain degree.

44. **A** This flow chart is asking you to think about the progression of ideas presented by the author. Based on the logic presented, the author implies that once enrollment increases, electives can return, and then students will want to remain at West Valley High School. It may seem that choice D is correct, but the flow chart represents a sequence of events that share a cause and effect relationship. If student electives come back, that does not necessarily mean that more athletic programs will be brought back immediately as well.

45. **C** This author states that she has had several of her children attend the high school and is therefore familiar with the problems that the high school is currently facing. Remember, an editorial is always an opinion; it is not a factual report. As a parent of a student, the author has information that she is using to formulate her opinion about what should be done to boost student enrollment. She does not need to be an expert on school policy to write an editorial. The fact that she is a parent of a student qualifies her enough to express her opinion.

46. **D** When you encounter questions that ask you to locate the best summary, read over each choice very carefully. Typically, each choice will accurately summarize a portion of the essay, story, poem, and so on. However, you are looking for the statement that summarizes the entire text. Choice D provides the most thorough summary of all the choices.

47. **C** The focus of this poem (or the subject) is the football player. When you are asked what the focus of a poem is, the question is asking you to name the central subject. The narrator of this poem is talking about a football player at his school. You may be tempted to select choice A, a geeky student, because he is the narrator of the poem. However, he is not the focus. The narrator is not focused on himself; he is focused on the football player.

48. **D** This statement is an example of an allusion because it compares the football player to Moses, the biblical figure. You first need to be able to identify that the statement is allusion, and then you can begin to piece together what the statement is implying. According to the Bible story, Moses parted the Red Sea with his hands and the sea cleared a path for him to walk through. This allusion implies that like Moses, the football player can walk through a crowded hallway and people move out of his way, clearing a path for him.

49. **A** It becomes clear at the end of the poem that the narrator respects the football so much because the football player defended him. Lines such as, "They call me 'geek' or 'retard' /Just to name a few," and "But you told them to stop / To back off and leave me alone," tell the reader that the football player kept other students from teasing the narrator. Since the football player stood up for him, the narrator now views him as a heroic figure.

50. **A** The statement contains the word "as," which makes it a simile. This statement is comparing the value of the high fives to hundred dollar bills, which implies that everybody wants a high five from the football player.

51. **A** By comparing the football player's number to a monument to the gods, the narrator is being reverent. To be reverent means to respect someone or something greatly. The narrator certainly respects the football player for his kindness.

52. **B** The last several lines of the poem cite names that both the narrator and the football player have been called. Each set of names represents a stereotype that the individuals are fighting. The narrator is obviously not "a retard," and the football player is certainly not a "meathead." Both the narrator and the football player are trying to counteract these imposed stereotypes.

53. **C** What has greatly impressed the narrator is the football player's kindness. According to the stereotype that the football player should conform to, he should have joined in the teasing. However, the football player stands up for the narrator, mak-

ing a huge impact on the narrator's perspective. He no longer sees the football player as simply a "roid rager" but as a kind, heroic person. The title is also important to note in reference to this question as well. The narrator of the poem has elevated the football player to the level of hero because he has been kind. This, in turn, makes a kind action even more valuable.

54. **C**   Pete's character evolves throughout the story, but he is always humorous. He makes jokes. Pete's humor is one of the things that Thomas seems to most enjoy about him. Pete also manages to make a joke at a time when he would be expected to be depressed. Choice B may sound correct as well because Pete does show an immense amount of dedication toward training for a marathon race, but that comes up at the end of the story.

55. **C**   Use the surrounding context to figure out that if something is "impending" it is approaching or will arrive without fail.

56. **D**   Finding the correct answer for this question may be tricky. Choice A is probably very tempting, but choice D does a better job of describing the theme. The boys obviously help one another through their problems. However, it is through dedication and perseverance that they manage to succeed. They help one another complete a marathon, an event that of course requires lots of dedication and perseverance.

57. **D**   The two friends share a supportive relationship that benefits both equally. Pete seems to have the more commanding personality, but he values Thomas's opinion and support. Their friendship is based on mutual respect and support.

58. **C**   To be nonchalant about something means that you are not interested. Context clues should help you figure out the definition. Pete is trying to antagonize Thomas by telling him Andrea was interested in him. As Thomas hears Pete's story, Thomas acts as though he does not care to get the real story from Pete.

59. **A**   Foreshadowing is a technique that authors use to build suspense. When Thomas thinks that they should have turned down another street, the reader becomes interested to know why they should have gone down another street. Foreshadowing usually tells the reader that something bad is going to happen, which in this story, is certainly the case.

60. **C**   The asterisks are used to show that time has gone by since the last event in the story. This is evident when the first set of asterisks appears right after Pete is stung by the bee. The story goes from the bee incident immediately to the hospital. The reader understands that events have occurred between that transition but that they are not vital to the understanding of the story. For example, the author has decided to leave out details concerning the ambulance ride to the hospital. The reader understands that the ambulance ride had to have taken place, but the details are not necessary. The asterisks simply tell the reader that time has passed.

PRACTICE TEST B ANSWER SHEET

Fill in the bubble completely.
Erase carefully if answer is changed.

1. Ⓐ Ⓑ Ⓒ Ⓓ   21. Ⓐ Ⓑ Ⓒ Ⓓ   41. Ⓐ Ⓑ Ⓒ Ⓓ
2. Ⓐ Ⓑ Ⓒ Ⓓ   22. Ⓐ Ⓑ Ⓒ Ⓓ   42. Ⓐ Ⓑ Ⓒ Ⓓ
3. Ⓐ Ⓑ Ⓒ Ⓓ   23. Ⓐ Ⓑ Ⓒ Ⓓ   43. Ⓐ Ⓑ Ⓒ Ⓓ
4. Ⓐ Ⓑ Ⓒ Ⓓ   24. Ⓐ Ⓑ Ⓒ Ⓓ   44. Ⓐ Ⓑ Ⓒ Ⓓ
5. Ⓐ Ⓑ Ⓒ Ⓓ   25. Ⓐ Ⓑ Ⓒ Ⓓ   45. Ⓐ Ⓑ Ⓒ Ⓓ
6. Ⓐ Ⓑ Ⓒ Ⓓ   26. Ⓐ Ⓑ Ⓒ Ⓓ   46. Ⓐ Ⓑ Ⓒ Ⓓ
7. Ⓐ Ⓑ Ⓒ Ⓓ   27. Ⓐ Ⓑ Ⓒ Ⓓ   47. Ⓐ Ⓑ Ⓒ Ⓓ
8. Ⓐ Ⓑ Ⓒ Ⓓ   28. Ⓐ Ⓑ Ⓒ Ⓓ   48. Ⓐ Ⓑ Ⓒ Ⓓ
9. Ⓐ Ⓑ Ⓒ Ⓓ   29. Ⓐ Ⓑ Ⓒ Ⓓ   49. Ⓐ Ⓑ Ⓒ Ⓓ
10. Ⓐ Ⓑ Ⓒ Ⓓ   30. Ⓐ Ⓑ Ⓒ Ⓓ   50. Ⓐ Ⓑ Ⓒ Ⓓ
11. Ⓐ Ⓑ Ⓒ Ⓓ   31. Ⓐ Ⓑ Ⓒ Ⓓ   51. Ⓐ Ⓑ Ⓒ Ⓓ
12. Ⓐ Ⓑ Ⓒ Ⓓ   32. Ⓐ Ⓑ Ⓒ Ⓓ   52. Ⓐ Ⓑ Ⓒ Ⓓ
13. Ⓐ Ⓑ Ⓒ Ⓓ   33. Ⓐ Ⓑ Ⓒ Ⓓ   53. Ⓐ Ⓑ Ⓒ Ⓓ
14. Ⓐ Ⓑ Ⓒ Ⓓ   34. Ⓐ Ⓑ Ⓒ Ⓓ   54. Ⓐ Ⓑ Ⓒ Ⓓ
15. Ⓐ Ⓑ Ⓒ Ⓓ   35. Ⓐ Ⓑ Ⓒ Ⓓ   55. Ⓐ Ⓑ Ⓒ Ⓓ
16. Ⓐ Ⓑ Ⓒ Ⓓ   36. Ⓐ Ⓑ Ⓒ Ⓓ   56. Ⓐ Ⓑ Ⓒ Ⓓ
17. Ⓐ Ⓑ Ⓒ Ⓓ   37. Ⓐ Ⓑ Ⓒ Ⓓ   57. Ⓐ Ⓑ Ⓒ Ⓓ
18. Ⓐ Ⓑ Ⓒ Ⓓ   38. Ⓐ Ⓑ Ⓒ Ⓓ   58. Ⓐ Ⓑ Ⓒ Ⓓ
19. Ⓐ Ⓑ Ⓒ Ⓓ   39. Ⓐ Ⓑ Ⓒ Ⓓ   59. Ⓐ Ⓑ Ⓒ Ⓓ
20. Ⓐ Ⓑ Ⓒ Ⓓ   40. Ⓐ Ⓑ Ⓒ Ⓓ   60. Ⓐ Ⓑ Ⓒ Ⓓ

Directions: Read the following essay and article and then answer questions 1–13.

Memories

"Fatty!" "Lardo!" "Lazy slob!" These were just some of the beautiful names that I was called while growing up. When it comes to adolescence, some people may remember their first kiss, the magical memories of prom, or winning their homecoming football game. Not me. My memories consist of crying in a bathroom stall, sniffing over the embarrassment that some jerk had made a beeping noise (similar to that of a semitruck) when I had finally gathered the courage to dance at Spring Fling. I remember hiding in the bathroom stall again (I probably spent half my of high school life in the bathroom), waiting until everybody had changed for P.E. so that no one would see my protruding naked belly or massive thighs. I remember always wearing clothes that were several sizes too big, just to make sure that nothing hugged my body too closely, showing every bulge or pocket of fat that thrived on my body. How many hours I wasted, worrying about how fat I looked, how ugly I felt, and imagining all of the nasty things that were being said behind my back.

Now that I am out of that nightmare known as high school, I can look back at those memories with a little more objectivity. I am no longer overweight, and I am physically active. Granted, I was not extremely active in high school. Trust me, the last thing I wanted was to be seen by a fellow classmate while attempting to jog through the neighborhood. I could just imagine the sound effects that would follow. My parents always ask me why I was so overweight in high school. They were both trim and enjoyed an active lifestyle. After lots of painful reflection on my part, I think

I finally have the answer to that question. I could have exercised more, not caring what my fellow classmates would think. However, that was not an option. I was already the brunt of every joke, and I really did not want to give my tormentors any more fodder.

The problem, I believe, was my massive consumption of junk food. I know every teenager loves to inhale Doritos, ice cream, and cheese whiz in mass quantities, but I could not get myself to control my junk food intake. Do you know who is to blame? My high school campus. That probably sounds ridiculous. The school was not forcing Twinkies into my mouth or demanding that I drink at least five Dr. Peppers every day. No, they did not force me. They just made sure to maintain a constant supply throughout every hallway and every courtyard. The vending machines—they were my nemesis. I battled them every hour between classes, trying not to become enthralled with the alluring candy bar wrappers, trying to disregard the temptation that chocolaty goodness was only fifty cents away. My nemesis usually conquered any willpower that I had. I would slowly walk to my next class, letting the flavors of caramel, chocolate, and nougat dance upon my tongue. For a brief moment, I was in my own universe; no taunts or jokes could penetrate my sugary bubble.

So it continued. It got so bad that I was literally buying some type of treat between every single class. That came out to about six pieces of junk food a day. I would alternate between chips and candy, usually buying a soda to accompany my chips. One day, after I got out of high school and no longer had to fight my battle with the vending machines, I added up all of the calories I would have theoretically eaten throughout my day at school. Averaging four candy bars, two bags of chips, and three sodas a day brought the grand total to 1,350 calories, just in junk food. That did not include the three meals a day I ate. No wonder I had turned into a human hippo.

As soon as I got out of high school, the weight began to fall off like layers of clothing. After several years of simply not eating junk food, I managed to lose fifty pounds. After realizing what was making me so overweight, I could not help but think, what if the schools had vending machines full of fruit instead of candy? What if sodas were replaced with water? If that were the case, I might have consumed four apples, two bananas, and three bottles of water every day instead. I might have avoided four years of locking myself in the bathroom, ashamed of what I had become. I do realize that it was upon my own free will that I fed myself that junk, but what if the tempting candy had never been there in the first place? It is a question that I ask myself constantly. I hope that another poor teenager is not being forced to face the same nemesis that I was never able to defeat, knowing that it was right down the hallway, constantly calling to me.

A New Silent Killer

Our nation is facing a new problem concerning adolescents. It is not drugs, and it is not the violence found in television or video games. It is obesity. Over the last twenty-five years, the rates of obesity in children and teenagers have tripled.

What is to blame for this current epidemic? For starters, many children log an excessive amount of hours anchored to the couch. Whether they are engrossed in their favorite TV program or blasting bad guys in the hottest video game, today's children do not get enough physical activity. Today's kids are perfectly happy spending an entire day watching TV, with never once giving a thought to going outside.

So how do we solve this problem? Several states across the nation have adopted their own solutions. For example, Arizona has set nutritional standards for all food and beverages sold on school grounds. California has banned the sale of junk food as snacks in schools starting next year. Kentucky now requires students to engage in vigorous physical activity for thirty minutes a day. These solutions are certainly a start toward a healthier adolescent population. Monitoring adolescents' junk food intake is crucial. Limiting their access to it by way of restricting the types of food sold at school should help many students.

However, one of the biggest responsibilities we have is to show children how satisfying physical activity can be. If parents and schools do not tell children how rewarding it is to be physically fit, we are creating a generation of obsessive dieters. If children are led to believe that food intake is the only method to curb weigh gain, they will be missing out on the joy of fitness. Several states have discussed cutting physical education courses due to lack of state funding. How can we cut a course that children need more desperately now than ever? If we are to raise a healthy, happy generation, it is our job to show our children the benefits of a healthy lifestyle, both by what we eat and by the satisfaction of fitness.

1 In the essay, *"Memories,"* which of the following statements reflects a sarcastic tone?
  A "Now that I am out of that nightmare known as high school, I can look back at those memories with a little more objectivity."
  B "These were just some of the beautiful names that I was called while growing up."
  C "The school was not forcing Twinkies into my mouth or demanding that I drink at least five Dr. Peppers every day."
  D "After several years of simply not eating junk food, I managed to lose fifty pounds."

2 Both the essay and the article are mainly about
  A the problems teenagers face in high school
  B how adolescents lack physical activity
  C the issue of weight gain in adolescents
  D battling an obsession with junk food

3 Within the sentence, "I was already the brunt of every joke, and I really did not want to give my tormentors any more <u>fodder</u>," from "Memories," the word <u>fodder</u> means
  A fuel
  B ideas
  C jokes
  D truth

4 Complete the web below according to the solutions presented in the article "A New Silent Killer."

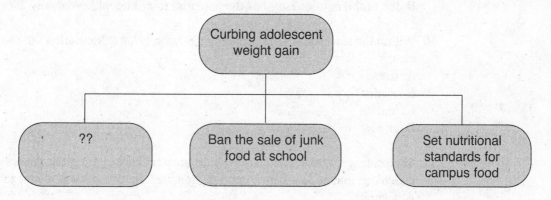

  A Educate adolescents about nutrition
  B Limit the amount of hours spent watching TV
  C Require all students to take a P.E. class
  D Require thirty minutes of physical activity a day

5 In "Memories," which of the following statements contributes to the humanlike quality of the vending machines?
  A "Trying to disregard the temptation that chocolaty goodness was only fifty cents away."
  B "I do realize that it was upon my own free will that I fed myself that junk."
  C "My nemesis usually conquered any willpower that I had."
  D "I was in my own universe; no taunts or jokes could penetrate my sugary bubble."

6 According to "A New Silent Killer," if we do not educate adolescents about physical fitness, we run the risk of creating adults who
  A will not care about being physically active
  B will only worry about what they eat, not about fitness
  C spend too much time watching TV instead of being outside
  D will be extremely unhealthy and overweight

7 Which of the following solutions do both the essay and the article agree upon?
  A limiting the number of hours watching TV and playing video games
  B forcing adolescents to exercise for at least thirty minutes a day
  C educating adolescents about the health issues related to obesity
  D removing junk food from all vending machines on school campus

8 Why does "A New Silent Killer" use the pronouns "we" and "our" throughout the article?
  A to recognize the variety of readers that may encounter the article
  B to make the reader begin thinking about other examples of obesity in America
  C to make each reader feel like he or she shares a certain degree of responsibility
  D to make the reader feel like he or she is part of the problem of adolescent obesity

9 Based upon the title, "A New Silent Killer," the reader can infer that
  A problems of violence are increasing among adolescents
  B video games and television have become increasingly violent
  C students remain quiet about how much junk food they actually eat
  D the problem of obesity has the potential to kill people eventually

10 Within the sentence, "They were my <u>nemesis,</u>" from "Memories," the word <u>nemesis</u> means
  A friend
  B victim
  C teacher
  D enemy

11 The sentence, "I would slowly walk to my next class, letting the flavors of caramel, chocolate, and nougat dance upon my tongue," in "Memories" is an example of
  A a simile
  B personification
  C a metaphor
  D imagery

12 Based on the statement, "I could just imagine the sound effects that would follow," from "Memories," the reader can infer that the narrator
  A hates to exercise and avoids it
  B makes a lot of noise when exercising
  C would have been teased for exercising
  D is excited to begin losing weight

13 The narrator's story from "Memories" supports the idea in the article "A New Silent Killer" of
  A requiring physical fitness classes at school
  B embarrassing teens who are overweight
  C stressing the importance of proper dieting
  D removing junk food from school campuses

Directions: Read the following advertisement and answer questions 14–20.

Calling All Writers!
Calling All Poets!
Calling All Lyricists!

Do you have a talent for expressing yourself on paper? Can you capture a feeling in words? Well, here's your chance to get recognized for your talent!

Fresh Ink Publishing Company is currently looking for young writers who can give a voice to today's teens. We are currently looking for the following:

- Short Stories (minimum of fifteen pages)
- Poetry
- Song Lyrics (minimum of two minutes sing time)

All approved submissions will be printed in next year's edition of *Voices of Today*, an anthology dedicated to young people. You will also be paid $500.00 if your submission is accepted!

If you have a piece you'd like to submit to Fresh Ink Publishing, we'd love to read it! Please send all submissions to

> Fresh Ink Publishing
> P.O. Box 4587
> Chatsworth, CA 91311

All submissions must be typed and double-spaced. Please include a self-addressed, stamped envelope so we may return your submission if we decide not to use it. If no envelope is included, all submissions become the property of Fresh Ink Publishing.

14 The purpose of this advertisement is to
  A make the publisher well-known to young writers
  B inform people about the upcoming book *Voices of Today*
  C provide information about the publishing company
  D acquire multiple written submissions from teenagers

15 Which of the following submissions is the publishing company NOT looking for?
  A essays
  B poems
  C stories
  D lyrics

16 If a submission is accepted
  A the writer's name will appear in *Voices of Today*
  B the writer will receive $500.00
  C it will be returned to the writer
  D it becomes the property of the publisher

17 The purpose of the upcoming book *Voices of Today* is to
  A showcase young writing talent
  B give teens a chance to become authors
  C highlight the current problems of teens
  D give a written voice to all teenagers

18 All submissions should include a self-addressed, stamped envelope because
  A authors of accepted entries need to be notified
  B the publisher cannot afford to buy lots of stamps
  C unaccepted entries will be mailed back to the authors
  D the publisher expects the need to send mail to the authors

19 Which of the following story topics would Fresh Ink Publishing most likely be interested in?
  A getting a car for a birthday present
  B battling stereotypes at school
  C how to take care of a new pet
  D current fashion trends and fads

20 Based on the needs of Fresh Ink Publishing, one can surmise that an anthology is a
  A collection of different writings from different authors
  B directory and listing of talented teenage authors
  C collection of poems all dealing with the same topic
  D magazine containing various articles by different authors

Directions: Read the following poem and answer questions 21–25.

SONNET 71
by William Shakespeare
(Reprinted with permission from Dover Publications)

No longer mourn for me when I am dead
Than you shall hear the surly sullen bell
Give warning to the world that I am fled
From this vile world with vilest worms to dwell;
Nay, if you read this line, remember not
That hand that writ it, for I love you so,
That I in your sweet thoughts would be forgot,
If thinking on me then should make you woe.
O, if (I say) you look upon this verse,
When I (perhaps) compounded am with clay,
Do not so much as my poor name rehearse,
But let your love even with my life decay;
Lest the wise world should look into your moan,
And mock you with me after I am gone.

21 This poem is focused primarily on the narrator's
   A eventual death
   B adult life
   C early childhood
   D adolescence

22 This poem was written for the narrator's
   A mother
   B love interest
   C funeral
   D sister

23 Which of the following statements best reflects the theme found in this poem?
   A Death is a painful part of life that we all must eventually face at some point.
   B It is best to live for the moment, not dwelling on what has happened in the past.
   C True love can last for an eternity, and not even death can kill true love.
   D It is best to forget those you loved because memories can cause pain and hurt.

24 Which of the following statements best represents the two central fears that the narrator has?

   A No one will care or notice when he has died, his love will quickly forget him and find new love.

   B Death will be a frightening experience, and he will have to lie in the ground with worms.

   C His love will be caused pain when remembering him, and she will be mocked by the world for loving him.

   D True love may not have the power to conquer everything, particularly death, and his true love may leave him.

25 Which of the following choices accurately summarizes the lines, "Nay, if you read this line, remember not / That hand that writ it, for I love you so, / That I in your sweet thoughts would be forgot, / If thinking on me then should make you woe."

   A The narrator would rather be forgotten by his love than have memories of him cause her any pain.

   B The narrator wants the reader to think of him every time she encounters this particular line.

   C The narrator hopes that his love will hold her memories of him close to her heart, making the pain easier to bear.

   D The narrator hopes that the reader will be so touched that she will want to cry and will reflect on life and death.

Directions: Read the following essay and answer questions 26–32.

Designer High

What do you wear each day to school? Are you the blue jean type paired with a simple T-shirt? Or do you like to dress up a bit, adding unique accessories? Where do you buy your clothes? Would you rather wear a pair of Wal-Mart jeans or a pair of Lucky's? How many of us do you think would answer "Lucky's" to the last question? I know I would. I am embarrassed to admit that I would rather spend eighty dollars on a pair of jeans that looks like any other pair of jeans except for one crucial factor: the label.

Everywhere you look at our school you begin to notice a common theme. Students look like walking billboards with words like Bebe, Sean John, Gap, North Pole, and Volcom plastered all over their shirts and jeans. What the actual article of clothing looks like does not even really matter anymore. It is all about the label that you can flaunt. You may be wearing the ugliest shirt in the world. As long as it says the right word, though, no one is going to criticize it.

Label mania is not limited to just clothes. Pop your head into any classroom at any time of day and you will notice another common trend. You start to see the same recurring element, sitting proudly on the desks of female students. It is not their schoolbooks or notebooks. Rather, it is designer purses. Logos boasting Dooney & Burke, Coach, Prada, and Louis Vuitton have the power to improve status overnight.

How have we become so completely label obsessed? Trust me, I am not above it by any means. I proudly wear my Baby Phat jeans and check the label before I buy any piece of clothing. However, I wish I could save myself some money and buy clothes at JC Penny's and wear them just as proudly. I know, though, that I would be the joke at my school. I would get the loser label just like all the other "no-brand" kids. So how are we supposed to cure this problem? I know the principals and teachers keep pushing for a dress code, but I do not think that is going to solve anything. Students will find a way to integrate designer elements into their outfits no matter what the dress code may be. Whoever has the newest Nikes or Uggs will be setting the bar for everybody else. I think the only real solution is to stop teasing students who maybe do not want to or cannot afford to keep up with the designer frenzy. If a student wants to impress everybody with his or her new hundred-dollar jeans, go right ahead. However, do not tease a student for not having hundred-dollar jeans. Students should not buy designer clothing so that they can feel better than somebody else. They should do it because they like the clothing. I have a feeling they could probably find something that looks just like it for much cheaper, sans label.

26 The intended audience for this essay is most likely
   A school teachers
   B students' parents
   C other students
   D school principal

27 This essay is mainly about
   A the importance of fitting in with others
   B the superficial value placed on designer clothing
   C how difficult it is to not care about what others think
   D how designer clothes have the power to impress others

28 What solution does the author propose for the label problem?
  A Students should have to obey a strict dress code when at school.
  B Students should disregard the intense pressures of trying to fit in at school.
  C Students should not be allowed to tease others for their clothing choices.
  D All students should buy clothing that has a designer label.

29 Which of the following details would be appropriate for the author to include in this essay?
  A providing examples of schools that have initiated dress code policies and their success stories
  B the amount of money teenagers across the country spend every year on designer clothing
  C the most common designer labels that are currently to be found on a high school campus
  D the number of bullying instances that are recorded every year on high school campuses

30 Based on the statement, "I would get the loser label just like all the other 'no-brand' kids," the reader can infer that
  A it is better to wear any kind of brand, even if the brand is not the most fashionable
  B all students are immediately judged by what clothing they are wearing
  C designer labels are a crucial component of success at school
  D wearing nondesigner clothing puts one into a lower social standing

31 Which of the following solutions would this author likely support?
  A having a no-label day at school where students cannot wear designer clothing
  B forcing students to turn their designer shirts inside out so that the label could not be seen
  C banning all designer clothing and accessories from the school campus
  D implementing no change at the school in hopes that the situation will improve itself

32 In the last sentence of the essay, the expression "sans label" means
  A identical label
  B unique label
  C generic label
  D without a label

| Directions: | Read the following letter and answer questions 33–40. |

1896 S. Wilson St.
Camp Verde, AZ 86366
(928) 567-3785

November 29, 2006

William Riven
Senior Director of Customer Relations
2638 N. Mountain St.
Phoenix, AZ 85051

Dear Mr. Riven,

My name is Thomas Banks, and I am writing to you with an issue that demands your immediate attention. I have just had the unfortunate experience of dining at a new restaurant called Paradise Grill, and trust me, my dining experience was anything but paradise. I have been told that you are the representative for the restaurant and handle all customer complaints. I feel that it is imperative that you know what happened to my wife and me when we dined at your restaurant last Friday evening.

To begin, we waited for nearly fifteen minutes in the waiting area. Normally this would not have bothered either my wife or me, but we had made reservations a week in advance. The hostess did not apologize for making us wait and offered no explanation as to why our table was not available. We eventually were taken to our table, only to wait *another* ten minutes for a server even to recognize our presence. Once a server finally decided to take our drink order, she was rude and completely unaccommodating. I simply asked for a slice of lemon in my water, and she rolled her eyes at me! Once again, we were left to wait. Our pleasant server finally returned with our drinks and begrudgingly took our dinner order. After *thirty* minutes, our food finally arrived. Once again, there was no apology offered, no explanation given as to why we had just wasted away thirty minutes of our lives . Frustrated beyond belief at this point, my wife and I began eating our dinners. However, the disappointment was not over. Not only was the food cold, my wife's chicken was not completely cooked. We immediately grabbed our server and complained about the quality of our dinners. She responded to our complaints with another eye roll and took our plates away. The next time we saw her was when she gave us the bill for the dinners that we had barely touched and that were not fit for human consumption! We were expected to pay full price for a dinner that had been absolutely horrendous. When we complained to a manager, he did nothing to correct the situation.

I am hoping that once you receive this letter, I will be sent a check reimbursing me for the worst dining experience I have ever had. I have enclosed the receipt from our dinner, and I look forward to hearing your response.

Thank you,

Thomas Banks

Thomas Banks

33 The purpose of this letter is to

    A inform the reader

    B express appreciation

    C demand a refund

    D issue a complaint

34 Which of the following events did NOT take place during Mr. Banks and his wife's dining experience?

    A They waited to be seated at a table.

    B Their food was cold and undercooked.

    C Their server was rude and unaccommodating.

    D They left the restaurant in the middle of dinner.

35 Within the sentence, "Our pleasant server finally returned with our drinks and begrudgingly took our dinner order," the word "pleasant" creates a _____ tone.

    A sincere

    B sympathetic

    C sarcastic

    D hostile

36 Complete the chart according to the events described in the letter.

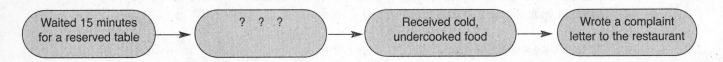

    A Paid full price for an uneaten meal

    B Received no apologies from management

    C Left the restaurant angry

    D Waited again for service

37 Once his letter has been received, Mr. Banks probably hopes that

    A the rude server will be fired

    B the restaurant will hire new managers

    C he will receive a refund for his dinner

    D his complaint will be given to the restaurant

38 Mr. Banks included the receipt with his letter because he wants Mr. Riven to

    A know exactly what they ate

    B know how much to reimburse him

    C believe that they dined at the restaurant

    D be able to identify the rude server

39 Which of the following details contributes to the rudeness of their server?
  A she rolled her eyes at Mr. Banks and his wife
  B she refused to take away their dinner plates
  C she did not tell a manager about the poor food quality
  D she did not ask them how their dinner was

40 Based on this letter, the reader can infer that Mr. Banks
  A will try to fire the rude server
  B will receive a reimbursement
  C will not return to Paradise Grill
  D will give Paradise Grill another chance

Directions: Read the following warranty and answer questions 41–45.

APPLIANCES 'R US REFRIGERATOR WARRANTY INFORMATION

Full one-year warranty on refrigerator
For one year from the date of purchase, when this refrigerator is operated and maintained according to the guidelines provided in the Owner's Manual, Appliances 'R Us will repair this refrigerator, free of charge, if defective in material or quality.

Full five-year warranty on sealed refrigeration system
For five years from the date of purchase, when this refrigerator is operated and maintained according to the guidelines provided in the Owner's Manual, Appliances 'R Us will repair the sealed system (consisting of refrigerant, connecting tube, and motor), free of charge, if defective in material or quality.

This warranty applies only to refrigerators that are used for private household purposes.

Warranty service is available by contacting your nearest Appliances 'R Us store location. For questions, please contact:
    Appliances 'R Us
    P.O. Box 568
    Albuquerque, NM 85647

41 Complete the Venn diagram according to the information found in the warranty.

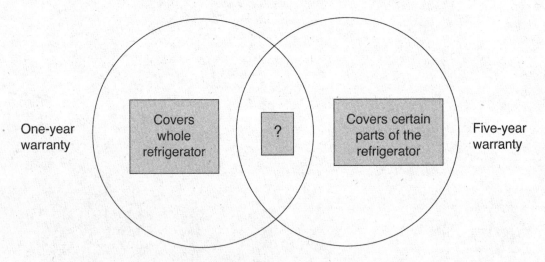

    A Warranty is valid for only one year from date of purchase
    B Warranty covers all possible damages to refrigerator
    C Refrigerator must be operated according to given guidelines
    D All warranty issues must be sent in writing to the company

42 Any questions concerning the refrigerator warranty should be
   A e-mailed to the company
   B called in to the company
   C directed to the store of purchase
   D mailed to the company

43 Both warranties are valid for only refrigerators that are used for
   A business purposes
   B household purposes
   C school purposes
   D commercial purposes

44 For warranty service, customers should
   A take the refrigerator to the nearest store location
   B describe the problem over the phone
   C telephone the nearest store location
   D wait for the refrigerator to be picked up

45 Which of the following refrigerator components does NOT fall under the
five-year warranty?
   A motor
   B exterior
   C connecting tube
   D refrigerant

Directions: Read the following recipe and then answer questions 46–50.

Creamy Mushroom Chicken

Ingredients

1 12-ounce package sliced portobello mushrooms

2-½ pounds chicken breast

Salt

Freshly ground black pepper

1 tablespoon unsalted butter (optional)

2 tablespoons olive oil

½ cup chicken broth

1 tablespoon fresh thyme leaves

2 tablespoons all-purpose flour

2 tablespoons heavy cream

Instructions

Dry the chicken with paper towels. Season liberally with salt and pepper on both sides. Heat the butter and oil in a large pot over medium-high heat. Saute the chicken in the oil, until nicely browned, about 3 to 5 minutes on each side When the chicken is done, transfer it to a plate. Add all of the portobello mushrooms to the pot, and lower the heat. Sauté for 5 minutes or until the mushrooms are soft. Add the ½ cup of chicken broth, scraping up the brown bits from the chicken. Return the chicken to the pot and sprinkle with the thyme leaves. Cover and simmer on the lowest heat for about 30 minutes or until the chicken is done and the juices run clear.

In a small bowl, whisk together ½ cup of the mushroom sauce with the flour, and then whisk it back into the pot. Raise the heat and slowly add the cream. Boil for 3 minutes. Add salt and pepper to taste. Serve the chicken on plates with any extra sauce spooned over the top.

46 The expression "season liberally" means to
   A measure the seasoning exactly
   B use very little seasoning
   C use a lot of seasoning
   D taste the sauce as you cook

47 Which of the following is NOT a necessary ingredient for this recipe?
   A unsalted butter
   B fresh mushrooms
   C heavy cream
   D fresh thyme

48 The chicken is done when
   A it has cooked for 3 to 5 minutes
   B it is seasoned with salt and pepper
   C the juices run clear
   D it is browned on each side

49 Based on the instructions in the recipe, to sauté something means
   A to be cooked in oil or butter
   B to be boiled with chicken
   C to add cream to a sauce
   D to season with salt and pepper

50 The expression "add salt and pepper to taste" means
   A to let each person season their own plate to his or her taste
   B to add however much salt and pepper you personally prefer
   C to measure the salt and pepper exactly according to the recipe
   D to omit all salt and pepper from the sauce

| **Directions:** | Read the following poem and then answer questions 51–60. |

Paul Laurence Dunbar was an African American who lived from 1872–1906. Dunbar's parents had been slaves in Kentucky. Dunbar has received acclaim for his poetry that deals with racism and inequality. His poem, "Sympathy," follows below.

SYMPATHY
by Paul Laurence Dunbar
(Reprinted with permission from Dover Publications)

I know what the caged bird feels, alas!
　　　When the sun is bright on the upland slopes;
When the wind stirs soft through the spring grass,
And the river flows like a stream of glass,
　　　When the first bird sings and the first bud opes,
And the faint perfume from its <u>chalice</u> steals—
I know what the caged bird feels!

I know why the caged bird beats his wing
　　　Till its blood is red on the cruel bars;
For he must fly back to his perch and cling
When he fain would be on the bough a-swing;
　　　And a pain still throbs in the old, old scars
And they pulse again with a keener sting—
I know why he beats his wing!

I know why the caged bird sings, ah me,
　　　When his wing is bruised and his bosom sore,—
When he beats his bars and he would be free;
It is not a carol of joy or glee,
　　　But a prayer that he sends from his heart's deep core,
But a plea, that upward to Heaven he flings—
I know why the caged bird sings.

51 The line, "And the river flows like a stream of glass," is an example of
A personification
B metaphor
C simile
D hyperbole

52 The caged bird is a symbol of
A inequality
B racism
C bravery
D slavery

53 Which of the following statements best summarizes the first stanza?

   A The narrator and the bird are very similar because they both enjoy being in the sunshine and fresh air.

   B Even if one cannot actually go outside, the memories of sunshine and fresh water can bring one through captivity.

   C Nature is a liberating force in itself—it has the power to bring dreams of freedom to both the bird and narrator.

   D The narrator, like the bird, understands the desire to go out and enjoy nature, yet he cannot because he is a captive.

54 Which statement best reflects the contrast found in the lines, "It is not a carol of joy or glee, / But a prayer that he sends from his heart's deep core?"

   A Traditionally a bird flapping his wings is looked upon as happiness. However, here it is the bird's way of begging to be released.

   B Through his flapping of wings, the bird is giving hope to all of those held in captivity; however, that message is not always heard.

   C The bird's flapping wings are representative of sending a prayer to heaven. However, not all of our prayers are answered

   D The bird may continue to flap his wings in his cage. However, the opportunity to fly away may never come.

55 This poem is entitled "Sympathy" because

   A the reader is supposed to feel sorry for the bird

   B the narrator understands how the bird feels

   C the bird understands the pain of the narrator

   D the narrator wants to release the caged bird

56 The line, "When the first bird sings and the first bud opes," refers to what time of year?

   A fall

   B winter

   C spring

   D summer

57 Which of the following statements best reflects the theme of this poem?

   A Just like a bird, a person cannot be kept against his or her will because it will result in misery.

   B Holding a person against his or her will deprives the person of fundamental rights and experiences.

   C One cannot be expected to be held in captivity because he or she will always find a way to escape to freedom.

   D Keeping a person against his or her will is similar to keeping that person in a cage because he or she is a captive.

58 Which statement best paraphrases the lines, "And a pain still throbs in the old, old scars / And they pulse again with a keener sting—"?

A Every time the bird's escape attempts are foiled, he is reminded again of how much he wants to leave his cage.

B The bird hurts himself worse every time that he tries to escape from his cage, leaving blood on the bars.

C No matter how hard the bird tries to escape, he will never be able to free himself from his captivity.

D It is not wise to keep birds in cages because they will be constantly looking for a way to escape, even if they are injured.

59 Within the line, "And the faint perfume from its <u>chalice</u> steals" the word <u>chalice</u> means

A vine

B petal

C cup

D bottle

60 Within the line, "Till its blood is red on the cruel bars;" the description of "cruel bars" is an example of

A simile

B imagery

C hyperbole

D personification

ANSWER KEY TO PRACTICE TEST B

1.	B	13.	D	25.	A	37.	C	49.	A
2.	C	14.	D	26.	C	38.	B	50.	B
3.	A	15.	A	27.	B	39.	A	51.	C
4.	D	16.	B	28.	C	40.	C	52.	D
5.	C	17.	B	29.	B	41.	C	53.	D
6.	B	18.	C	30.	D	42.	D	54.	A
7.	D	19.	B	31.	A	43.	B	55.	B
8.	C	20.	A	32.	D	44.	C	56.	C
9.	D	21.	A	33.	D	45.	B	57.	B
10.	D	22.	B	34.	D	46.	C	58.	A
11.	B	23.	D	35.	C	47.	A	59.	C
12.	C	24.	C	36.	D	48.	C	60.	D

EXPLANATION OF CORRECT ANSWERS

1. **B**   When the author refers to being called beautiful names such as "fatty," she is obviously being sarcastic. No one likes to be called names such as that. By calling them beautiful, she lets the reader know that she did not appreciate being called those names. She is not being serious when she calls the names beautiful, and therefore the reader is able to detect sarcasm.

2. **C**   Both of the pieces focus on the issue of weight gain in young people. Some of the OTHER choices do come up in either the article or the essay, but they do not come up in both. For example, the article spends more time discussing the value of physical activity for children, but the essay does not focus on that issue. Once again, the wording of the question itself is very important because it asks you identify what both the article and the essay are *mainly* about. Even though the article mentions fitness, it is primarily about childhood weight gain.

3. **A**   Technically the term "fodder" means food that is fed to animals. However, it is also used to mean fuel or material. For example, within the context of the story, the author does not want to give her fellow classmates any more fuel or material to make fun of her, which is a large part of the reason why she does not exercise.

4. **D**   You need to complete the web based on the information presented in the article only. It is not asking you about the essay. If you look back at the article, it lists three solutions that different states have implemented to help curb weight gain. The missing part of the web needs to be completed with the idea of requiring students to be active for thirty minutes every day.

5. **C**   By calling the vending machines a "nemesis," the author manages to make the vending machines sound like a human enemy. They are an actual force that she has to combat every day. By making the vending machines seem like a real, breathing enemy, the reader begins to feel that the vending machines are powerful beings, not just machines.

6. **B**   The article cites the worry that if children are taught about only nutrition, they will not care about the benefits of being physically active. When you have questions that are asking you to compare two different pieces of text, make sure to read the question carefully. It may be asking you to evaluate both pieces or each piece individually. In this case, the question is asking you to focus on only the article.

7. **D**   Both the article and the essay propose the solution of removing junk food from school campuses. The author of the essay feels that if the junk food had not been available on campus, she would not have gained so much weight. The article suggests that the removal of junk food would be very beneficial. The article also provides an example of a school that has done just that. The article does suggest requiring students to participate in thirty minutes of physical activity, but the essay makes no such suggestion. Remember to select an answer that accurately reflects both pieces.

8. **C**   The word "we" comes up when the author begins mentioning solutions at the end of the article. The purpose of using the word "we" makes the readers feel like they share a certain degree of responsibility for solving this problem. By using "we," the author may hope to inspire readers to help because they might feel responsible.

9. **D**   In order to answer this question, you have to think of the title within the context of the article. Just looking at the title itself will not point you in the right direction. By calling the problem of obesity a "silent killer," the reader understands that being extremely overweight has the potential to kill people. The reason why it is labeled as a "new" killer is because the problem of obesity in children is a relatively new development.

10. **D** The author of the essay gives plenty of clues as to what a nemesis is. We know it is something she has to fight with because she gives descriptions of having to resist the vending machines and then give in to them. A nemesis is a formidable enem. For the author, the vending machines certainly fall into that category.

11. **B** The idea of flavors being able to "dance" is personification because flavors cannot dance. The flavors are given humanlike qualities, which of course makes the sentence personification.

12. **C** Since this author is constantly teased for her weight, she is afraid that if she exercises, people will make more fun of her. By saying that she can imagine the sound effects that will follow, she is implying that her classmates will make noises as she tries to exercise. Since she is afraid of being teased, she decides not to exercise.

13. **D** This question is similar to a previous question, but it is worded a bit differently. It is asking you to recognize which solution both texts agree upon, which is of course to remove junk food from schools. Do not be surprised if you get questions that resemble one another on the actual exam. Many times the exam will ask the same question but in a slightly different format just to make sure you have understood what you read.

14. **D** The flyer aims to get teenagers interested in sending in their written material. It provides the needed information for individuals who are interested in submitting material. Therefore the publisher hopes to receive submissions for publication.

15. **A** Based on the list in the flyer, the company is not looking for essays.

16. **B** The flyer clearly states that if a submission is accepted, the author will be paid $500.00. Choice A is certainly logical because if a piece is submitted, the author's name will probably appear in the book. However, that is not explicitly stated. On the other hand, the information concerning the $500.00 is made very clear to the reader.

17. **B** The purpose of the book appears to be that of giving young people a chance to be authors and to voice their opinions. It is not necessarily for the opportunity to showcase writing talent, as provided in choice A. Instead, its primary focus is to let teens have the experience of being published authors.

18. **C** The flyer clearly states that unaccepted submissions will be mailed back to the authors only if they include a self-addressed, stamped envelope. If an envelope is not included, the submission becomes the property of the publisher.

19. **B** The publisher seems to be advertising the book as something that focuses on the problems and issues that teens face today. If the company is looking for submissions that deal with teen issues, it would probably be most interested in a story that dealt with battling stereotypes.

20. **A** Since the publisher is putting together a book comprised of multiple submissions from multiple authors, you can determine that an anthology is exactly that. Any book that holds a collection of text from different authors is usually considered an anthology.

21. **A** As mentioned in Practice Test A, dealing with older text can be challenging. However, if you simply focus on the words and read the poem several times, you should begin to understand the meaning of the text. In this case, the bulk of the poem is concerned with the eventual death of the narrator. Lines such as, "No longer mourn for me when I am dead," tell the reader immediately that the narrator is talking about his own death.

22. **B** This poem is addressed to the narrator's love. He refers to her several times throughout the poem with lines such as, "Remember not / That hand that writ it, for I love you so." This tells the reader that the narrator is writing this poem for the person that he loves.

23. **D**   The lesson contained in this poem seems to be one of painful advice. The narrator does not want his love to be upset after he dies, and he is afraid that his memories of him will cause her pain. Throughout the poem he is telling her to forget about him after his death so that she is caused no misery. Therefore, the theme of the poem becomes the message that it is best to forget those that we have loved because memories can cause much pain.

24. **C**   This question connects directly to the theme presented in the previous question. The narrator states that he fears his death will cause his love pain when he says, "That I in your sweet thoughts would be forgot, / If thinking on me then should make you woe." He is also afraid that the world will make fun of his love because she chose to love him. When he states, "Lest the wise world should look into your moan, / And mock you with me after I am gone," he is telling his love that it is better to forget him so that the world cannot tease her for loving him.

25. **A**   This particular question focuses on the central theme of the poem. The lines mentioned in the question simply state that the narrator feels it is better if his love forgets him after his death. He has loved her so much; he does want to hurt her by causing her to think of painful memories.

26. **C**   The way in which this essay is written makes it appropriate for a student audience. Elements such as mentioning designer labels are important to note because adults may not be as familiar with them as other students. Clues such as that let you know who the intended audience is supposed to be.

27. **B**   The author of this paper is focusing on how superficial it is to care so much about wearing a certain label. She mentions that students who do not wear designer labels get picked on and how buying cheaper clothes is not accepted by other students. She wishes that students at her school would not care so much about what type of clothes a person wears. She does not like the status and emphasis that designer clothing is given.

28. **C**   The author thinks that a solution to the problem is not to let students make fun of one another for their clothing choices. She clearly states that she does not support a dress code as a solution because she feels that students will still figure out a way to integrate designer elements into their outfits.

29. **B**   Since the author is so bothered by the superficial value placed on clothing, integrating a statistic that shows how much money teenagers spend on designer clothing would be helpful. It would help to show that teens spend a lot of money on clothing and that it is becoming excessive.

30. **D**   The author implies that by not wearing designer clothes, one gets knocked down into a lower social standing at school. The students who do not wear nice clothes are picked on and teased, something the author is not willing to be a part of.

31. **A**   Based on the opinions of the author, he or she would most likely support a day where students were not allowed to wear designer clothing. She does not like the idea of a dress code. However, having one day where students were put on an equal standing with one another would probably appeal to the author.

32. **D**   The word "sans" means without. Based on the context clues, it should be fairly clear that the author thinks a person could purchase cheaper clothing elsewhere that probably looked similar to designer clothing. They do not get the label, but they get an article of clothing that looks like nice and is much cheaper.

33. **D**   Even though Mr. Banks is requesting a refund at the end of the letter, the central purpose of the letter is to complain about his dining experience at the restaurant.

34. **D**   Mr. Banks and his wife did everything the choices provide except leave the restaurant in the middle of dinner. They were probably both angry enough to leave the restaurant, but they did not.

35. **C** Referring to the server as pleasant is of course sarcastic. Their server has been nothing but rude, and Mr. Banks is not being serious when he calls the server pleasant.

36. **D** Remember that flow charts show a sequence of events. According to the letter, Mr. and Mrs. Banks waited for a table, waited again for service, and received bad food, and then he wrote the complaint letter. If you are unsure how to fill in flow charts, just look back at the text and begin to sequence the events in order.

37. **C** Mr. Banks wants to receive a refund for the poor dinner that he paid for. He asks Mr. Riven to issue a refund at the end of the letter.

38. **B** The purpose of any receipt is to show how much you paid for something. Mr. Banks is sending his receipt to Mr. Riven to let him know how much his refund needs to be.

39. **A** The only detail that Mr. Banks provides is that of the server rolling her eyes at him. The other choices are not correct because they are not mentioned in the letter.

40. **C** Based on Mr. Banks's horrible experience, the reader can be fairly confident that he will not return to the restaurant, even if he does receive a refund. He probably does not have much interest in getting the server fired. He simply wants his refund and probably will not risk going to Paradise Grill again.

41. **C** The one stipulation that applies to both warranties is that the refrigerator has to be operated according to the provided guidelines. A refrigerator that has not been used properly will not be covered under either warranty.

42. **D** The warranty clearly states that any questions need to be mailed in to the company. You can tell because the only contact information they give is a mailing address.

43. **B** The warranty covers refrigerators used for household purposes only.

44. **C** Like the previous questions, the answers are stated plainly in the text. If you cannot recall an answer, just look back to the warranty. The warranty tells customers to call the nearest store location for warranty service.

45. **B** The only portion of the refrigerator not covered by the five-year warranty is the exterior.

46. **C** When directions tell you to "season liberally," they mean use a lot of seasoning. To use a liberal amount of anything implies that you need to use a lot.

47. **A** The unsalted butter is not a necessary ingredient for this recipe because it is labeled as being optional. Optional means that it is not required.

48. **C** The recipe states that the chicken is done when the juices run clear. This tells you that the chicken has cooked completely through.

49. **A** This is just like using context clues. The only time the word "sauté" comes up is when something is being cooked in oil or butter.

50. **B** To season something to taste means that you add however much salt and pepper that you as the chef personally desire. If you do not want to add any, you do not have to. If you want to add a lot, you may add a lot.

51. **C** The key word in this statement is "like," which makes it a simile.

52. **D** Based on the quick biography that you get of this poet, you know that his parents were slaves. When people are kept as slaves, they lose their right to freedom. Just like the bird in the poem, the slaves are "caged" and are not allowed to fly freely away.

53. **D** Both the narrator and the bird understand the desire to be free. The elements of the breeze and fresh air only add to their torment because they are reminders of the things that the narrator and bird cannot freely experience.

54. **A** The contrast here is what people typically believe versus what the bird is actually doing. People usually see a bird flapping his wings as an expression of joy. However, the poet is implying that the bird is flapping his wings is an expression of grief, begging to be released.

55. **B** The narrator feels sympathy for the bird because the narrator understands how the bird feels. He can sympathize with the feelings of being held against one's will because he has had that experience himself.

56. **C** The poet is implying that it is springtime because the first flower is blooming and the first bird is singing.

57. **B** In the poem, the bird is robbed of experiencing freedom and is therefore robbed of experiencing his life. The narrator is making a statement that the same thing happens to people if they are caged or held against their will; they cannot experience their lives the way in which they are supposed to.

58. **A** That particular line is emphasizing how painful it is to be reminded again of being held against one's will. Every time that the bird tries to escape through the bars, he is reminded again of how he is caged.

59. **C** A chalice is typically defined as a type of cup. In this case, the flower is the cup, letting out a sweet fragrance or perfume.

60. **D** The bars of the cage are described as being cruel. This is giving an inanimate object being given humanlike characteristics, which makes the statement an example of personification.

PRACTICE TEST C ANSWER SHEET

Fill in the bubble completely.
Erase carefully if answer is changed.

1. Ⓐ Ⓑ Ⓒ Ⓓ
2. Ⓐ Ⓑ Ⓒ Ⓓ
3. Ⓐ Ⓑ Ⓒ Ⓓ
4. Ⓐ Ⓑ Ⓒ Ⓓ
5. Ⓐ Ⓑ Ⓒ Ⓓ
6. Ⓐ Ⓑ Ⓒ Ⓓ
7. Ⓐ Ⓑ Ⓒ Ⓓ
8. Ⓐ Ⓑ Ⓒ Ⓓ
9. Ⓐ Ⓑ Ⓒ Ⓓ
10. Ⓐ Ⓑ Ⓒ Ⓓ
11. Ⓐ Ⓑ Ⓒ Ⓓ
12. Ⓐ Ⓑ Ⓒ Ⓓ
13. Ⓐ Ⓑ Ⓒ Ⓓ
14. Ⓐ Ⓑ Ⓒ Ⓓ
15. Ⓐ Ⓑ Ⓒ Ⓓ
16. Ⓐ Ⓑ Ⓒ Ⓓ
17. Ⓐ Ⓑ Ⓒ Ⓓ
18. Ⓐ Ⓑ Ⓒ Ⓓ
19. Ⓐ Ⓑ Ⓒ Ⓓ
20. Ⓐ Ⓑ Ⓒ Ⓓ

21. Ⓐ Ⓑ Ⓒ Ⓓ
22. Ⓐ Ⓑ Ⓒ Ⓓ
23. Ⓐ Ⓑ Ⓒ Ⓓ
24. Ⓐ Ⓑ Ⓒ Ⓓ
25. Ⓐ Ⓑ Ⓒ Ⓓ
26. Ⓐ Ⓑ Ⓒ Ⓓ
27. Ⓐ Ⓑ Ⓒ Ⓓ
28. Ⓐ Ⓑ Ⓒ Ⓓ
29. Ⓐ Ⓑ Ⓒ Ⓓ
30. Ⓐ Ⓑ Ⓒ Ⓓ
31. Ⓐ Ⓑ Ⓒ Ⓓ
32. Ⓐ Ⓑ Ⓒ Ⓓ
33. Ⓐ Ⓑ Ⓒ Ⓓ
34. Ⓐ Ⓑ Ⓒ Ⓓ
35. Ⓐ Ⓑ Ⓒ Ⓓ
36. Ⓐ Ⓑ Ⓒ Ⓓ
37. Ⓐ Ⓑ Ⓒ Ⓓ
38. Ⓐ Ⓑ Ⓒ Ⓓ
39. Ⓐ Ⓑ Ⓒ Ⓓ
40. Ⓐ Ⓑ Ⓒ Ⓓ

41. Ⓐ Ⓑ Ⓒ Ⓓ
42. Ⓐ Ⓑ Ⓒ Ⓓ
43. Ⓐ Ⓑ Ⓒ Ⓓ
44. Ⓐ Ⓑ Ⓒ Ⓓ
45. Ⓐ Ⓑ Ⓒ Ⓓ
46. Ⓐ Ⓑ Ⓒ Ⓓ
47. Ⓐ Ⓑ Ⓒ Ⓓ
48. Ⓐ Ⓑ Ⓒ Ⓓ
49. Ⓐ Ⓑ Ⓒ Ⓓ
50. Ⓐ Ⓑ Ⓒ Ⓓ
51. Ⓐ Ⓑ Ⓒ Ⓓ
52. Ⓐ Ⓑ Ⓒ Ⓓ
53. Ⓐ Ⓑ Ⓒ Ⓓ
54. Ⓐ Ⓑ Ⓒ Ⓓ
55. Ⓐ Ⓑ Ⓒ Ⓓ
56. Ⓐ Ⓑ Ⓒ Ⓓ
57. Ⓐ Ⓑ Ⓒ Ⓓ
58. Ⓐ Ⓑ Ⓒ Ⓓ
59. Ⓐ Ⓑ Ⓒ Ⓓ
60. Ⓐ Ⓑ Ⓒ Ⓓ

Chapter 10

Reading Practice Test C

A Test of Conscience

I looked at myself in the mirror with pride. My crisp, white, button-down shirt screamed sophistication and my pressed black pants hit the top of my shoe, right above the toe. My maroon-colored apron completed the ensemble. The entire outfit seemed to ask (in a very classy voice no less), "How may I serve you tonight?" Tonight was my first night at Keegan's, one of the hottest restaurants in town. I was so excited to begin waiting tables at this popular eatery because my best friend, Tina, could not stop raving about how much money she was making night after night. Keegan's was definitely designed for the teenage consumer. However, it was designed for the teenager customer who had a lot of extra cash. They served the best gourmet pizzas, had amazing custom sodas, and always had the hottest new DJ's for after-hours dancing on the weekends. It had a reputation for hiring only the best, You can imagine my excitement when I finally got the call from Ross, my new boss, that I had been hired as a server. The best part of the whole deal was that I was going to get to work with Tina. We have been best friends since the second grade, so working together just seemed like it should be part of the plan. I know that I owe a lot of the decision to hire me to Tina. I am pretty sure she was putting in the good word for me every time she saw Ross.

I did one last check as I walked out the door. I had plenty of extra pens and pads of paper, and my apron was on straight. My mom made sure to give me a good-luck kiss en route to the driveway. I am just grateful she did not stop me and take my picture in my new work uniform. My mother is notorious for documenting every single nanosecond of my life.

"Good luck, honey! You're going to do just great! I know it!" my mom called after my car taillights. I gave a wave as I cruised down the street toward Keegan's, my mom's beaming face disappearing from the rearview mirror.

"Ice teas are here, silverware is here, and here's straws and napkins."

I followed around Tim, my trainer for the night, trying to remember where everything in the server stations was kept.

"Make sure to keep an eye on people who order soda. A lot of the time, a person orders one soda and four people drink from it. You do not want that, especially when Ross catches you. He'll really lay into you."

"OK. Thanks for the tip." I replied, trying to store that information away as well.

Sensing that I was becoming a little overwhelmed, Tim said, "Do not get stressed. By next week, you'll have everything down pat and it will be as easy as breathing. You ready to follow me to our first table? Looks like table five just got sat."

"Sure, sounds great," I replied enthusiastically.

"All right, just stay behind me and watch how I talk to the customers and the questions that I ask concerning their orders. Remember, do not stress."

Our first table was a group of girls from our high school. I recognized them only from the times I had seen them in the hallways, but they seemed nice enough. I could tell that I was quickly going to become familiar with students who had money to burn. All four girls ordered the most expensive items on the menu and did not bat an eye.

"Wow, that's going to be a great tab," I said quietly to Tim as we headed back to the kitchen.

"Which hopefully means a great tip," he replied.

The night continued to proceed smoothly. I felt like I had learned about a million new things in the time span of just a few hours.

"Well, that's it for me tonight. You're going to be training with Tina to learn how to close down. Any questions?" Tim asked as he removed his apron.

"No. Thanks for all of the great tips. Are you working tomorrow?"

"Sure am. I'll be supervising you as you take your own tables."

"All right, see you tomorrow then."

As Tim proceeded to count his tip money for the night, Tina came bustling over in a flurry of excitement.

"Did you hear? You get to train with me the rest of the night!"

"I know! That's awesome!"

"All right, well, let's get started so we are not stuck here until midnight."

Tina walked me through all of the details on how to close down the restaurant. It did not seem too difficult, just a lot to remember.

At around 10:00, the last customer finally left. In contrast with the bustle of servers and kitchen cacophony, it became eerily calm. Tina and I flopped down in a booth to do her cash out. "This is the best part of the night," Tina began as she started pulling out twenty-dollar bills from her apron. She walked me through the cash-out process, going over details like how to sort credit card slips, money that had to be given back to the restaurant, and then finally, tip money. By the time all the money was counted and divided up into its respective piles, Tina declared that she had made two hundred dollars for the night. I knew the money at Keegan's was supposed to be good, but I had no idea that I would be making that kind of money.

"Tina, are you sure that's right? That seems really high," I asked tentatively.

"Well, let me clue you in on a little secret of mine," began Tina, leaning over the table. "Technically, I should be bringing home only about a hundred dollars, but I've figured out some pretty sneaky ways to just about double my tip money every night."

"What are you talking about?"

"Let's just say, do not upset me during a shift because you might find your tip money disappearing."

"I don't get what you're saying."

"It's really simple. You know how people just leave cash on the table for tips, right? Well, I just make sure to grab it before the other server gets to it."

"You mean to say that you're taking other servers' tips?" I asked in disbelief. I had known Tina for years. I would have never even suspected she was capable of such a thing.

"Don't act so shocked, Madison. The first time you get stiffed on your own table, you'll start looking for ways to make up the loss."

"Tina, what you're doing is stealing from people who are working just as hard as you. I cannot believe you'd do this to someone else. And how do you keep other servers from suspecting you?"

"Just like you said Madison, you cannot believe I'd do such a thing. I've got every person here thinking I'm an angel. They'd never accuse me of doing something like this. And besides, they do not have any proof. The servers just think that the table was a bunch of jerks that did not tip. I've got to head out of here. I'll see you tomorrow, right?"

I nodded slowly, avoiding Tina's eyes. "Yes, I'll be here tomorrow."

"Hey, I know I don't have to say this, but don't tell anyone. I wouldn't be doing this if I was not in a desperate situation. I really need the money."

"That doesn't make what you're doing any better," I replied quietly.

"Whatever. Bye."

I watched Tina disappear into the kitchen office. What could she possibly need money for so badly that she was stealing? I leaned my head back against the vinyl covering of the booth and closed my eyes. What would prevent Tina from stealing from my tables when I was done with my training? How long had this been going on?

My thoughts were suddenly interrupted when Robert and Joyce, two other servers, came out of the kitchen.

"What a night. I'm almost positive I should have made at least thirty more dollars. And I had several tables who didn't tip me at all," said an exasperated Joyce.

"I know, same here. The last few nights, I haven't made as much as usual. Same number of tables and customers. I don't get it," replied Robert. "And I'm really stressed now because my cell phone bill is due and I'm going to have to ask my mom to help me out. I hate doing that, especially when it's not usually a problem."

Unnoticed, I watched Joyce and Robert leave the restaurant through the front doors. I knew exactly where their money was going. I did not know what to do. Tina was my best friend. Part of me wanted to think that she was taking the money because she really was in some sort of desperate situation. However, I knew that that did not excuse the fact that she was stealing. If she needed money, she should ask somebody to help her. Another part of me could not help but wonder if Tina's "desperate situation" didn't include the need for designer clothes.

"So, Madison, how'd your first night go?"

I did not even notice that Ross, my boss, had approached the booth I was sitting in.

"Oh," I began, sitting up straight. "It went just fine. Tim taught me a lot of helpful things, and Tina just finished showing me how to close."

"Good. Hopefully, if we're on schedule, you'll start taking your own tables on Wednesday. Did you have any questions that Tim or Tina didn't cover?"

I looked at Ross and was silent for what felt like an hour. I took in a deep breath, unsure of what I was about to do. "No, I don't have any questions. But I need to tell you something really important. And please don't tell anyone."

1 The statement, "My crisp, white, button-down shirt screamed sophistication" is an example of
A simile
B metaphor
C hyperbole
D personification

2 At the end of the story, the reader can infer that Madison
A is going to quit her job at Keegan's
B is going to tell Ross about Tina's stealing
C will keep Tina's secret safe from Ross
D will remain best friends with Tina

3 Madison is most excited to be working at Keegan's because
A she will make lots of money in tips
B she will be working with Tina
C it is a popular restaurant among teens
D the food is of high quality and delicious

4 Based on the conversation that Robert and Joyce have, the reader can infer that
A they have both waited on tables that did not tip
B they both suspect Tina of stealing money
C Tina is stealing their tips from their tables
D Robert and Joyce do not get along with one another

5 The theme of this story can best be defined as
A it can be difficult to watch friends make mistakes, especially when one knows that what they are doing is wrong
B a person may have to battle the loyalty they feel for a friend when it comes to doing the right thing
C a person learns many new things when starting a job and may quickly become overwhelmed
D strong friendships can survive through any obstacle and will come out more stable in the end

6 Within the sentences, "At around 10:00, the last customer finally left. In contrast with the bustle of servers and kitchen <u>cacophony</u>, it became eerily calm," the word <u>cacophony</u> means
A glare
B smell
C mess
D noise

7 The sentence, "My mother is notorious for documenting every single nanosecond of my life," is an example of
A metaphor
B simile
C hyperbole
D imagery

8 Based on inferences made by the reader, Madison's character can best be defined as
A honest
B hardworking
C deceitful
D loyal

9 The sentence, "Another part of me could not help but wonder if Tina's 'desperate situation' didn't include the need for designer clothes," tells the reader that Madison
A can now understand why Tina needs money so desperately
B is thinking about stealing money as well so she can buy new clothes
C is going to tell Robert and Joyce why they are not making as much money
D thinks that Tina does not really need the money for anything important

10 Within the sentence, "'Tina, are you sure that's right? That seems really high,' I asked <u>tentatively</u>," the word <u>tentatively</u> means
A softly
B hesitantly
C loudly
D accusingly

Directions: Read the following article and then answer questions 11–20.

How to Raise a Great Puppy

So you are thinking about getting a puppy? Congratulations! Getting a new pet is a very exciting decision, and the rewards that come with raising a pet are many. However, along with those rewards come lots of responsibility. As your pet's owner, it is your job to teach your new puppy proper behavior, how to listen to you, and how to respond appropriately to your commands. This may sound like a lot of work, and it certainly is. However, if you commit yourself to raising a great puppy, you will enjoy the rewards of having a grown dog that you can share a memorable relationship with.

Making your new puppy feel welcome

The most important thing you can do when you bring your new puppy home is have your home ready for him. Remember that your new friend is undergoing some substantial changes. He will know that your home is not the store or pound where he just came from. He will be missing his puppy friends, and this may be the first time that he has had to spend the night without other dogs. It is your job to make sure that you have his food and water dish out, a new bed, and maybe a toy or two for him to play with. Let your puppy sniff around his new setting and belongings. Remember that dogs evaluate new situations through smell, so make sure to let your puppy sniff his new home. If your puppy seems intimidated by his new surroundings, he may feel better if you get down on all fours and coax him to come explore. Even though you are probably excited to show off your new friend, keep the number of people present at your house to a minimum. Adapting to a new environment is stressful enough without the added element of noisy and excited friends.

Setting a feeding schedule for your puppy

It is extremely important that your puppy adjusts to a feeding schedule as soon as possible. Most puppies will need to eat a small cup of food three times a day. You want to make sure to give your puppy his meals around the same time every-

day. This is extremely important if your puppy is going to realize that you are the boss! He needs to understand that his food comes from you and is not simply always sitting in his bowl, waiting for him. Begin training your puppy to sit for each meal. This may take several days or several weeks, depending on your puppy. However, the most crucial element during feeding time is that your puppy sees that you are providing him with nourishment. This gives your puppy a reason to listen to you and, more importantly, a reason to please you.

Training your puppy to obey basic commands

The most important thing when it comes to training is to be consistent! If you are trying to get your puppy to sit, make sure you use the same command every time. Do not alternate between *sit*, *stay*, and *heel*. This will only confuse your puppy and prolong the training process. Choose one command for a specific action, and stick with it. Initially, your puppy may need some physical guidance. For example, if you want your puppy to sit, gently push his bottom down while saying the command. If you remain consistent, your puppy will eventually come to understand what you want from him based on the command. Remember, your puppy looks to you for guidance. It is your job to teach him proper behavior.

Giving your puppy exercise

Even though you may think of your puppy as your best friend and begin to see almost humanlike characteristics emerge, you must remember that your puppy is still an animal. All animals need some type of physical activity. As your puppy's owner, you have the responsibility of making sure that your puppy gets enough exercise. When puppies are very young, they typically do not need walks for exercise because playing and exploring supply enough exercise. Your puppy is still a baby, so he does not need any exercise beyond play. However, as your puppy begins to grow, you must provide activity for your dog. You may want to take him on a walk, to a dog park, or play fetch. Whatever method you select, your dog needs at least forty minutes of physical activity each and every day. This may seem like an awful lot, but most dogs are kept in a confined area for the majority of their day. They need exercise to release all of that energy. If you do not give your dog enough exercise, you will most likely see problem behaviors beginning to emerge. For example, your dog may become destructive, ruining things in the house and chewing things to shreds. Instead, your dog may become aggressive or unwilling to listen to your commands. In order for a dog to be happy and healthy, you need to make sure to give him the opportunity to be active.

Of course, these are not the only issues that you need to be concerned with when raising a puppy. As your puppy grows, you will notice things that need to be addressed such as eating habits, vet checks, and so forth. However, this information should get you and your new puppy off to a great start!

11 This article covers all of the following topics *except*
   A obeying basic commands
   B potty-training methods
   C exercising your puppy
   D setting a feeding schedule

12 The central purpose of this article is to
   A educate new dog owners about the responsibilities of owning a puppy
   B inform new dog owners about how best to raise their new puppy
   C evaluate the pros and cons of owning different dog breeds
   D discuss the different methods for providing a dog with exercise

13 What function do the bold-faced headings placed throughout the article serve?
   A to draw the reader's attention to that information
   B to make reading the article more difficult
   C to highlight the central topic of each section
   D to emphasize important details and information

14 According to the article, the most important issue concerning training your dog to obey commands is to
   A use physical force
   B use multiple commands
   C teach your dog slowly
   D always be consistent

15 According to the article, if a dog does not get enough exercise he will
   A potentially become destructive
   B lose his healthy appetite
   C be aggressive to other dogs
   D lose levels of physical fitness

16 According to the article, a dog should get at least _____ minutes of physical activity every day.
   A thirty
   B forty
   C twenty
   D sixty

17 According to the article, setting a feeding schedule for a puppy is important because it
   A helps to establish a routine for the puppy
   B helps a puppy to learn basic commands
   C makes the puppy value and appreciate his owner
   D forces the puppy to earn his daily meals

18 In order to make a puppy feel welcome in his new home, an owner should do all of the following *except*
   A have his food and water dish out
   B invite friends over to meet the puppy
   C let the puppy smell and explore
   D have toys out for him to play with

19 Very young puppies do not need structured exercise because
   A they are too young to understand what you want them to do
   B they could get sick from getting too much activity
   C puppies do not like structured activities such as walking
   D playing and exploring provide enough daily exercise

20 Which of the following topics might a reader of this article also be interested in?
   A dealing with aggression and bullying in older dogs
   B adjusting a dog's feeding schedule as they age
   C introducing your dog to young children
   D toys that encourage development in puppies

| **Directions:** | Read the following poem and answer questions 21–28. |

I WANDERED LONELY AS A CLOUD
by William Wordsworth
(Reprinted with permission from Dover Publications)

I wandered lonely as a cloud
That floats on high o'er vales and hills,
When all at once I saw a crowd,
A host, of golden daffodils;
Beside the lake, beneath the trees,
Fluttering and dancing in the breeze.

Continuous as the stars that shine
And twinkle on the milky way,
They stretched in never-ending line
Along the margin of the bay:
Ten thousand saw I at a glance,
Tossing their heads in sprightly dance.

The waves beside them danced; but
    they
Out-did the sparkling waves in glee:
A poet could not but be gay,
In such a jocund company:
I gazed,—and gazed—but little thought
What wealth the show to me had
    brought:

For oft, when on my couch I lie
In vacant or in pensive mood,
They flash upon that inward eye
Which is the bliss of solitude;
And then my heart with pleasure fills,
And dances with the daffodils.

21 The lines, "When all at once I saw a crowd, / A host of golden daffodils," are an example of
  A personification
  B imagery
  C allusion
  D metaphor

22 Within the line, "In such a <u>jocund</u> company" the word <u>jocund</u> means
   A merry
   B lonely
   C excited
   D lovely

23 The theme of this poem can best be described as
   A the joy of being outside
   B the beauty that is found in nature
   C the pleasure to be found in being alone
   D the simple pleasures that make life meaningful

24 The mood of this poem can best be defined as
   A reflective
   B appreciative
   C whimsical
   D lighthearted

25 The line, "The waves beside them danced;" is an example of
   A imagery
   B allusion
   C personification
   D metaphor

26 The lines, "Which is the bliss of solitude; / And then my heart with pleasure fills, / And dances with the daffodils," supports the idea that
   A solitude can bring happiness and joy to an individual
   B memories can be very powerful on multiple levels
   C people desire to be alone in order to appreciate nature's beauty
   D people will never fully be able to recognize the value of solitude

27 Within the lines, "Continuous as the stars that shine / And twinkle on the milky way," the two things being compared are
   A stars and shining
   B daffodils and stars
   C stars and twinkle
   D daffodils and milky way

28 The line, "In vacant or in pensive mood" means that the narrator is
   A remembering the daffodils
   B feeling lonely and abandoned
   C wishing he were out in nature
   D in a thoughtful mood

Directions:	Read the following ad and letter and answer questions 29–35.

Are you good at communicating with others? Do you enjoy being on top of what's hot in music? Would you like to hear your voice on the radio?

KPRD Radio is currently looking for a few good DJs. Our station plays today's hottest hits. We are looking for people who will project a fresh, contemporary image.

Applicant Requirements:
- A bachelor's degree in broadcasting, public relations, or consumer science
- Previous DJ experience through either past employment or internships
- Must have a clean driving record
- Be able to attend radio functions outside of normal work hours

Job Requirements:
- Must be willing to work both days and evenings, alternating throughout the week
- Must project a professional image in and out of work
- Must have good communication skills and enjoy being in a social atmosphere

If you are interested in working for a great station, please send a letter explaining your qualifications to:

Katherine Reed
KPRD Station Manager
P.O. Box 587
Tucson, AZ 85735

1658 S. Mountain View St.
Flagstaff, AZ 86004
(928) 226-1897

December 14, 2006

Katherine Reed
KPRD Station Manager
P.O. Box 587
Tucson, AZ 85735

Dear Ms. Reed,

"Well good morning, Tucson! My name is Samantha Stone, and I'd like to introduce myself as KPRD's newest DJ. I'll be in charge of sharing today's hottest hits with you each morning as you make your way to work. I'll also be keeping you posted on traffic developments and events that are making the morning headlines. But enough about me, how about Smash-mouth's latest hit?"

Ever since I saw KPRD's ad, I have been practicing what I could say as one of the station's DJs. I feel that I would fit in perfectly at your radio station. Not only do I actually listen to the station every day, I have had several years of DJ experience in Chino Valley and Cotton-wood. I feel that I am ready to make a move to a large-city radio station and share my talents with a bigger, more diverse audience. I also feel that a move would enable me to use my degree in broadcasting to its fullest potential.

Not only do I have experience in the world of DJing, but I pride myself on the fact that I am always up to date on the latest music and fashion trends. I believe that if you want to be able to relate to your audience, you need to know what is really going on. I would love attending broadcast functions outside of work because that gives DJs the opportunity actually to meet their listeners and talk with them face to face. I know that I would project the fresh image the station is looking for, both in and out of the DJ booth.

I would love the chance to come and speak with you further about this great opportunity. I have also enclosed a tape of several of my past broadcasts. If my qualifications sound like they would be valuable for your station, please feel free to call me for an interview.

Thank you for your time,

Samantha Stone

Samantha Stone

29 According to the ad, qualified applicants must meet which of the following criteria?
   A be able to discuss current events and traffic conditions each morning
   B be able to move to the city in which the station is located
   C have a bachelor's degree in broadcasting, consumer science, or public relations
   D have current knowledge concerning the hottest fashion trends and fads

30 What function does the first paragraph of Samantha Stone's letter serve?
   A It shows that she can communicate well with a radio audience and that she has
     had DJ experience.
   B It lends a creative touch to her letter, helping her potential boss to see that she
     can visualize herself working for the radio station.
   C It shows that she knows about current music trends and she wants her potential
     boss to see that she has that knowledge.
   D It shows that she can discuss things beyond simply music, such as traffic and
     current events.

31 Why is it important that the radio station's DJs project a fresh image?
   A In order to report accurately on current events, they need to be up to date and
     informed of events taking place within the community.
   B Radio listeners want DJs who know what is currently going on within their
     communities.
   C The station plays contemporary music, and the DJs should resemble both in
     actions and appearance the music that is played.
   D The radio station does not want to have to provide additional training on the
     image that the DJ should project.

32 Complete the chart according to why Samantha Stone feels she would be a good DJ.

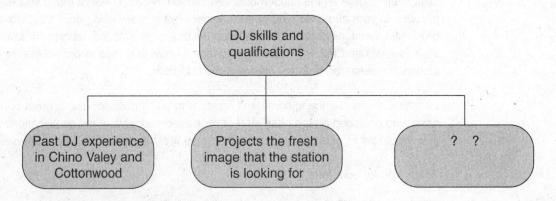

   A Bachelor's degree in broadcasting
   B Can work different shifts and hours
   C Has a clean driving record
   D Has great communication skills

33 Samantha feels that she is ready to move to a large city because
  A her talents as a DJ are being wasted in a small town
  B she wants to share her fashion knowledge
  C she would enjoy the move from a small town
  D she wants to deal with a larger, more diverse audience

34 Samantha includes a sample tape of her broadcasts because
  A she thought her potential boss would appreciate her thoughtfulness
  B she wants people at the station to hear how she sounds on the radio
  C she wants to brag about how great she is as a radio DJ
  D she wants to provide proof that she has had DJ experience

35 According to the ad, an applicant can meet the experience requirement through
  A internships
  B education
  C on-site training
  D conferences

Directions: Read the following essay and answer questions 36–45.

Video Games and Violence

"Finish him!" These famous words precede the death of an imaginary foe in the legendary video game, *Mortal Combat*. After these fateful words are spoken, you can choose to finish your foe in a number of ways. Maybe you feel inclined to tear his spine out, or maybe you are more in the decapitation mood. Whatever method you decide, the game has guaranteed that it will be violent, filled with unimaginable blood and gore. Games such as this contribute to the growing idea that violent video games are contributing to an ever increasingly violent youth. If a child has the opportunity to tear out someone's spine, what kind of message is our society sending about the value of human life? It is really any big surprise that today's kids are becoming more violent than ever?

From the early days of *Mortal Combat* to the evolution of games such as *Far Cry Instincts* and *Vice City*, today's kids are not only receiving a <u>barrage</u> of violent messages, but they are also receiving questionable moral guidance. Today's games not only include acts of extreme violence, they also integrate foul language and drug use. Granted, a ratings system is now in place to indicate the level of objectionable material. However, it does not seem to be helping in reducing the amount of violence we witness every day among young people. There have been several acts of horrendous violence where a reference to a video game has been made. For instance, at the tragic high school shooting in Columbine, the killers were rumored to be obsessed with the game *Doom*. The weaponry used to murder their fellow students was reminiscent of the guns used in *Doom*. What is society supposed to think when something as tragic as Columbine occurs and it appears one of the few explanations available is a video game?

Certainly not all violence among youth can be blamed on video games. Issues such as broken homes and poverty all contribute to violence. However, it is hard to ignore the fact that along with an increase of graphic violence in video games, America has seen an increase in real acts of violence. Is it possible for young people to play these games without it affecting their perspective on some level? Granted, many older children are able to distinguish the difference between reality and fantasy. They understand that they cannot run <u>amok</u> with a shotgun, killing everything in sight. However, even if video games do not inspire every child to kill something, they certainly numb a child's response to witnessing acts of violence. Reports of murder and abuse are simply a cornerstone of the evening news. These reports do not make us cry. Instead, they are simply part of the day's events. Children do not see them as out of the ordinary. When compared with the ways that characters can die in video games, the stabbing of an individual seems fairly tame. It is hard to avoid the idea that maybe children would be more sensitive to actual violence if they did not desensitize themselves through video games.

As in all things a child learns while growing up, the parents have the primary responsibility of teaching the difference between right and wrong. In order for a child to understand the severe implications of violence, he needs his parents to tell him the consequences of inflicting violence on others. Video games do not pause to tell a child that blasting someone's head off with a shotgun is not morally acceptable. If we want to see acts of violence decrease among America's youth, parents need to be the pause button, providing a clear moral compass for our children.

36 The purpose of this article is to
A inform readers about different video games
B argue that violent games contribute to real violence
C persuade readers to limit the types of games children can play
D prove that American children are desensitized to violence

37 Within the sentence, "Today's kids are not only receiving a <u>barrage</u> of violent messages but are also receiving questionable moral guidance," the word <u>barrage</u> means
A debatable topic
B influx
C high amount
D decrease

38 The author states that in addition to violent games, actual violence can also be blamed on
A lack of education
B lack of compassion
C lack of proper role models
D lack of parental guidance

39 Which of the following elements could this author integrate into the article to make a stronger argument?
A interviews from children expressing their opinion on whether or not violent games desensitize them to real violence
B statistics such as percentages showing how violence among children has risen over the last several years
C providing more specific names, examples, and instances that occur within violent video games
D explaining how a video game is made from the initial design stages to the marketing stages

40 What would be an appropriate replacement title for this article?
A "Increasing Acts of Violence"
B "Video Games and American Culture"
C "How a Child Becomes Violent"
D "Our Desensitized Gaming Youth"

41 Within the sentence, "Parents need to be the pause button," the author is saying that parents
A should turn off a video game that is violent
B need to take time to explain things to their children
C need to ask children questions about the games they play
D should discourage acts of violence among children

42 The author states that in addition to foul language, video games have also integrated elements of
 A car chases
 B drug use
 C realistic violence
 D illegal activity

43 Which of the following articles would this author most likely be interested in reading?
 A "Successful Single-Parent Families"
 B "Improving Coordination Through Gaming"
 C "The Creation of a Successful Video Game"
 D "The Connection Between Poverty and Violence"

44 Which of the following statements reflects a sarcastic tone?
 A "Parents need to be the pause button, providing a clear moral compass for our children."
 B "They understand that they cannot run amok with a shotgun, killing everything in sight."
 C "Maybe you feel inclined to tear his spine out, or maybe you are more in the decapitation mood."
 D "Reports of murder and abuse are simply a cornerstone of the evening news."

45 Within the sentence, "They understand that they cannot run <u>amok</u>" the word <u>amok</u> means
 A wildly
 B nervously
 C frantically
 D happily

Directions:	Read the following play excerpt and answer questions 46–55.

The following is a short excerpt taken from William Shakespeare's tragedy, *Macbeth*. *Macbeth* is a story about a Scottish lord by the name of Macbeth who through supernatural occurrences learns that he is to be the king of Scotland. Once Macbeth learns of his fate, he begins to plot how to make it a reality. The current king of Scotland, Duncan, still lives, and Macbeth believes that killing Duncan will open up an opportunity for himself to become king. Macbeth is unsure about what to do because Duncan is a good friend of his. However, Macbeth decides that he values being king more than friendship. This excerpt takes place immediately after Macbeth has murdered Duncan in his sleep. Macbeth's wife, Lady Macbeth, also plays an important role in the murder of Duncan.

Macbeth
by William Shakespeare
(Reprinted with permission from Dover Publications)

Lady Macbeth: Why, worthy thane,
You do unbend your noble strength, to think
So brain-sickly of things. Go get some water,
And wash this <u>filthy witness</u> from your hand.
Why did you bring these daggers from the place?
They must lie there. Go carry them, and smear
The sleepy grooms with blood.

Macbeth: I'll go no more.
I am afraid to think what I have done;
Look on't again I dare not.

Lady Macbeth: Infirm of purpose!
Give me the daggers. The sleeping and the dead
Are but as pictures; 'tis the eye of childhood
That fears a painted devil. If he do bleed,
I'll gild the faces of the grooms withal,
For it must seem their guilt.

Exit. Knock within.

Macbeth: Whence is that knocking?
How is't with me, when every noise appalls me?
What hands are here? Hah! they pluck out mine eyes.
Will all great Neptune's ocean wash this blood
Clean from my hand? No; this my hand will rather
The multitudinous seas incarnadine,
Making the green one red.

Enter Lady Macbeth

Lady Macbeth: My hands are of your color; but I shame
To wear a heart so white. *(Knock)* I hear a knocking
At the south entry. Retire we to our chamber.
A little water clears us of this deed;
How easy it is then! Your constancy
Hath left you unattended. *(Knock)* Hark, more
Knocking.
Get on your night-gown, lest occasion call us
And show us to be watchers. Be not lost
So poorly in your thoughts.

Macbeth: To know my deed, 'twere best not know
Myself.

                                                    Knock

Wake Duncan with thy knocking! I would thou
Coulds't.

                                                    Exit

46 Throughout this excerpt, Macbeth appears to be battling with
   A his wife's fearless attitude toward murder
   B whether or not he truly wants to be king
   C the fear of being caught for the murder of Duncan
   D his feelings of guilt over murdering Duncan

47 Within the statement, "And wash this <u>filthy witness</u> from your hand," <u>filthy witness</u>
   is a metaphor for
   A blood
   B guilt
   C disguise
   D the crown

48 When Macbeth says, "Will all great Neptune's ocean wash this blood / Clean from
   my hand?" he is suggesting that
   A he needs divine forgiveness for the act that he has committed, otherwise he will
      be plagued by guilt
   B the act of murdering Duncan was so bloody that he is going to need a lot of water
      to clean up the evidence of his crime
   C he feels so guilty for murdering Duncan that not even an ocean would remove the
      blood from his hand
   D his wife is just as guilty as he and they will be battling feelings of guilt for years
      to come

49 When Macbeth says the lines, "Wake Duncan with thy knocking! I would thou /
   Coulds't," the reader understands that Macbeth
   A regrets murdering Duncan
   B is excited finally to become king
   C feels like he is living in a nightmare
   D wishes that he had never learned his fate

50 When Lady Macbeth says, "I'll gild the faces of the grooms withal, / For it must seem their guilt," the reader learns that
A Lady Macbeth has no fear concerning the act of murder
B the Macbeths are trying to frame Duncan's guards for his murder
C the guards were in fact responsible for the death of Duncan
D Macbeth also murdered Duncan's guards

51 When Lady Macbeth says, "My hands are of your color; but I shame / To wear a heart so white," the reader understands that Lady Macbeth
A feels that she is innocent of committing any wrongdoing and that the blame falls on her husband only
B is equally as guilty as her husband, however, she feels no remorse in committing murder
C wishes that they could undo the act of murdering Duncan and that she is extremely regretful
D is joyous that the murder is over with because now she and her husband will rule Scotland

52 The line, "Will all great Neptune's ocean wash this blood / clean from my hand?" is an example of
A personification
B allusion
C metaphor
D simile

53 Throughout this excerpt, Lady Macbeth can best be defined as
A remorseful
B sympathetic
C commanding
D cowardly

54 Throughout this excerpt, Macbeth can best be defined as
A remorseful
B sympathetic
C commanding
D cowardly

55 Based upon Macbeth's behavior after the murder of Duncan, the reader can predict that
A he will soon put the murder behind him and will happily reign as king
B he will confess his murderous acts and bravely face the consequences
C Lady Macbeth will betray her husband to escape any punishment
D he will continue to face a battle with regret and a guilty conscience

Directions: Read the following flyer and answer questions 56–60.

Are you looking to get in the best shape of your life? Sammy's Gym has your answer!

Come join Sammy's Gym today and become a part of a community where people like to be healthy, make new friends, and encourage others in their fitness pursuits.

Sammy's Gym offers:
- full cardio room with treadmills and elliptical trainers
- full weight room with both free weights and machines
- lap pool
- jacuzzis in both men's and women's locker rooms
- wide variety of aerobic, yoga, and dance classes
- personal trainers ready to help you realize your potential
- child care Monday through Friday

If you join now through the month of March, you will receive:
- one month membership FREE
- your choice of either a personal training session or body fat analysis
- FREE initiation (a $200 savings)

Come into Sammy's Gym today and start reaching your fitness goals!

56 Sammy's Gym offers all of the following services *except*
  A yoga classes
  B personal training
  C weight room
  D spa treatments

57 Benefits of joining Sammy's Gym now include
  A making new friends
  B free nutrition program
  C free initiation
  D free spa service

58 Which of the following pieces of information would be helpful to include in the flyer?
  A monthly cost of membership
  B qualifications of personal trainers
  C list of all aerobic classes offered
  D hours and days of operation

59 According to the flyer, Sammy's Gym wants to project an image of a gym that is
  A a support system for elite athletes and competitors
  B a group of people helping one another reach their goals
  C interested in individuals who have over fifty pounds to lose
  D competitive and encourages individuals to be their best

60 An individual interested in joining Sammy's Gym might also be interested in information concerning
  A a competitive running club
  B tanning services
  C food and nutrition
  D available spa services

ANSWER KEY TO PRACTICE TEST C

1.	D	13.	C	25.	C	37.	C	49.	A
2.	B	14.	D	26.	A	38.	D	50.	B
3.	B	15.	A	27.	B	39.	B	51.	B
4.	C	16.	B	28.	D	40.	D	52.	B
5.	B	17.	C	29.	C	41.	B	53.	C
6.	D	18.	B	30.	B	42.	B	54.	A
7.	C	19.	D	31.	C	43.	D	55.	D
8.	A	20.	D	32.	A	44.	C	56.	D
9.	D	21.	B	33.	D	45.	A	57.	C
10.	B	22.	A	34.	B	46.	D	58.	A
11.	B	23.	C	35.	A	47.	A	59.	B
12.	B	24.	D	36.	B	48.	C	60.	C

EXPLANATION OF CORRECT ANSWERS

1. **D** Because the shirt is described as "screaming" something, you should recognize that you are looking at personification. Clothing obviously is not capable of making sounds. In personification, an inanimate object is given humanlike characteristics.

2. **B** The last several lines of the story let you know what Madison has decided to do. The pause, the looking at Ross, and the drawing of a deep breath let you know that Madison has decided to do something difficult, which in this case is telling on her best friend. She also finishes the story by telling Ross that he must not tell anyone what she is about to say.

3. **B** At the beginning of the story, Madison mentions that the best part of working at Keegan's is going to be that she will work with Tina.

4. **C** Paying attention to details such as both servers noticing that their nightly intake has been less and that they both waited on tables that did not tip is important because it lets the reader know that Tina stole from them. The placement of this conversation is important as well. If it occurred at the beginning of the story, the reader would probably think that both servers simply did not get a tip from a table. However, since it follows Madison and Tina's conversation, the reader has a pretty good idea about what is happening to the other servers' tips.

5. **B** The reader learns that Madison and Tina have been good friends for many years. However, at the end of the story, Madison chooses to turn in Tina rather than keep her secret for her. Even though Madison morally does the right thing by telling Ross, she is risking losing Tina forever. The other themes presented are not as strong as choice B. Remember that when determining the theme, you have to find a statement that directly relates to the events within the story.

6. **D** For all vocabulary-oriented questions, use context to help you figure out the correct definition. For instance, Madison mentions that the restaurant is now calm because there are no longer servers running around and there is no more cacophony, or noise. A good technique for figuring out the meaning of vocabulary words is to substitute each choice within the context of the sentence to see which makes the most sense.

7. **C** Documenting every single nanosecond of someone's life is obviously an exaggeration and could never be the truth. Since Madison uses this description to dramatize how much her mother enjoys taking pictures of her, it is an example of a hyperbole.

8. **A** Madison's character is ultimately defined by her actions at the end of the story. She is willing to sacrifice a meaningful friendship in order to do the right thing. Since Madison cannot be labeled as either deceitful or loyal, the only remaining choices are hardworking and honest. Madison is certainly excited to be at her new job, but there is not enough evidence given throughout the story to make that her strongest characteristic.

9. **D** The key clue in that sentence is that the term "desperate situation" is put in quotation marks. This tells the reader that Madison is viewing Tina's desperate situation as something that is not to be taken seriously. Another clue is that Madison views Tina's desperate situation in a somewhat sarcastic light. Needing designer clothes does not fall into the category of a desperate situation, and Madison is questioning Tina's motives for stealing the money.

10. **B** Once again, use context clues and substitute answer choices until you find one that fits within the context of the sentence. At this part in the story, Madison begins to wonder how Tina could be making so much money. She does not want to come right out and accuse her of miscounting or some other error. Therefore, Madison asks in a hesitant voice.

11. **B** This answer can be determined by simply eliminating the topics that are covered in the article. The bold-faced headings also help you answer this question because there is no section labeled "potty training." When you read informational text, make sure to go back and locate the answer if you cannot recall some of the information that you read.

12. **B** The central purpose of this article is to tell people about training methods and how to raise a puppy. Choice A may seem tempting because it mentions educating people, which this article certainly does. However, the entire article is not dedicated to that purpose. Pay attention to key words within questions such as "central" or "main." The question wants you to determine what the article, story, or essay is primarily dedicated to.

13. **C** The headings serve as a summary for each section so that the reader is aware of what is going to be covered. This way, a reader can quickly locate information that he or she may need.

14. **D** The author clearly states that being consistent with a puppy is crucial in order to have successful training. If you cannot remember the correct answer, locate the section labeled "training your puppy to obey basic commands" and reread that section. Always keep in mind that there is no reason to rush through the test questions; you have all the time that you need.

15. **A** Within the section discussing how to exercise a dog, the author names some potential side effects if a dog does not get enough exercise. Three answer choices might make logical sense, but the question is asking you find the correct answer according to the article itself. It is not asking you to answer the question based on what you personally think.

16. **B** Simply go back through the article to locate the correct amount of time to exercise a dog.

17. **C** The author states that setting a feeding schedule is important so that a puppy can begin to see who he has to thank for his full belly.

18. **B** In the section that covers bringing a new puppy home, the author mentions that you should do all of the answer choices except have friends over.

19. **D** Within the exercise section, the author provides information both about older dogs and puppies. Simply reread the section to the find the answer for "very young puppies." It says, "When puppies are very young, they typically do not need walks for exercise because playing and exploring supply enough exercise."

20. **D** This is the only answer choice that relates to puppies. Any reader who is interested in the given article would be interested in other material that deals with puppies, their development, and training.

21. **B** Since these lines describe something that the narrator is seeing, you should realize that it is an example of imagery. Anytime that you encounter a description relaying color, the author is using imagery.

22. **A** In order to figure out that jocund means merry, simply analyze how the narrator feels when he is outside, seeing the daffodils. The flowers themselves seem to be celebrating and are in a merry mood. He also mentions that he cannot help himself from becoming happy as well, considering the merry company of the daffodils.

23. **C**   The narrator clearly values the beauty of nature and how it affects him. However, the narrator is stressing how valuable it is to witness things such as the daffodils in solitude. The title of the poem is a good clue for finding the theme of this poem. His wandering and being alone are not presented as bad things, rather, they provide peace and calm for the narrator. The narrator of the poem wants the reader to understand the value and joy of solitude.

24. **D**   As the narrator relates his experience outside with the daffodils, he himself seems to be lighthearted and enjoying the beauty found in nature. The choice of whimsical may be a tempting choice. However, whimsical means to be fanciful, which does not accurately relate what is occurring throughout the poem.

25. **C**   Describing the waves as dancing is clearly giving an inanimate object (water) humanlike characteristics (the ability to dance).

26. **A**   Those particular lines certainly support the idea that solitude can bring happiness to an individual. This question may help you answer question 23 because you look at specific lines that support a thematic concept. The concept of nature is mentioned through reference to the daffodils, but the central message is that of the joy in solitude.

27. **B**   In order to answer this question correctly, make sure to look back at the poem to understand what is being compared. The question pulls the simile out of context and does not tell you what is being compared to stars. You need to reread several lines ahead of the quoted lines to see the daffodils are being compared with stars.

28. **D**   When someone is being pensive, he or she is behaving in a thoughtful manner.

29. **C**   The ad clearly states, that to be qualified for the job, an applicant must have a degree in one of the areas asked in choice C. The other choices are things that Samantha lists in her letter as qualifications that she feels would add to her success as a DJ.

30. **B**   The main purpose of the first paragraph is to show her potential employer that she is creative and that she sees herself as a station employee. The first paragraph gives her letter some creativity is because it is a unique way to begin a business letter. It should catch her employer's attention and set her letter apart from the other letters that the station will receive.

31. **C**   It is fairly logical that a radio station that played new music would want its DJs to resemble its listening population. Their DJs should be in touch with current trends in music, but they should also be able to relate to the audience.

32. **A**   In her letter, Samantha mentions her educational qualifications. She does not mention what hours she can work or the status of her driving record. However, the advertisement for the job does mention issues such as hours and driving record. Do not let yourself get confused when you are comparing two pieces of text. Make sure that you are focused on the one that the question is referring to.

33. **D**   Samantha specifically states, "I feel that I am ready to make a move to a large-city radio station and share my talents with a bigger, more diverse audience." Just reread the letter to find the answer.

34. **B**   In order to answer this question, you need to think logically about why a DJ applicant would include a tape. Obviously, a DJ works on the radio and people listen to that individual every day. It would be beneficial for an employer to be able to hear how an applicant actually sounded on the radio before hiring that person.

35. **A**   The advertisement informs applicants that even if they have not actually worked at a radio station yet, they may count an internship as DJ experience.

36. **B** This article is definitely presenting an argument that centers around the violence found in video games and how video violence contributes to real violence. Choice C mentions persuading a reader, but the article is not attempting to persuade the reader about which video games that children should play. Essentially, this article presents an argument that the author hopes the reader will evaluate.

37. **C** A barrage simply means a lot of something. Once again, substitute the provided choices to determine which makes the most sense within the context of the sentence.

38. **D** The author realizes that violent video games are not the only source for inspiring actual violence. The author states that lack of parental involvement also contributes to real violence among children.

39. **B** As with most arguments, this one could be made more convincing if it included concrete proof to support the author's ideas. Being able to integrate statistics and numerical proof is a valuable resource for arguments because it gives the author a good foundation for her argument.

40. **D** The author mentions that due to the violence in video games, children are becoming desensitized to real violence. "Our Desensitized Gaming Youth" combines two key elements mentioned in the article: being desensitized to violence and playing video games.

41. **B** According to the author, acts of violence among children might be curbed if parents took the time to explain exactly what children were witnessing when playing a video game. The author explains that parents have to be "the pause button," meaning that they have to be the ones responsible for interrupting a child's game if they feel it is too violent.

42. **B** The article states that video games "also integrate foul language and drug use."

43. **D** Based on the author's perspective concerning violence, he would likely be interested in other articles that dealt with the issue of violence and its cause. Although the other choices may mention video games, they do not mention any correlation to violence.

44. **C** Choice C certainly has a sarcastic tone because typically people are not in a decapitation or spine-ripping mood. Sarcasm is used to emphasize the concept of desensitization because the sentence makes it sound like ripping out someone's spine is not a big deal.

45. **A** Within the context of this sentence, substituting "wildly" for "amok" retains the intended meaning.

46. **D** Through numerous line references, such as wanting to wash the blood from his hands, Macbeth is clearly battling with extreme guilt. He feels awful for what he has done and shows no indication of wanting to celebrate the fact that now he will be king.

47. **A** When Lady Macbeth tells her husband to wash his hands, it is clear that he has blood all over them. Using the term "filthy witness" is metaphorical because at this point, blood is the only testament to the crime that Macbeth has committed. In a sense, the blood is a witness. Once Macbeth has washed the "filthy witness" from his hands, there will be no witnesses to the crime with the exception of the Macbeths themselves.

48. **C** These lines express the idea that Macbeth feels he needs all the water in an ocean to clean his hands. This indicates that he feels he is covered in blood even though simply plunging his hands into a bowl of water will wash the blood away. Macbeth is so guilty that he feels he is drenched in Duncan's blood and that no amount of water will ever erase his feelings of guilt.

49. **A**   Once again the reader sees that Macbeth feels guilty for the murder of Duncan. In those particular lines, he is saying that he wishes the knocking on the door would wake Duncan from sleep or, in this case, death.

50. **B**   This line gives the reader important information about Duncan's assassination. In order to be seen as innocent, the Macbeths have planned to smear Duncan's blood on his guards, making them appear guilty. This is a crucial part of their plan, otherwise they risk being blamed for murdering the king.

51. **B**   In order to understand this statement fully, you need to notice the reference to color. Lady Macbeth's hands are now of her husband's color, which is red from blood. However, she feels her heart is white, or pure and innocent. She is therefore saying that she does not feel guilty for committing murder because she has a heart so "white."

52. **B**   Any time that a reference is made to a piece of literature, historical figure, or in this case, a mythological figure, remember that you are looking at an allusion. When Macbeth says that he will need Neptune's ocean to wash his hands, he is making a reference to a Roman god.

53. **C**   Lady Macbeth is certainly in control of this situation. While her husband wallows in guilt, she manages to frame the guards and to help Macbeth pull himself together. She gives Macbeth orders and tries to help him feel better about what they have done. She is without a doubt in clear command.

54. **A**   Unlike his wife, Macbeth feels horrible for what he has done. He is unable to think clearly and is already lamenting his choice to murder Duncan. Nearly every line spoken by Macbeth in the excerpt shows his guilty conscience.

55. **D**   Macbeth does not show any indication of being able to cope with his guilt quickly. An accurate prediction based on Macbeth's behavior is that he will continue to battle his guilt.

56. **D**   Among the services listed on the flyer, spa treatments are not mentioned.

57. **C**   The flyer informs prospective clients that if they join now, they receive free initiation. The other answer choices are not mentioned in the flyer.

58. **A**   Individuals interested in joining Sammy's Gym would probably like to know how much it will cost them each month to be a member.

59. **B**   The flyer clearly states that the gym is focused on helping individuals reach their fitness goals and providing a comfortable environment for their members. The gym is not advocating competition or intimidation between members. Rather, it wants everyone to feel comfortable.

60. **C**   A person interested in joining a gym that has a philosophy like Sammy's Gym, would most likely be interested in nutrition information. For example, if an individual is not looking for a competitive atmosphere, that person would not want to join a competitive running club.

| # AIMS Writing Practice Tests

WRITING PRACTICE TEST A

| Directions: | Read the prompt below and use the space provided for your prewriting/planning. Then write your draft. |

As of late, the community in which you live has seen increased acts of vandalism, such as graffiti and destruction of public property. Your community is blaming its teenagers for this destruction. In an essay, persuade members of your community that the vandalism could be decreased by adopting your proposed solution.

Your essay should include:

- An introduction, body, and conclusion
- An explanation of your proposed solution to the vandalism
- Specific, supporting details that make your argument clear

Remember to proofread your paper, checking for spelling, grammar, and punctuation.

Prewriting

Directions: Use the prewriting space below for outlines, webs, freewriting, or any other method that might help you to plan your writing.

Draft

Directions:	Write your draft in the space provided. Make sure to look back at your prewriting as you write your draft.

Revision

Directions:	Now revise your final draft. As you read over your draft, ask yourself the following questions. If you answered "no" to any of the above questions, make the necessary changes to your draft. Then write your final copy on the following pages.

- Is my paper written for the correct audience?
- Does my paper contain a strong main idea?
- Does my paper stay focused on my main idea?
- Does my paper contain specific ideas that support my main idea?
- Does my paper have a clear beginning, middle, and end?
- Are my ideas logical and easy to follow?
- Does my paper contain interesting and meaningful words?
- Does my paper contain varied sentences that are clear?
- Does my paper contain correct spelling, punctuation, and grammar?

Final Copy

| Directions: | Write your final copy on the following pages. Remember, your final copy cannot exceed two pages. |

_____

_____

_____

_____

_____

_____

_____

_____

_____

_____

_____

_____

_____

_____

_____

_____

_____

_____

_____

_____

_____

_____

_____

_____

_____

_____

Sample Essay

The following is a sample of a strongly written essay that answers the prompt about vandalism and provides a proposed solution to the problem. This essay includes a strong introduction that grabs the reader, a strong thesis, and supporting examples.

Today in our community, we see destruction everywhere we look. Playground equipment is tagged with graffiti, and car windows are broken every night. This describes just a few of the instances of vandalism that occur in our community. Right now, teenagers are being blamed for the problem. Unfortunately, the majority of the vandalism is probably caused by teenagers. However, I believe that I have a solution that I can offer to our community. The current vandalism in our community could possibly be curbed if we began community art projects. Community art projects would give teenagers the opportunity for several things. Art projects would give teenagers a reason to value and respect community property and would give them the opportunity to use their spare time effectively and productively.

Before I begin explaining my solution in more detail, let me first explain what a community art project would entail. Teenagers would paint murals, plant park gardens, and do other projects that would help to beautify our community. If teenagers took part in these projects, they would not want to vandalize or destroy things because they would value the community they had helped to create. If teenagers felt that they had provided the community with something of importance, they would not take pleasure in destroying things. There is a lot to be said for the power of pride.

The second reason why art projects would be effective is because they would be a good way for teenagers to use their spare time productively. I know a lot of students who do not have anything to do once they come home from school. Having something to do would curb a lot of the vandalism that results from boredom. If we had adults who were willing to volunteer with the project, teenagers would have adult supervision and would not be given the opportunity to destroy things.

Art projects would solve a lot of the problems of vandalism that our community faces. I know many adults think that any program for teenagers is a waste of time, but art projects would help focus a lot of energy and dedication. Our community could be proud of the great things teenagers would create to decorate our neighborhoods.

Community art projects would greatly benefit our surrounding area. Teens would be given the chance to take pride in their neighborhoods and would be able to spend their time in a productive manner. I think if we put this plan into action, we would see a vast improvement.

WRITING PRACTICE TEST B

Directions: Read the prompt below and use the space provided for your prewriting/planning. Then write your draft.

Due to problems that have occurred in past years, your high school is currently discussing getting rid of their homecoming celebration. In an essay, explain why or why not your high school should be able to celebrate homecoming.

Your essay should include:

- An introduction, body, and conclusion
- An explanation of your proposed solution
- Specific, supporting details that make your argument clear

Remember to proofread your paper, checking for spelling, grammar, and punctuation.

Prewriting

Directions: Use the prewriting space below for outlines, webs, freewriting, or any other method that might help you to plan your writing.

Draft

Directions:	Write your draft in the space provided. Make sure to look back at your prewriting as you write your draft.

_____

_____

_____

_____

_____

_____

_____

_____

_____

_____

_____

_____

_____

_____

_____

_____

_____

_____

_____

_____

_____

Revision

| Directions: | Now revise your final draft. As you read over your draft, ask yourself the following questions. If you answered "no" to any of the above questions, make the necessary changes to your draft. Then write your final copy on the following pages. |

- Is my paper written for the correct audience?
- Does my paper contain a strong main idea?
- Does my paper stay focused on my main idea?
- Does my paper contain specific ideas that support my main idea?
- Does my paper have a clear beginning, middle, and end?
- Are my ideas logical and easy to follow?
- Does my paper contain interesting and meaningful words?
- Does my paper contain varied sentences that are clear?
- Does my paper contain correct spelling, punctuation, and grammar?

Final Copy

Directions: Write your final copy on the following pages. Remember, your final copy cannot exceed two pages.

WRITING PRACTICE TEST C

Read the prompt below and use the space provided for your prewriting/planning. Then write your draft.

Due to a lack of appropriate funding, your school is currently discussing whether or not they should keep Physical Education (P.E.) courses as part of the curriculum. Available money is the school's biggest concern. In an essay, explain why your school should or should not keep P.E. classes.

Your essay should include:

- An introduction, body, and conclusion
- An explanation of your proposed solution
- Specific, supporting details that make your argument clear

Remember to proofread your paper, checking for spelling, grammar, and punctuation.

Prewriting

Directions: Use the prewriting space below for outlines, webs, freewriting, or any other method that might help you to plan your writing.

Draft

Directions:	Write your draft in the space provided. Make sure to look back at your prewriting as you write your draft.

_____

_____

_____

_____

_____

_____

_____

_____

_____

_____

_____

_____

_____

_____

_____

_____

_____

_____

_____

_____

_____

_____

_____

_____

_____

_____

_____

_____

_____

_____

_____

_____

_____

_____

_____

_____

_____

_____

_____

_____

_____

_____

_____

_____

Revision

Directions:	Now revise your final draft. As you read over your draft, ask yourself the following questions. If you answered "no" to any of the above questions, make the necessary changes to your draft. Then write your final copy on the following pages.

- Is my paper written for the correct audience?
- Does my paper contain a strong main idea?
- Does my paper stay focused on my main idea?
- Does my paper contain specific ideas that support my main idea?
- Does my paper have a clear beginning, middle, and end?
- Are my ideas logical and easy to follow?
- Does my paper contain interesting and meaningful words?
- Does my paper contain varied sentences that are clear?
- Does my paper contain correct spelling, punctuation, and grammar?

Final Copy

Directions:	Write your final copy on the following pages. Remember, your final copy cannot exceed two pages.

_____

_____

_____

_____

_____

_____

_____

_____

_____

_____

_____

_____

_____

_____

_____

_____

_____

_____

_____

_____

_____

Index